HOMEWORKS

HOMEWORKS

The complete guide to
displaying your possessions

ROBIN GUILD

VAN NOSTRAND REINHOLD COMPANY
New York Cincinnati Toronto London Melbourne

$6⁰⁰

Printed in The Netherlands
by Smeets Offset BV, Weert

Published in 1979 by
Van Nostrand Reinhold Company
A division of Litton Educational
Publishing, Inc.
135 West 50th Street, New York,
NY 10020, USA

Van Nostrand Reinhold Limited
1410 Birchmount Road
Scarborough, Ontario M1P 2E7, Canada

16 15 14 13 12 11 10 9 8 7 6 5 4 3 2 1

Homeworks was conceived,
edited and designed by
Marshall Editions Limited,
71 Eccleston Square,
London SW1V 1PJ, England
Editor Penny David
Art Editor Bridget Heal
Picture Editor Zilda Tandy
Associate Editor Ruth Farnsworth
Assistant Editor Lewis Esson
Designer Simon Blacker
Editorial Consultant Susan M. Norris
Production Hugh Stancliffe

**Library of Congress Cataloging in
Publication Data**
Guild, Robin.
 Homeworks
 1. Interior decoration – Psychological
aspects.
I. Title
NK2113.G83 747'.01'9 79-14421
ISBN 0-442-24576-9

Qualities that matter to me
and people to whom I'm grateful

Taste:	David Bishop
Colours:	Tricia Guild
Conviction:	Terence Conran
Patience:	David Millard
Perfection:	Bruce Wolf
Confidence:	E.K.
Proportion:	Angelo Donghia
Discrimination:	Giorgio Saporiti
Arrangement:	David Hicks
Texture:	Jack Lenor Larsen
Simplicity:	Syrie Maugham
Originality:	Karl Springer
Interpretation:	David Jessel
Style:	Fluff

And Bruce, John, Penny, Bridget,
Zilda, Simon and Ruthie at
Marshall Editions

This is a book about Things.

Things you treasure, and Things you had half-forgotten up in the loft. Things you have spent your life collecting and Things you've never had the heart to throw away. Prized possessions and junk, heirlooms and clutter, the flotsam of the years. Things the builders left behind. Things you borrowed years ago but forgot to give back and Things which now you couldn't bear to part with. Things that say something about you and Things that matter to you. Things that belong to you and Things you belong to. Things that are part of your life and part of your home.

They are the kinds of Things you hardly ever see in those crisp and tidy books about interior design. I sometimes wonder where they keep everything, those families whose elegant and empty rooms you see in the design magazines. There's usually one solitary, self-conscious collector's item in the middle of the room, but where are the toys, the set of china you inherited in your aunt's will, the driftwood and shells picked up on the beach? And why does every glossy magazine's kitchen hide the ketchup bottle as if it were a guilty family secret? Your things turn a room into *your* room. You may have picked the paper with care, matched the fabrics, got the proportions of the furniture right, but really all you've done so far is to colour the surface of the room and to fill in a few blocks of space. So far, there is no detail, no clue as to the identity of the individual who lives in this room. Without Things, even the best-designed room is as anonymous as most hotel suites.

For too long, designers neglected the basic human need we all have – to belong in our own homes. Birds lay claim to their patches of territory by singing out their individual tunes: we should make our homes as individual as birdsong. Every room should directly or obliquely reflect the kind of people we are. By putting our belongings on display we are not simply making a statement about ourselves for the benefit of our visitors, nor just flaunting what we own, but we are also reminding ourselves that this is the place we come home to, and these are the things we cherish.

I don't know what things *you* have, so how can this book help? I think it can help in what every designer knows is the best way of all: to give you the inspiration for your own ideas, and the courage of your own creative convictions. This isn't a book for copy-cats. You won't find any instant design blueprints in these pages – you can find those in the magazines. Nor is this book a grim grammar of good taste. (Good taste is what I think *I* have, you know *you* have and we both agree *they* haven't got.) There aren't any rules when it comes to individuality – except, perhaps, that it's very important to be honest; if you strive to create an artificial personality for a room you will feel an uncomfortable fraud every time you enter it.

The best ideas – the ideas that matter most, the ideas you cherish – are always the ideas you have yourself. This book, which addresses itself to the designer in you, is intended to set in motion the wheels of that exciting, intuitive process of self-discovery. It's the first link in a chain of thought which will end in as many different, original, creative ideas as there are readers of these words. That's why this isn't a book of answers – it's a book of questions to ask yourself.

The book contains a large number of photographs. Some are of my own arrangements, and some are of other people's work which I've chosen either because they make a specific point or simply because I like them. Don't be intimidated: judge for yourself whether or not a picture achieves what it is meant to. You may not like all the pictures. That's not surprising, because design is for individuals and we are all different people. But don't just leave it at that: look especially hard at the ones you don't like and work out for yourself why you feel they don't work for you. What's the essential difference between the pictures you hate and the ones you like? What would you do to change things to make them right for you?

Answer those questions and you are on your way to doing it.

Don't be daunted by displays of other people's things. Some of them are very lovely and very valuable, but most of them are really very ordinary. They're on display because they are important to the people who own them. You've got things which may or may not be valuable in money terms, but which are important to you because of what they mean to you. Everything you have is special in one way or another. If I just look around me I find things that matter to me: my pinboard is a riot of different coloured bits of paper – tickets, photos, postcards, stamps – which, together, form a constantly changing mosaic. On my desk I have a glass paperweight from a wedding anniversary long ago, some pheasant feathers (souvenir of a cold November walk), a pewter mug I keep pencils in (some school prize once important for what it represented, now important for what it is), a bottle of ink (a brand I always buy because the label is nice to look at). They wouldn't fetch anything in an auction, but they are valuable to me, and an integral part of the random landscape of my desk. And there's an old Leica which I hardly ever use, but I leave it out because it's been a good friend and still looks good.

We are all collectors whether we know it or not. Things accumulate; the problem is how to display them. If you heap everything into the middle of the room it will look like a garage sale that nobody came to. Make a start by sorting it all out into contrasting or complementary categories. Put all glass things together, whether they are ancient or modern, functional or decorative. Put wooden things together. Put smooth things together; or put rough things with smooth things. Put colours together: put everything blue together and remind yourself how many blues there are. Put together things that you've always been told don't go together and be surprised at how often they do.

Once you have found an arrangement that pleases you, the next question is where to put it. Ask yourself how prominent you want it to be. Position means a lot – the context in which an object or collection of objects is displayed, and the effect on the overall balance of the room. See how it catches the light, and how the whole feel of the arrangement can change subtly as the sun moves round. Start to see not just objects themselves, not just the relationship between the objects, but the spaces created between the objects. Don't cram everything in; even things need air.

There will come a moment (with a bit of luck) when you achieve something beautiful and satisfying. This is the time to change it. Your life isn't static and your home shouldn't be unchanging like a museum. Moods change. Monday isn't Saturday. Seasons change, demanding fresh perspectives. When you've found a set of clothes which suit you to perfection, you don't have to wear them every day. Juggle things around. Break up arrangements and mix them up together. Put things away and bring out new things. Play games with your things to keep up with your interest in them, because once you get bored with them they lose their reason for being there. Introduce a new focus of attention – let's say a vase of flowers – and see what new relationships are created. Buy a few grammes of pink-and-white sugared almonds just for the pleasure of seeing them on a pink-and-white china plate. If it doesn't work – you can eat them.

In random or contrived arrangement, my possessions give me pleasure by the contribution they make to the feel of my home. But there is extra satisfaction in being constantly reminded of the interest inherent in the things themselves. All too often you buy something because it's interesting, fun or attractive – and then lose interest and put it away at the back of a drawer. It's still just as attractive, but it has grown stale in your sight. Put it with other things and keep changing its context, and it will keep all its original freshness and friendliness.

Right at the end of the book there is a section designed to help you rediscover the value of your things. There are tips on restoring objects and on how to bring out the best in them. There is also practical advice on lighting and methods of display to help create the right backgrounds for your things.

I began by saying that this is a book about things. It is also a book about ideas. The best ideas have yet to come. They are the ones you're about to have.

Enjoy them.

Robin Guild

This room says a lot of the things I believe in. In the first place, it is a very personal room: it bears the very individual imprint of its owner.

I like the unhesitating confidence with which periods and styles have been thrown together – the high-tech windows reflected in the mirror, and the 'thirties carpet, for instance. Some of the things here are quite valuable, but others might have been picked up in junk shops for next to nothing. Like the best of design, it is classless; a room like this could be a small studio apartment where ideas have been the biggest investment, or a corner of some opulent, sprawling mansion.

A lot of thought has gone into the room: it's a room for sitting or lying down in, so the pictures are at the relevant height.

The shelves arouse my curiosity – an apparently random arrangement is much more intriguing than a formal display case: it is like the difference between reading someone's diary and reading their autobiography.

This room seemed to give me hundreds of clues about the personality of its creator, while at the same time making me more and more interested; I was intrigued to discover that it is in the Paris apartment of designer Jacques Granges, whose work I have always liked.

LIVING WITH THINGS

We are all collectors whether we know it or not, and
we all collect in different ways. Some people collect
at random like magpies; others take endless time
and infinite pains to seek out the one thing they're
looking for. My own tastes are so catholic that I am
an incurable accumulator. I sometimes think that
it's the things that collect me.

Don't worry if at first you can't see any coherent
theme in your possessions. Almost anything will
flatter anything else. A marble-topped table doesn't
insist on an ormolu clock and a pair of candlesticks;
a tin bucket full of ferns might make a refreshing
change – as long as it's a nice tin bucket. What
matters is the conviction with which you put things
together. They've at least got one thing in common
already – they're all things you like.

SETS AND MATCHES

Everybody, but everybody, has *some* china and glass. Some of it was designed explicitly for display, some purely for function, some with both purposes in mind.

All of it can become display – even the last surviving couple of saucers from a twelve-piece coffee set, the ink bottle emptied by a contemporary of Dickens, or the modern ribbed-glass bottle that only last week contained maple syrup or olive oil.

Arrange a piece with others that match, pieces different in shape but related in colour, or different shapes designed to do the same job. Let light show off the translucence of glass or the texture of china. And if you like it, enjoy it and be proud of it – whether it is a collector's piece or something you can throw away tomorrow without a second thought.

Pre-war china looks good in sets, and in oddments. Tricia Guild mixes patterns on her dresser (left); I arrange odd pieces so that light reflected from the window sill throws the surface into relief.

The natural, Pre-Raphaelite lily and the machine-age glass serve each other well. Part of Christopher Vane Percy's collection of Lalique pieces demonstrates the icy, translucent textures of glass.

Empty bottles are usually thrown away; here they have been kept for their attractive shapes, colours and labels. Crowd them together, or select a group that has characteristics in common – don't just display one on its own; there's no single star turn in this cast.

CAN DO

The packaging collection need not dominate the whole room, but can make a colourful corner. Trivial objects gain importance by being brought together and arranged interestingly.

Printers' typecases make simultaneous storage and display cases for collections of small objects when the drawers are kept open. There is plenty of scope for varying the show from day to day.

It is an absurd truth about present-day house-proudness that we give star billing to things that their original owners threw away. In the age of built-in obsolescence we resuscitate bygones.

Packaging, for instance. It has always had as its *raison d'être* the need to be eye-catching and attractive (and the known appeal of the old has caused the most modern designers to reproduce old, loved forms). Consider collecting modern packaging for mass effect; it's as easy to keep drinks cans as it is to throw them away – and they will be on show before they reach the prices of collectors' items.

Small groups work better with tight control of colours and shapes, and work best of all with mellow, old pieces. But as the pictures on these pages show, combinations of old and new, special and trivial, work surprisingly well. And where collections can be displayed on harmonious old wooden shelves as in the village stores of yesterday, the nostalgia is complete.

Packaging in quantity
makes pattern:
uniform sizes, uniform
labels, or the
kaleidoscope effects
of mixing colours and
motifs. Stacks of
drinks cans grow up
the walls like
stalagmites. They
make good anchor
points for the more
scattered exhibits on
the walls – and are a
modern counterpart
of the real collectors'
items on the floor.

Shelves that were
once shop fittings
house the containers
they were designed
for. Each section of
the shelves contains
its own little
arrangement of
shapes and colours.

THE SOFT TOUCH

Linda Garland used batiks from Bali to make a tent effect under the sloping roof of her top-floor apartment. Cushions in appropriate plain colours enrich the scheme but accord full importance to the batik patterns.

Since the days when the walls of the castle were lined with arras, the reasons for hanging fabric on walls have changed; nowadays textiles are hung less for heat insulation than for their effect in softening the acoustic, and for sheer decoration.

Textile collections may be hung in panels as in a picture gallery, may form part of the soft furnishings like cushions and quilts, or may camouflage walls and ceilings like a tent. The pieces themselves dictate what you do with them. Here the hangings had a legitimate start in life. But last year's spinnaker, the wedding-present bath towels that seem too fancy to use and the tablecloths found in grandma's trousseau chest all have their possibilities.

These rooms have in common a commitment to colour and pattern, and the softening effects of the fabrics. Together, the photographs share the same muted, rich tones; they work together on the page just as different patterns work together in each room. But although each room has a variety of patterns, they have sufficient elements in common to harmonize.

Different patterns work together if there
are enough of them, and if they have
something in common: materials,
colours, maybe scale of design, like this
confusion of embroidered cushions on a
background of traditional blackwork and
quilting.

Somak rugs are given the height they
need on the lofty brick wall of this
Kuwaiti house, against a complementary
background texture. Their shape echoes
the patterns of the pictures and the hi-fi
equipment. A rug on the floor tops – or
tails – the rectangular and colour effects.

Indian cotton
bedspreads make an
exotic wall-covering
whose panels
emphasize the
proportions in a
Victorian house. Huge
cushions bring
related designs into
the room, but large
areas of plain colours
provide a necessary
astringent.

IT'S A STICK-UP

A colourful printed frieze from a greengrocer's shop window goes once round the room and no more. It brings welcome colour to a cool blue-and-white kitchen. The same position would suit a collage of can labels, fruit wrappers or crate labels.

Framed labels have bold shapes and colours, like a chart of the world's flags. The empty space could be suggesting that the framed choice is not definitive.

How does a collection grow? Some people choose things selectively; others just can't throw anything away. Wall-coverers see every surface as a space to fill – like a mountain to climb – because it's there.

Collections *can* over-run a home like a plague. There's nothing wrong with that; but if they threaten the peace of mind of inhabitants, it may be time to decide that enough is enough, to display a *selection* from a collection and put the surplus out of sight . . . at least for the moment.

Setting a collection to work: the patchwork of Victorian, Edwardian and modern tiles that makes the bath area so cheerful would need careful planning to make the collection fit the space and distribute the different colours and patterns to best effect.

Many of the postcards
on the wall behind
Alan Fletcher's dining
table are heart- and
stomach-felt
acknowledgements
that his wife Paola is
among the best cooks
in London. Thus the
pleasing pattern on
the cork wall has
cherished overtones
for the hosts.

Grandma's sewing
corner shows a
collection growing
into a display, as a
handful of button and
elastic cards and
needle packets is
given a deep frame
and becomes a low-
relief picture.

A SHOW OF HANDS

Heads, hands and feet – originally functional forms, now collectors' pieces – are coveted for their smooth wooden texture and their fascinating shapes. I chose to group these things together in pure display; I could have used them in greater number, but this was enough, and kept the message simple.

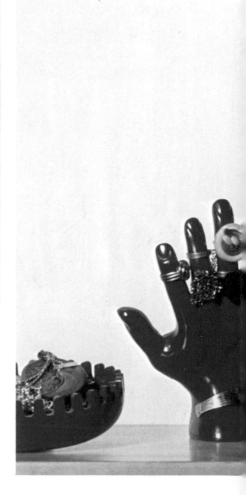

The hand theme is confined to the candlesticks, but the whole grouping works well in more than just its colour relationships. Shapes in the painting reflect those in the group, and the hands are in proportion to the head, too.

Functional display hands of different sizes and epochs work together to hold a ring collection. Note the finger-like fringe around the bowl on the left.

People collect all sorts of things, for all sorts of reasons and in all sorts of ways – from barbed wire to toastracks. Sometimes collections begin around a theme, when something with a simple, almost universal shape attracts – egg forms, sea shells; in wood, minerals, even plastics. Then you begin to notice all the paintings, advertisements and trinkets that feature them.

Collection on a theme may begin for some sentimental reason, or as a joke; the word gets around and the collection snowballs as people give presents inspired by the theme.

Or the collection may have had a visual basis, when two shapes were put together because they enhanced each other. Once someone starts noticing shoe lasts or sunburst motifs, scouring junk shops for relevant bric-à-brac is often habit-forming.

But it is sometimes necessary to make a conscious choice between the intellectual idea of the theme, and how it looks. It's a good idea to store the majority of the collection and make selected displays of *some* of the items, changing them round and keeping their impact fresh. It can be more effective to keep the greater part submerged, like an iceberg, and only show the tip.

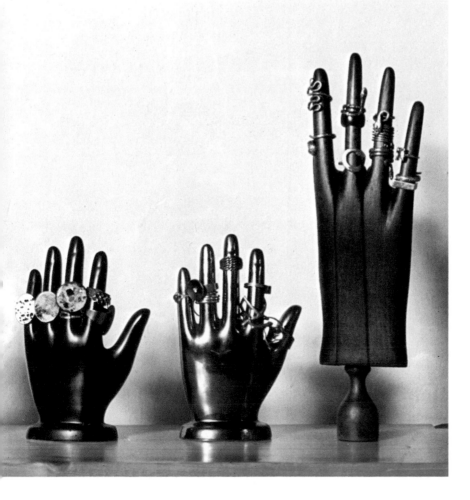

STILL LIFE

*Surrealistic padded
dolls lurch life-sized
in an abandoned way
across the furniture –
an exotic vulgarity
against the discreet
nude reflected in the
mirrored wall behind
them.*

*A doll collection
(below) which seems
thoroughly at home.
When displaying
dolls it is not
necessary to go to
this length, but one or
two scale accessories
help establish the
context.*

*Not so much a collection of dolls as of
ecclesiastica, of which some happen to
be figurines. Religious kitsch benefits
from straight display presentation on
simple shelves.*

Dolls are only human, after all. They don't
look good in a neat row; unless they are
very studied forms, they need the ambience to which imagination would ac-
custom them – in strait-laced composure or
kapok floppiness. Most sorts of doll dictate
their own terms, requiring the companion-
ship of others, agreeable surroundings
and a comfortable place to sit.

Other bygones – the parasol, the seat –
give this clutter of dolls the nursery-
corner ambience they would have
known in their salad days.

NOSTALGIA

Some of it exotic, some junk, interesting bits and pieces offer an invitation to poke around and discover what's there on the marble washstand.

In the dining end of Tricia Guild's kitchen, French beaded lampshades over the long table light a group of 'thirties pottery. Similarity of colouring and style make the shades work together; being hung at different heights makes a more interesting shape.

Glossy Victorian advertising signs on a matt brick wall enhance a stylish but austere modern counter top. The predominating browny-yellow and gold make the atmosphere mellow and welcoming.

Chrome and glass shelves make a sympathetic background for a collection of glittering Art Deco, with angular shapes and a preponderance of silver and glass materials.

A taste of nostalgia can infuse one corner of a room or the whole house. Nostalgia is a theme whose concern is with time rather than a kind of object. It may be specific, it may be just enough to give a non-specific 'atmosphere' or 'character' to a room. Or it may go for scrupulous historical accuracy – and could border on the manic.

Nostalgia is likely to create relaxed, harmonious arrangements, because it is based on affection rather than some external dictate about what goes with what, and conformity with some recognized style. It is often personal, because its founding focus may well be an intimate artefact, like a treasured trinket from childhood. Certainly it tends to encourage visitors to observe closely – maybe because of such affectionate overtones.

Nostalgia can be a self-contained display, period things on a period bookshelf, perhaps; but it often looks good against a modern context. Without being anything very special, like an original piece of art or a valuable antique, it tends to encompass those things that were *not* bought yesterday, and made the day before that. And it can embrace objects with the tell-tale signs of having been loved in the past.

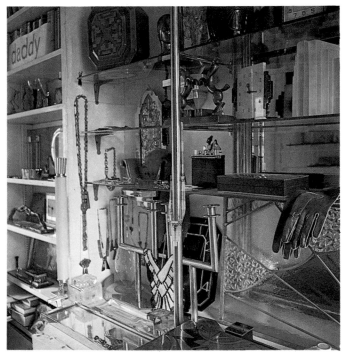

Why should a bathroom be clinical and cold? Why not lie in the bath looking with pride and enjoyment at a collection of things – like this royal flush – instead of at plain tiles? And in a bathroom with room to spare, it could provide just the space that's needed for an overflow collection.

STYLE

When designing a room, which comes first – the fabric of the room (the carpet, wall covering, curtains and lighting), or the objects within the room itself? Should one design the shell and then go out to find the props? Or are there possessions waiting for a room to be designed for them?

I firmly believe that objects and their background should interrelate. That interrelationship does not, however, have to be a harmonious one, creating an established 'look'. The objects may suit a textural background of similar quality, or alternatively may contrast with a totally different background.

On these pages some of the objects have been chosen for the rooms, and some of the objects have taken over the rooms. In any event, the result is a sense of style. This may be anything from high baronial through high tech to high camp.

The style in Sir Cecil Beaton's drawing room is classical and strictly symmetrical taking its cue from this graceful and elegant architectural balance; only the arrangement on the table prevents one half being a mirror image of the other.

Silks and satins sustain the Hollywood extravaganza atmosphere set up by a monumental Egyptian-style mirror. You almost expect to see a kohl-eyed Cleopatra reclining on those cushions.

The antlers and stags' heads echo the architectural lines of the roof of Glen Tanar House, in Scotland – and the lines of the roof dictate their positioning.

*In a way the artificial
window created on
the far wall is the only
deliberate and
self-conscious piece of
arrangement in
Andrew Logan's
apartment; everything
else seems to have
just happened. Like
Topsy it 'just growed'
a growth as organic
and energetic as that
of the Monstera
wandering up the
wall in the
background.*

*The colour of the
walls holds together
the accumulation of
kitsch objects dotted
about: a bathroom is
often just the place to
let good taste go
berserk.*

COURAGE AND CONVICTION

Conviction . . . that
enough is never
enough. Painter
Duggie Fields fills up
every available space
between his plaques
and oddments with
period pin-ups. Only
a couple of sensible
workaday gadgets
bring you down to
earth.

Conviction . . . that
the sun will never set
on the British Empire.
There's a dignity and
an indeterminate
nostalgia pervading
this room with its
mellow tones and
formal arrangements.
A place for the stiff
upper lip to relax a
little, maybe.

Schools can be mixed when it's done with conviction: the very deliberate arrangement of pictures, couch and rug (all with their honey-gold tones) has its formal abstraction challenged by the surrealist hand-chair.

Strict period accuracy is less important than that things mix well; this combination of the objects of yesterday and the day before works in terms of colour, materials and weight.

It takes nerve to paint the whole room blood-red, but having taken the plunge, anything goes – a mixture of the exotic and the mundane creates a kitsch extravaganza. However, the temptation to paint the ceiling red was resisted, and the walls' gloss surface is light-reflecting.

These courageous rooms, utterly different from one another, have one thing in common: single-minded devotion to a concept. Their designers have committed themselves to idiosyncratic visions (and they have to live there); they have totally trusted the value of the joke, the style, the intended mood – and gone the whole way. They have made the rooms into the backgrounds for the objects; they selected the ingredients – and then these took over the decoration. Because of the designers' personal assurance, the things they have put together work together. There is no shortage of character in these very personal places – wish we could all have such assured conviction about our tastes.

Maya Bowler, shoe designer, seems convinced that there were blue skies behind those nineteen-forties clouds. Wartime period atmosphere is sometimes so convincing that you can almost hear the voices of the Andrews Sisters over the wireless . . .

SECOND TIME AROUND

A room of objects certainly not intended to be where they are. We wanted to show that recycled things, used in the right combination and context, can create unexpectedly appealing environments.

Here we used mostly coarse textures: rough brick walls, stained wooden floor, clay chimney pots, basketweave chairs, hessian sacks; we cleaned an ordinary galvanized dustbin and gave it a thick glass top for a change of texture. The scale is established by the sack seats and the tables on the lower plane, with the giant plants and the huge umbrella giving it height (and colour, as an antidote to drabness).

The key to recycling is to be disciplined enough to use only objects you really like – not just ones that are cheap.

TURN THE TABLES

There is physical balance as well as balance of shape with these glass-topped plant-pots. The terra-cotta and bamboo tones are picked up in the colourful cushions against a neutral background. Several items are in pairs – but not symmetrically.

The golden-honey tones of wood in different forms and textures pervade this room: the tea-chest blends in, but its markings make interesting pattern, and its metal edging gives it definition.

*Slabs of concrete –
like the base of the
metal sculpture –
make a sound, square
table which is low
like the furniture and
has the same
angularity and hard
lines. This could be a
forerunner of the
'high-tech' school.
Smooth-edged blocks
of glass stacked in the
same way would
make an alternative
table material.*

*A cardboard and
plywood cable drum
should give a
season's use on the
terrace; give it a
pretty top to go with
its surroundings, but
be prepared to
jettison it when it
begins to collapse.*

*Empty cola cans glued together make a
six-sided table; the three-sided ashtray
in the same idiom is at home on top.*

Almost anything up to knee height has the
potential to be a table – but don't take the
concept of recycling too far. Here only the
tables are unexpectedly styled; they look
positively respectable in their surroundings and yet their essential character has
not been changed. An object should look
good in its context (here you could use the
flagstones without the sculpture, the cable
drum without the cloth) – but don't recycle
for the sake of it, don't introduce inappropriate things whose only *raison d'être*
is their shock value. Choose them because
their colour, shape or texture helps the
room. And not necessarily because of
economy: a thick plate-glass table-top to
put on your dustbin, plant-pot or paving
stones may well cost as much as the
average coffee table.

COME AGAIN

You can do a lot with cans – especially the sort that have removable lids, and hence smooth lips. These are attached end-on to a bathroom wall. And they haven't earned a status that makes them too grand for a coat of paint.

The chimney pots as umbrella stand and jardinière are just right, because they 'belong' with the raw brick wall and the quarry-tiled floor.

Choose whatever pot your flower arrangement needs: for shape first, and then colour; if it means using something unexpected – and the result looks all right – it's worth while.

The same applies to cache-pots: use shopping baskets, any baskets. The different weaves make variations on a theme, the wooden shelves tone in and the colour element is subtly pretty, too.

It's a question of 'useful until proved useless'. The object is to find new roles for unlikely things. Start by considering their shape. Is there a job they can do? Then, is their material/texture/colour appropriate to the environment that you imagine putting them in?

As a general rule, if the object is going to add anything to its intended environment, it should work on its own. If you find

yourself wanting to take a coat of white paint to a handsomely weatherbeaten chimney stack before you stand it in the hallway, forget it. And resist the temptation to paint the bucket – just clean the galvanized steel.

But I believe that over-cleaning is worse than no cleaning at all. I far prefer to see the patina of time to the shine produced by detergent or by lacquer.

At the most you might increase the shine on galvanized buckets with a fine wire wool – and maybe it would not be sacrilegious to lacquer them. But had you ever noticed before now how good they can look?

MUCH OF NOTHING

The simplicity of the shelving means the packaging stands out, and the way it is neatly arranged shows how even a sauce bottle can have its own visual dignity.

Why not a graceful bunch of shapely umbrellas in place of the usual dried grasses and seed heads? If the display is presented with sufficient confidence it will be respected as such.

Lately, homemaking has come out of the closet. No longer is it a dictum that work-aday things should be hidden behind walls full of blank, sterile cupboard doors.

Why not see the decorative potential of everyday objects – see them as shapes and colours to be worked with into pattern, and start building them into a display. Packaging is a good example. Ever since Campbell's Soup became respectable as an art form, there has been no excuse for not enjoying the appearance of packaging. For example, sometimes the cupboards in our kitchens and larders contain three or four bottles of washing-up liquid. The one in use is out on the work surface within hand's reach. Use display techniques. Bring all the bottles out and stack them together as a colourful block and leave the cupboard free for the storage of some less visually interesting item.

It is order and imagination that elevate storage into display. Not just tidying but arranging objects is what makes the difference: making sure that everything is carefully positioned, aligned along the front of the shelf; that labels face forwards; that things look good in proportion to one another. Make sure the shelf itself is not so deep that things get into a muddle instead of being displayed effectively.

Often we put away things just because we are trained to do so. Why not question whether a thing needs to be put away – immediately? Why not hang a favourite dress or hat on view, like a picture, for a while? If you're not superstitious, stand a new pair of shoes on the dressing table, side by side like pieces of sculpture.

Open eyes and an open mind can enhance the pleasures we derive from the things we own – however unlikely – when they look good.

Harness delinquent urges and allow graffiti to decorate the telephone wall. If an unlimited expanse of white wall is too tempting, circumscribe the area with a frame, provide a board, or make the wall washable.

Nails evenly spaced out all over a board (right) make a useful display of sewing-thread reels, with a border of scissors.

Photographer Jessica Strang's daughter (below) enjoys seeing her shoes as well as wearing them. They are framed in divided fruit crates and displayed on the wall like pictures within easy reach.

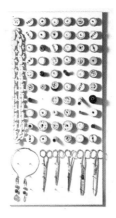

SHOW OFF

Now that we appreciate the surprising scope of the objects and collections we never realized we had – how best do we display them?

The following pages take you on a Grand Tour of the great debates of design – harmony versus contrast, naturalism versus artifice, symmetry versus imbalance, and choosing colours and textures – while we continue the fascinating process of putting things together to see how they look.

Don't abandon your intuition: react to the pictures, but then sit back and work out in exact detail the reasons for your reactions, and precisely what changes are needed to make a room or an arrangement right for you. Try to do the same thing another day when your mood has changed – and check that the same things hold true for you then.

WHITE ON WHITE

In these two pictures I've chosen to group objects that are shiny in contrast with the rope-covered table and the rough brick wall. See how the yellowness of the light alters the white.

People and plants look marvellous in a pure white room. Somehow the natural things don't cancel out the whiteness.

White and white equals boring? Only when it's a colour scheme chosen because it doesn't offend, or when it's the safe colour the builders have used because no one can decide on an alternative. I so often hear 'We're going to paint everything white until we've got the feel of the house.' After the effort of moving, repainting is seldom undertaken. This kind of half-heartedness leads into the temptation of picking out 'features' and introducing colour to break the monotony. DON'T.

Enjoying white-and-white needs conviction, though not necessarily to the extent of taking a paintbrush to the sharps and flats of the piano keyboard. Interest must be strong in the textures if it is not there in terms of colour. Contrast shiny things with matt, soft with hard, smooth with rough, natural with artificial. Just make a deliberate choice: enjoy whiteness – or choose a colour.

The white shade card from a good paint shop – or a row of white cars of different makes – is a reminder of how many different whites there are. Remember, oil-based paint goes yellow more rapidly in a room without good sunlight: use acrylic or

Night brings contrast naturally to the monochrome scheme – making it black-and-white instead.

emulsion for the blue-whiteness the soap ads tell you to strive for.

But there's nothing sacrosanct about virgin whiteness: in a predominantly white room rich colours, paintings, sculptures and objects will be the jewels of the setting.

NEUTRAL GROUND

Neutral is often synonymous with natural, involving pattern that is subtle rather than obvious, and with a strong tactile element. Natural and neutral objects – and rooms – may seem simple, but they needn't be naïve.

Sophisticated neutrality: uncompromisingly modern materials and style are in daring contrast with ancient clay and with a monumental column of firewood.

Neutral doesn't mean negative. If all-white schemes are labelled 'safe', neutral ones could seem equally unadventurous. But these three rooms demand a response that is as much tactile as visual. With the primary and secondary colours used as accents, it's often the sheer surface colour that gets noticed – before shape, texture or any other qualities. In the absence of accent colour, objects have to speak much more emphatically. Aspects other than colour become far more significant.

Much that is neutral is also natural – and nature is always challenging in its forms and its textures. Animal, vegetable and mineral elements bring neutral rooms to life. Plants and plant forms (wood, bamboo, basketwork), animal hides and horns, un-bleached fabrics, unpainted surfaces are the starting points. Bone-white and light-reflecting shine help the mixture of neutral things to take off. And as in white rooms, green plants enrich without seeming to introduce colour.

John Dickinson reverses the normal process: he leaves the plaster walls of his old firehouse raw and reproduces this finish on the two new walls built to divide off the kitchen; but he paints the 'airport junk' wood carvings so they almost become sculptural. In their 'natural' colour they would have had importance as colour accent; now the emphasis is on shape.

Nature in a state of armed neutrality. Plain, simple white sofas 'work': you don't need to spend a fortune on expensive, elaborate upholstery. Spend some on cleaning instead: the more they are worn and cleaned, the softer and nicer they get, like jeans?

SUGAR CANDY

What colour? Personal colour tastes may be acquired in childhood: prints that were around us at home, the sweet candy colours of the confectioners', of flowers or country greenness. Any of these preferences can contribute to choosing an object to be the focal point of a room and the starting point for a total colour scheme.

Pastels work naturally together; their effect is gentle, feminine. The sharper citrus tones are lively without being strong. Different colours of the same tonal value mix naturally – but they need to be carefully managed to become interesting. While an over-cautious approach is tame, an excess of candy colours may be sickly. But it all comes down to a question of taste.

Colour choice and texture in my arrangement are dictated by the satin patchwork background. The vases are late-'thirties lustre, the cloth satin – and the flowers silk, arranged in a natural way.

Colour has been introduced into a white room; it is subtle, but almost incomplete; waiting, perhaps, for a bowl of cornflowers – or even brilliant red poppies.

Red poppies would devastate this room. First came the painting, then the cushions, then the flowers (which will always be chosen from the established colour range).

The stronger-coloured cushions, whose contribution is necessary to give the whole scheme some bite, are partly hidden behind the paler ones so that they do not dominate.

PRIMARY SCHOOL

The primary colours are separated with plenty of white and pale blue, which helps them to work into a mural. A plain, if not neutral, floor would be normal: here stripes across the floor summarize the colour scheme and offer pattern to play on.

Bedspread, pillows and walls are all covered with the same fabric. White wall units work as panelling round the bed, give welcome relief from pattern and make a good background for a display of toys.

Because primary colours are intense, they must be used with conviction. Their effect in equal amounts is in no way natural (even in summer gardens there is a predominance of green). Just as in fashion, coordination is the key.

I prefer working with rich neutrals and subtle colour schemes. When choosing a bold design in bright primaries, have the courage to see it through. Use it on walls, floors *and* ceilings. Team it with something of matching intensity if a break is needed. Don't end up with a half-and-half effect.

When strong colours are put together, the individual colour values are initially far less important than the fact that they contrast. Blue-plus-yellow is noticed, rather than the exact shade of lemon or buttercup or sunshine yellow. But the different colours have to be equal in strength: try a more muted combination of primaries, and you find out how hard it is to dilute the different colours equally.

Angelo Donghia was inspired by an Afghan patchwork tent to design this printed fabric – which is used to make a Paris room look like a tent. Imagine how much less dramatic it would have been to have painted either the walls or the ceiling a safe white. The floor picks up the little-used blue from the tented walls; white relieves the fabric pattern of some of its hot intensity.

RICH AND DARK

You might walk past this market-stall group if the wall behind was white or grey: as it is, the tone value of the colours is the same, and the lack of contrast makes it interesting.

The background neither helps nor hinders this pretty group; it holds together because of the predominance of blue, and because of a pervading simplicity in its ingredients.

Everywhere white walls, light backgrounds, reflect contemporary preoccupations with space and light. Objects and pictures hung on them remain the separate parts of a series, like words and pictures on the white of the printed page. A dark background makes a room look smaller, and dark objects stand out in contrast. And dark objects placed against a dark background have their colours enhanced and enriched, whether they are shiny plastic boxes, pieces of elaborate chinoiserie – or common-or-garden vegetables.

Like every colour choice, it is a matter of taste. The dark red walls that I find womb-like and secure you may find stifling and claustrophobic. It is also a question of texture. Avoid flat ones that absorb the light: use gloss-finish paint rather than matt; dark velvet rather than hessian (but make sure the pile runs downwards to reflect light and repel dust). Choose and position lighting so that objects don't get lost. Place shiny objects so that they reflect light, and use a leavening of gilt, chrome or mirror to avoid drowning in darkness.

Simple plastic boxes, like lacquer-work, have texture and rich colour. If the shelves and background were white, shape as well as colour would become more significant.

Gore Vidal's home has the opulence of red and gold, and reflective texture. I find the brilliant arrangement and the painting detract from one another: the table should have bare wall behind it.

The common elements in this collection of chinoiserie, old masters, Art Deco objects, Persian carpets and tapestries are their elaborate ornamentation and their exoticism. The royal red of the walls is almost the only possible background for objects this sumptuous.

51

IN THE PINK

The dusky rose petals of the pot-pourri are the finishing touch, but their colour is the starting point: almost everything either contains or reflects this pink. Objects are not self-consciously arranged. The glass-covered table is a good size, the colour is beautiful, and the substantial braiding gives it depth.

A favourite colour leads to acquiring favourite objects in that colour; combine these and you have a colour theme. In general, it is harder to marry together different elements in a monochrome scheme, because tones vary subtly, but if you are consistent in your colour tastes when choosing things, they will work together.

A single basic colour changes as it is incorporated in different materials; which may be matt, light-reflecting, smooth, uneven, pearly or translucent. Use large amounts of the colour in the background, both to establish the theme and to contain the variations as it appears in different materials. Reflective surfaces will pick it up. Try to keep the theme within a broad band of colour: perhaps blushing warm pinks instead of frosty ones, or *vice versa*. Finally, use lighting, lamp-shades and window treatments that will sustain the colour bias that you want: just as the photographer and the printer have brought out the warmth of the pinks in these photographs.

The Art Deco figurine combines rose pink and flesh pink; with its reflective surfaces it would fit into any pink context.

Tricia Guild's bathroom combines a vast range of textures: quilted tiles, 'thirties glass, lustre vase and mirrors, shell frame; and soft absorbent ones like the carpets, rag rug and towels. For a theme like this even the soap has to be the right colour. But Tricia has resisted the temptation to use pink sanitary ware: she never chooses anything but white.

BLUE AND GREEN

Colour themes are made personal in dozens of different ways; their effect depends on the objects themselves and on their owners' tastes. They can be stark, pretty, graphic, soft, simple or contrived.

A colour theme begins when you put forget-me-nots into a blue-print vase: it may or may not lead you to paint walls, floor, ceiling and furniture. It implies the preponderance of one colour, so that you think of it as 'the blue room'. When you look closely there may be less blue than other colours, but it is the blue that makes the memorable statement. This is a subtle matter of quality rather than quantity – don't be afraid of using other colours, especially white or neutrals, as a relief.

This Philadelphia kitchen has retained and revitalized its original fittings. There is plenty of relief from the predominant blue: matching ceramic tiles, for example, would be too much. Blue painted stripes darkening towards the midnight ceiling make the room less lofty. The picture seems to contain all the blues used elsewhere in the kitchen.

Green is Tricia Guild's favourite colour – because it is the colour of plants and nature. It is everywhere, and she finds it easy to live with. The message from her bedroom is of light and greenness; the deep, rich colour of the plants strengthens it. Fabric everywhere makes a soft, feminine atmosphere: the room has no hard lines, no hard textures.

The tiles probably came first, and the plates were collected to match – but it could be the other way round. The plates disguise the stark white walls and marry with the tiles' glaze. Not all the plates need be old or rare: with a cover-all theme, the more the merrier.

A blue-and-white theme in microcosm; have miniature colour themes on shelves within the wider context of a room.

PAINT IT

Painted plumbing is acceptable as a frame for Ann Sutton's knitted sculpture – but there has to be a good reason for drawing anyone's attention to pipes and radiators.

The solution to plastic pots: hide them – with cache-pots, or with paint. Blue and green here give greater uniformity to the group than would a collection of cache-pots of the appropriate sizes and colours.

Paint it to make it stand out (fire-fighting apparatus), or for camouflage.

Strong paint colour must be used with conviction, sometimes a difficult decision. The Pompidou Centre in Paris throws discretion to the winds, displays all its service-carrying conduits on the exterior and boldly colour-codes them in primary colours. Conviction: a far cry from the inhibited 'picking out' in contrasting colours of the traditional radiator and single plumbing pipe. Unless it's justified by quantity, by some significance in the use of colours, or by something in the context, never use paint to make a 'feature'.

Solitary painted objects may stand out like a sore thumb. Use paint to introduce accent colour, but only when this relates to whatever else is around. Paint a chair yellow because there's plenty of yellow about, because you've painted all the other

Reaching for the rainbow at Alan Fletcher's dining table. Eclectic mealtimes can be fun (it's tragic to forgo the pleasures of company for a lack of matching sets); if classic consistency is out, go for as many different shapes and colours as possible. But maybe colour is superflous to a good set of bentwood chairs.

The sort of junk carvings they sell in airports and tourist traps is already a travesty and John Dickinson does no disservice in painting it white for consistency in his San Francisco apartment.

chairs yellow – or because you are painting them orange, red, purple, blue and green as well.

Paint changes more than the colour of an object. We have to decide whether this kind of cover-up is beneficial, or if in some way it devalues an object. Paint clay-coloured plastic plant pots (because they are nasty imitations of the original material) in other colours – but not earthenware ones. Paint cardboard boxes to harmonize with the room's colours – but not a good wooden tea-chest. Paint mass-produced, machine-smoothed, ready-varnished tourist fodder, but not original carved-wood sculptures. Paint shelves of chipboard or blockboard or whitewood – but think twice before hiding the fine grain of teak or mahogany.

When all is said and done, the solution may be not to paint it at all: but to strip it.

MATERIAL FACTORS

Take a long look at these photographs. Feel. Imagine the textures. Think what sensations they provoke. Some are hard, some soft. Some feel cold, others seem warm. Some repel, others invite. Some make patterns. You respond to some more than to others.

Look at your environment. What elements there resemble these pictures?

Look at other photographs in this book. Which ones appeal? Which would you feel comfortable with? Uncomfortable? Why?

As a professional decorator on a new commission I often open the wardrobe as if to assess the amount of space needed for storage. But more likely, I am seeking insights into the client's character: just as tastes in colour and pattern are indicated by clothes, so preferences in texture are expressed here: a predominance of wool and tweed, silk and lace, linen and twill, synthetics or naturals, rough or smooth.

The objects people collect sometimes offer these clues, too.

Loosely spun fibres look soft and warm; when tightly spun and woven they become harder.

Glass contrasts with most textures and stands out in almost any display because of its light-reflecting qualities.

Fur-backed textiles give luxurious softness.

Palm fronds have hard lines and texture, in contrast with most plants.

Two mosaics in contrast: the stonework façade is rough-textured and unsympathetic; the smoothness of wood is inviting.

Then there is the question of putting these textures together. Contrast or harmony? Wrong or right? Are there any rules?

It depends. Hand-thrown pottery would normally 'go' against coarse-weave fabric, wood with a pronounced grain; fine porcelain against fine linen, French-polished wood. To reverse either combination is not impossible – but needs conviction.

The flower arrangement in a galvanized bucket on an ormolu table needs to be good; the metal needs to have a gleam reminiscent of the table's gilt – and the room should have an element of eclecticism. It is difficult to get away with just one kitsch object in a pure classical environment.

When you choose harmony in materials: marble on marble, wood on wood, there has to be interest of shape, positioning, colour – and excellent lighting to bring out these subtleties. Objects that contrast must have something in common to relate them to each other or to the context: their purpose, shape, colour, or their source.

Cold and light-reflecting like the glass opposite, the raw minerals and shells are rough rather than smooth. You could add metal and even plastic 'eggs' to these objects if they were the right colour.

The classic modern texture of steel: these cogs make a pattern of dull sheen and shadow.

THE ROUGH WITH THE SMOOTH

Combine materials and textures in different ways – mixing like with like, or creating contrasts. Often you notice colour or shape first, textural subtleties later.

Responses to the pictures here will depend partly on tastes in colour and style, but one of the aspects that will emerge as you contemplate them is the textural quality of the objects. Which invite handling or stroking? On a wider scale, which materials would make your environment more comfortable and sympathetic?

Then examine how textures are used: whether they are put with things that harmonize or contrast, in period or style, as well as in shape and colour. Imagine alternatives to the objects in these rooms or arrangements: what could be substituted and not upset the harmonies? What new objects would create a completely different effect: sometimes it's the incongruous things that go together – an exotic table can make ordinary things look special, or special things can make a mundane piece of furniture out of the ordinary.

It helps to hold an arrangement together if objects are placed so that they balance and overlap. For this table-top group I chose objects which, because of their colour and shape, bridge the gap between the clean modern painting and the baroque gilt table. Trace the characteristics that link the elements: the colours in the marble, the curving encrustations of the shell and the table, and pure whiteness in different materials. The plant's grey colour, plastic-like leaves and curving shape make it right for inclusion in the group. Apart from this, all the textures are hard, cold, but not unsympathetic.

The colours and the strong horizontal lines of this restful room give it an Oriental simplicity. Immaculately smooth surfaces hold objects that are matt, incised or mosaic-textured. The mirror on the left of the fireplace wall contrasts strongly with the adjacent stone texture, thrown into relief by the recessed lights set close above it.

There is natural harmony in the elements here: the warm colour and texture of wood and stained basketware. The intricate pattern made by the Boston fern contrasts with the clean lines of the polished branch, but the weight of the plant balances the height of the wood.

Fine glass, in contrast with chunky wood, is cold and icy. Shapes and textures in the glass contrast: it is smooth, curved or faceted. Blue or white flowers would be more obvious in this context ('cold' colours) but the warm yellow makes a good contrast, and will harmonize when the candles are lit.

The smooth, hard surfaces of the uncompromisingly modern materials are softened only by the shaggy white rug and the upholstery and cushions; the plants are almost the only 'natural' objects. No room for nostalgia here. The disorientating effects are increased by the vast mirror on the left-hand wall, and by the mirror-lined cubes in which the kinetic light sculptures sit. Perhaps a room for modernists only.

ALL THAT GLITTERS

Glitter can mean Christmas-time fantasy, or it can signal ostentatious luxury – the crystal chandelier brigade. The mistake the conspicuously affluent often make is to think first about thick carpets, silk walls and curtains, and then add the chandelier and objects (often, too, calling them 'accessories'). One of my basic rules of interior design is that the environment should be the context for the things, and should be planned with them in mind. At best, room design should be done as an organic whole, so that objects and environment interrelate and enhance each other. In these three rooms, I aimed to use glitter subtly, boldly – and experimentally.

Too much glitter is overwhelming. The satin-and-mirror room (right) needed those two comforting kelims on the silver-foil floor to bring you down to earth.

I based this scheme on a beautiful tufted wall fabric by Jack Lenor Larsen. The French upholstery fabric is similar in colour but has a gold thread running through it. The gold theme is sustained in the lamé-lined display shelves, and makes a fitting background for an Indian chest of brass and wood, and the Art Deco clock and gilt bull figure.

The twin theme of one of Homeworks' most elaborate rooms is represented by the multi-faceted ceiling covered with panels of smoky mirror, and the thick sculptured carpet: hard, reflective surfaces teamed with luxurious softness. Between the two extremes, details in the creamy colours of the furnishings sustain the glittering element: the glass beading in the modern Italian furniture, the mother-of-pearl inlay in the lacquer cabinet, and the brass frames around fireplace and picture.

Satin patchwork covers the walls and is in 3-D on the ceiling. The angled walls are mirror, with squares of silvering etched away and fabric covered. Glass tables hold silvery objects.

LIGHT OF DAY

Daylight influences the way arrangements are planned in a room in three ways. Daylight usually comes into a room from the outside; we can filter it to reduce its intensity, and to lessen the contrast between the window and surrounding wall, but we can't position it at will as we can artificial light; even if we position objects in relation to daylight, in any room that is not north-facing, the colour of things alters in relation to the movement of the sun.

How to use daylight effectively? Choose window treatments that filter the daylight gently: lace, Venetian blinds, pinoleum, slatted bamboo. I feel you should not use curtains to hide from the outside world; where privacy is necessary, in the bathroom, for example, avoid the ubiquitous frosted glass. To retain privacy and get the benefit of the light, try plain white roller blinds: lowered, they give pure white light; when they are raised you get the view back.

Tricia Guild's bedside table contains a collection of objects lit by the cool, diffused natural light from the window on one side. Compare the night-time effects of top-lighting this group in the photograph overleaf.

Only when the sun's low rays accent things momentarily does natural lighting spotlight objects. In this photograph the low shaft of sunlight throws the fruit-bowl into sharp relief, like a sculptural mass.

Lace at the window diffuses the daylight gently. At night the contrast of a dark background against the white lace can show up the pattern even better.

SEE THE LIGHT

These lighting examples combine the two prime requisites for lighting: they are both functional and decorative. This is achieved by placing a decorative shade in a functional position.

Use accent lighting to display treasured things, but don't be afraid to use light itself as an object: a halo glow around an arrangement, or a pattern reflected on a wall. And enjoy the light fittings themselves. Ceiling ones can benefit by splendid isolation; others look good when they form a group, or when they are put together with other congenial things.

Purely decorative lighting makes good atmosphere for relaxing, and diffused background lighting, but usually needs to be supplemented with functional fittings for specific purposes. There can never be too many lighting variations and alternatives in a loved and comfortable home.

A parasol is being used for its intended purpose: to shield against the light and gently filter its rays. The diffused light bounced back off the light-coloured ceiling is sufficient to illuminate the hallway and stairs.

A happy marriage of shape and texture (scallop shapes, the texture of brass and of brittle white shell and bone) is pleasant when the light is off, but striking when it is turned on. Light bounced onto the wall bathes the group in a halo and prevents excessive glare on the top of the bell-jar dome covering the delicate shell.

Goose lights make interesting illumination, all the wittier for being at floor level, and in a gaggle. But most homes would need to find a solution to prevent the trailing cords from becoming trip-wires.

Tricia Guild often uses decorative lighting as an integral part of a group: in this case, three old gas-lamp shades converted for electricity are hung low at the end of brass chains in a way never possible in the days of gas. It is good to see items that are similar but not identical being used together. The weaker bulbs show off the glass shades and demonstrate that three 40-watt bulbs can have more impact than a single more powerful one.

When lit by lamps hung immediately above it, the table-top and the objects on it show up more distinctly than in daylight.

SHINE ON

Use a dimmer of appropriate wattage so that the intensity of the light can be varied to the occasion.

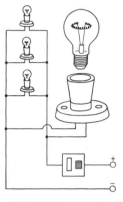

Don't try to make one light fitting perform all functions. I like best sharp accent types of lighting, but I also like variety. Work on the principle of five-way flexibility: movement in a vertical or a horizontal plane, swivelling for accurate change of direction, alteration of intensity by the use of dimmers – and alternative systems to turn on or off at will.

Build in enough control over lighting to create and maintain the atmosphere you want: from the sort of spotlighting used in exhibitions to late-night dimness. Make lighting work for you: just as you choose colours that flatter in decoration, make sure the colour of light is what is intended. I find that low-voltage tungsten halogen spotlights become less yellow when

'Hollywood' lights originated for making up for intense stage lighting, but at home the light should be flattering for painting on confidence. Back-up from overhead lighting is needed for doing your hair.

The light (and its shadows) makes a picture just as much as it illuminates the hallway. The variety of types of lighting define different planes and textures in a monochromatic colour scheme.

Glass shelves running through the alcoves and the chimney breast itself in a divided living room provide plenty of display space. The enlarged fireplace space has a concealed downlighter. The continuous lines of the shelves are good, but perfection would entail keeping a consistent strong line at the bottom, with the lowest shelves being at the same height all along.

dimmed than do regular tungsten, which means that subtle colour differences can be maintained.

One type of lighting I use a lot is the uplighter: a cylinder that sits on the floor and contains crown-silvered spotlights with integral reflectors. Used in corners or behind plants, uplighters throw interesting upward shadows. David Hicks has a masterly understanding of lighting. I particularly like the way he uses floor uplighters underneath plate glass tables.

You should never be bored with light. Give objects importance by spotlighting them. Distract attention from parts of the room that are not attractive by focusing light elsewhere. Fill empty space with interesting play of light and shadow. Create wall pattern with beams and shadows. Use angled lighting to emphasize texture in a rough wall or in textiles.

Plan flexible lighting so that at a flick of a switch the mood of a room can be totally transformed.

Adjustable angled lights are not used nearly enough at home. Clamped on, their bases take up no space; they can focus downwards for work or for eating, but optionally turn upwards for bounced lighting. They make the perfect wall-mounted bedside light, leaving the sides free for a chest or table.

Generally diffused light in the background comes from the kitchen area where the functional strip lighting is concealed by the pelmet effect of the partial room divider. It lights the cooker, sink and work surfaces without causing glare in the dining area.

CANDLEPOWER

Lining up before the party begins: a bank of candles, at the back of the table, are inviting but out of the way.

The candles almost match the lamps in luminosity, but there are enough flames to contribute a flickering glow to the cool, elegant atmosphere in this room.

Candlelight is living light, both decorative and functional – when candles are used *en masse*.

Candles in quantity, and at a distance, are magical compared with the uncompromising glare of the single statutory candle on the restaurant table, which is often too close for comfort and at the wrong height. (Move it aside to the edge of the table.) Distant candles give the reflected light that is flattering.

Arrange areas of candles: group them. Have matching ones together, or put short ones with tall ones. Replace each as it gets low at its own pace. Think of church prayer candles at different heights as they burn away, or of the menorah.

It needn't be exclusively candlepower. Combine candlelight with artificial light – used to accent features in the room. But keep this low: use dimmers or gentle wall wash. And be sure to let the candles predominate, or at least hold their own with the electricity.

Candlestick-makers' parade – like a line of musical notation. The line of light above the dark candles brings alive the slab of bare wall – necessarily bare since this quantity of candles could harm a painting or shelf above them.

At its brightest, candlelight still gives a yellowish cast to its surroundings. The warming process can be exaggerated by choosing yellow, orange and red candles together until there's a fire-like glow. Bearing in mind the ever-presence of yellow, choose candle colours like everything else: with the context of the room in mind. (In the same way, the scale and shape of the candles themselves can be as important as the colours.) But for me there's nothing to beat the waxy whiteness of the traditional candle.

And as the evidence on these pages shows, candlesticks are optional. It's a rare candlestick that is beautiful enough not to be eclipsed by the hypnotic effect of the burning candle flame.

Here Bruce Wolf has captured the mood I created by using candles in holders, by themselves, and also as part of the flower arrangement.

A pretty, traditional use of candles, but fireproof the tree.

TABLE TALK

It is good to keep to stark simplicity on a small round table where there is not much room for elaborate arrangements. The adjustable lamp can cast a pool of light at the desired intensity and height.

Eight sets of everything certainly proclaim that you had generous relatives and wedding guests – but lack of them should not rule out dinner for eight. And nowhere in the home is a better place to re-examine attitudes to enjoying things than the darker recesses of kitchen storage: place settings purchased two at a time until the pattern was discontinued; cutlery whose long-deceased colleagues died in the waste disposal; surviving crystal glasses from formerly full teams.

Take out all the survivors, dust them off – and enjoy. For if ever there is an opportunity to enjoy 'things' it is at mealtimes. If you like it, use it: most of the china we collect was meant to be used. Handling it (carefully) and seeing it in different lights and situations will renew acquaintance and affection more than keeping it respectfully on some high dresser shelf. Don't let a preoccupation with symmetry and uniformity inhibit your enjoyment: be eclectic in your table setting, and you need not turn away the extra guest.

The table setting I arranged (opposite) at my Ditchling house sums up my attitudes not only towards table settings themselves but also towards any display using a combination of unlikely things. An oak refectory table surrounded by odd pairs of chairs holds a bizarre collection: pewter and silver, traditional Limoges, 'thirties English china, Spanish pottery, French coffee cups, Art Deco jug, crystal glasses; there are Designers Guild napkins, but no tablecloth.

The table is not laid symmetrically: the candle and flower arrangements are not in the centre, and the places are laid towards one end of the long table. It is an asymmetric grouping within formal confines – and it is inviting.

I used plastic grapes and artificial flowers to take the solemnity out of a formal table setting in Homeworks' showroom. Fine porcelain and glass is unexpectedly backed by bare pine, instead of the cold white linen of custom.

Strong and unusual colours and shapes give this table setting a different look and, as in any display, the formal repetition of the groupings makes a pattern. It takes more than visual impact to make a meal a good experience, but an attractive table is a promising start.

FLOWER SHAPES

Roses, roses . . . for once artificial and alone. The bowl alongside contains shredded paper packing from chocolate boxes. The key to the grouping is in the pink.

Simple shapes, nothing contrived, for a simple context.

Nothing makes a room come alive like flowers. On a budget I would rather cut down on the cost of the background – the room's fabric and furniture – than miss out on regular supplies of fresh flowers.

Use artificial flowers, as long as they are well made. Flowers of finest silk are things of beauty and of joy – if not for ever, at least longer than the ones that grow in hothouses. Don't be afraid to mix real and artificial flowers together in an arrangement; treat the false ones like real ones. They should be beautiful enough to behave like the real thing.

I seldom make arrangements composed of artificial flowers on their own, except perhaps when the whole situation is contrived. And *never* use false greenery. Whether the flowers are real or artificial, always put them with real leaves. Use real leaves in fruit arrangements, too.

Greenery without any flowers at all is preferable to a miserable arrangement of poor imitations. Better to enjoy an empty vase than a bunch of leaves or flowers that aren't saying anything. An arrangement has to work all the way, whatever its ingredients.

Always arrange flowers to suit their position and the light in the room – as I have done in these arrangements.

Let flower shapes do what nature intended them to – but make an overall grouping that will please the eye.

Fill the dining-table when no one is coming to dinner. Do all-round arrangements in the round: make them look good from all angles. Don't aim for a regular, preconceived shape – this should evolve as the flowers build up. The lilies, tulips and greenery in this group grew – all the rest are man-made.

FLOWER GROUPS

Take a leaf from the florist to give an impression of abundance: separate bunches, each of a different kind of flower, are an alternative to making large mixed arrangements. But the vases need something in common.

An arrangement is more than just a bunch of flowers. Look outside the ingredients themselves and see the possibilities of arranging the arrangements. Try five different bowls containing bunches of the same flowers. Let the bowls make the group, not the flowers. Alternatively, take five matching bowls and fill each with a different sort of flower.

Flower arrangements have to work in context. Be sensitive to their environment, perhaps parodying a classical arrangement in a formal setting. Be casual or witty according to the flowers and the room, and make play with the pots and the objects round about, too. Some flowers or containers suggest a mood. Go along with this, take it all the way. But let the flowers play themselves.

I don't like flowers to do what nature didn't intend, but I often cut the stems really short to make a cushion shape with a mass of chrysanthemums, for instance: small flat containers or baskets packed with short-stemmed blooms become cushions of fresh flowers.

*Tricia Guild groups
small numbers of
flowers with the
immaculate
casualness that marks
all her arrangements.
Don't always make
one arrangement say
everything: let the
message sometimes
come over in a
chorus.*

*Springtime plants and
things in a kitchen
corner show Tricia at
her natural best.
When flower
arrangements are this
strong, put them in
place and bring
things to them to
make up the group –
not the other way
round.*

As the changing seasons bring new
varieties to arrange, so the whole mood of
a setting can alter. From the budding twigs
and graceful bulbs of spring through the
summer blooms of the herbaceous border
and the classic luxuriance of roses and
peonies, the shape and the character of the
arrangements in any one place must
change – demanding a reappraisal of the
group as a whole. And the objects that are
placed in relation to the flowers will need
to be chosen with their compatibility of
shape, material and colour in mind.

*Here I have filled six of the eight glass
jars with similar flowers to make an
arrangement of jars and flowers. The
empty jars add form; the lamp adds
balance.*

FLOWER-POT

When the pot has a lid, don't reject it: here I've used it as part of the arrangement.

Flowers growing in a garden aren't symmetrical and neat – so when you see them that way in traditional arrangements they look uncomfortable. Flowers shouldn't *seem* arranged – they need to obey the laws of nature by which they grew. I seldom use wire and never contort the stems with effort to make them into preconceived shapes.

Florists' contraptions – from chicken wire to the foam stuff they sell to keep the stems in place – are often limiting. The only constraint should be the character of the flowers themselves. If you need artifice to hold the flowers up in the pot you have chosen, either add more flowers or use a smaller pot.

The salvation here is greenery: use it to establish the basic shape and support before adding the flowers as accents.

Roots – in earth and in art. Bulbs are happy in containers without drainage.

Second-time-around pots, this time for flowers.

Playing with whites and with rising, swirling lines in a tall, narrow frame.

Blooms pay their respects to their container in a nostalgic arrangement – flowers in context.

CUT AND DRIED

Daisy impact is doubled when fresh ones are in bloom: in winter, it's just a pretty picture.

This crowded window gives an impression of garden profusion. But quantity is not essential: a single arrangement can be striking if it's the right one.

This heaped-up arrangement of wreaths, cushions and sprays has been carefully compiled. Nevertheless it's reminiscent of country hedgerows in shape and content.

Flowers don't have to be living to be enjoyed. Dried flowers are natural and look best in arrangements echoing nature, like all blooms; but they're also often seen in tight knots hung up to dry, so that this, too, seems an appropriate way to display them.

While fresh flowers speak primarily of colour, dried ones suggest shape. Use compact cushions of flower heads, spiky clusters of seedheads, twisting garlands and wreaths – on shelves and surfaces, or hanging.

Dried flowers defy the seasons but don't defy dust, and should not be in one place for too long. Before they get too tired-looking shake them out (at the risk of scattering seeds) and rearrange them.

Preserving the taste of summer. The group is pleasing to look at in the window, but direct sunlight will harm oil and vinegar, and damage the flavour of dried herbs. They need to be kept cool.

CONSUMING INTEREST

*Tropical harvest suggests plenty –
almost excess. But the effect of this
monumental group could be echoed on a
smaller scale, and with vegetables
instead of fruit.*

The bowl of fruit is almost one of those
arrangement clichés rivalling the three
flying ducks on the parlour wall. But like all
clichés, it is based on sound good sense:
fruit is beautiful. Rather like plants and
flowers, fruit does something positive towards making an empty room seem less
inanimate.

How to get away from the clichés? In a too
small, or too carefully contrived, arrangement of fruit, the temptation to take the
apple will precipitate the fall of the whole.
Fruit-bowls must be large enough, relaxed
enough, for some of the contents to be
removed without spoiling the effect.

I take the greengrocer's trick and always
buff up the fruit to a glossy shine so that it
looks its best however much is there.

Cheat: use window-display fake fruit to
bulk out the bottom of the bowl, where real
fruit usually goes bad. At the risk of disap-
pointing the greedy, mix it in with the real
thing just as with flower arrangements. It is
a tongue-in-cheek solution for the people
who say 'but I can't afford *that* much fruit.'
Remember old-time Harvest Festivals,
Thanksgiving, greengrocers' shops and
market stalls. Think big and bountiful.

And for fruit, read vegetables throughout. Between bringing them home from
market and preparing them to eat, let the
vegetables sit where you can see them,
and enjoy their shapes and colours.

*Fruit, like plants,
brings life into a
room. The yellows in
this fruit-bowl
naturally sustain the
room's colour theme.*

*Here I have used
three red apples, five
green ones, one
orange, five
tangerines – and
blooming peaches
that are fakes. I add
leaves as a rich,
natural background,
and flower heads for
the occasion.*

A bouquet of cabbages can have as much colour subtlety and give the same visual pleasure as the more conventional roses – though without the scent.

Arrange vegetables as you would flowers: pack them tightly together, but let their shapes form their own patterns. These look neither arranged, nor static. I have used a rich mixture here, with lots of complementary reds and greens, but a much smaller number can still be effective.

ROBIN'S ROOM

The grandfather clock looked heavy until it was balanced by the dark Elizabethan portraits. You can use much larger pictures than you might think. Although these are heavy, they don't dominate; they hang low, relating to the sofa rather than hanging in isolation.

Instead of placing the kelim in its 'usual' position underneath the coffee table, I placed it beneath the large table which defines the working area.

In one of my favourite areas in Homeworks I always try and assemble mixtures of antique and modern objects. The scheme is based on contrasting textures of creamy beige carpet, soft glove-leather upholstery from Saporiti, and parchment-type wallpaper buffed to a soft sheen with wax.

The old and new objects play variations on colour and texture themes: the ivory-white handles of the magnifying glasses and the simulated ivory-lacquer surface of the tables; the rich red background colour of the kelim; the lacquer-red tray.

Taken separately, the items might seem to make an incongruous collection, but each has some aspect that justifies its inclusion. In fact, this room exemplifies a successful combination of old and new from east and west.

Arrangements need to look good from different heights and angles. At a distance, things should make a pattern; they can be appreciated individually when you get close to them. Choose things that look good in the round when displaying them on a coffee table or in the centre of a room.

DOVE GREY

It takes strong tones, textural excitement, and a good lighting script to keep an all-grey room from looking monotonous. There are strong shapes in the structure and in the furniture, lighter grey accents – and a giant plant to bring life into the room when no one's there.

The arrangements on these shelves deliberately make a grid. The obvious horizontal lines are opposed by vertical groupings of objects – as if there were four invisible uprights.

Alan Dempsey's dove picture is the Homeworks logo, and the sculpture is Tricia Guild's Christmas present. Once the grey room was established, friends gave objects to go in it – like Harold Wood's portrait in the bottom picture.

Why is my office grey?

When so much of my working time is spent in places festooned with colour swatches and pattern samples, it's a relief to have a retreat where I don't have to be constantly 'thinking colour'. This room is functional above all else – I decided there should be nothing in it that I'm not currently working on. Its absence of colour makes it functional for me – its peaceful calm is the perfect place for making a seasoned judgement on individual colour samples.

Grey can be very cold, though: it needs to be leavened by texture. Matt emulsion on the walls of my room would prevent its being alive, so I've chosen a very glossy paint finish. It and the other shiny objects make the most of the play of the afternoon sunlight from the windows – and the constantly changing patterns being made by shadows from the Venetian slatted blinds.

Tones of grey vary considerably and in the same medium it's very difficult to get the 'right' combination of different ones. The varying greys of the carpet, walls, suede upholstery and stained wood would jar if they weren't saved by textural contrast – and if they each weren't present in such large quantities.

Grey seems a functional choice: as a good neutral, it is often the background used by exhibition designers as unobtrusive – but an art collector would be unlikely to choose it as the most favourable colour for a permanent collection. Although grey often works very well with brown, it can be a difficult colour to put together with natural objects, or with the sorts of thing that most people have in their homes: old china collections, carvings, textiles, bits and pieces. Grey doesn't provide a sympathetic environment to hold different things together: it merely tolerates them.

ON THE MANTELPIECE

Tricia Guild brings alive her mantelpiece with plants and plant forms. The off-centre picture creates interest. Movement is intrinsic in the grain of this marble – not added in the carving.

The arrangement I like best defies the strong symmetry of the central mirror and ornate fireplace, but the two separate groups balance.

Try, try, try again. Build up arrangements of objects like flower arranging or painting. It is not an instantaneous process like a photograph – it is done by trial and error. There are no rules about working from one end to the other, from the outsides towards the centre, or *vice versa*. It can be different each time: work in your own way, and time, with whatever materials you have.

Experiment with objects, shapes, groupings. Add things. Take them away. Move them around. To the litany of the colour/texture/harmony creed, add your own vision. The secret ingredient in an arrangement that works could be harmony of ingredients, rhythm in the placing of them, overall shape – or it could be surprise. Be traditional, experimental, shocking – but be convinced.

Spacing is crucial: too much, and a group separates into fragments; too little and it is overcrowded. The eye needs some guidance as to what you mean to be seen as a group of objects, and what is its counterweight. You need to 'read' an arrangement

The three alternative arrangements I made also 'work', but that's all. The candelabra are 'officially' compatible in style, but look both stark and predictable.

The coffee pots have scale, shape and colour in their favour, and on a white painted mantelpiece would be strong, but they feel too light for this marble.

Marble on marble – a harmonious combination of objects and environment – is somewhat predictable, but play with shape, repetition and grouping. It becomes all the more important to make interesting patterns in the positioning. Pairs don't have to be symmetrically separate.

on a mantelpiece: compare the pauses and the emphasis in a spoken sentence.

Show some respect towards the context of your arrangement. Not that a Victorian whatnot must have Victorian objects on it. But strong shapes like marble mantelpieces need strong objects.

PLANT LIFE

Everything informal and natural, if not actually growing: wood, bamboo, basketry, with pinoleum blinds and daylight as the natural backdrop. Even the subtle cotton 'log cabin' patchwork on the table sustains the theme. For all the casualness of the arrangement, there is good contrast in the plants' scale.

The plant chosen to dominate this Paris studio is as simple and monumental as a pillar. Its clean lines suit the stark, uncluttered elegance of the rest of the room. Anyone with the ceiling height should take advantage of the scope it offers for plant drama.

A room takes on life when its contents are introduced – arranged to answer the requirements of day-to-day living. The finishing touch to most rooms is the addition of living things: flowers and plants. Although these are often left to the end of the arranging process, their position should be planned from the outset, but with a degree of flexibility. Plants can dot i's and cross t's: ferns and palms in a cane-furnished Somerset Maugham set; an aspidistra to confirm that this is an Edwardian *jardinière*; an array of geraniums to make a mellow kitchen cottage.

Some plants need to be placed where they will not be disturbed, and others have specific requirements for light and warmth. Besides, an old favourite plant or a large, beautiful specimen will need to command a space of its own, like a treasured piece of furniture or a good painting. Otherwise, make groups combining plants, pictures and other objects. When changing the plants' position for light, for example, take the opportunity to alter the whole display.

Leaf through this book and look at photographs of rooms containing plants. Try masking out the plants, and see how rooms are deprived of a living element.

While I often use false flowers with real ones, I never use false plants.

Tricia Guild's bay window was deliberately left free for plants, but the actual arrangement of them was the last thing to be done within the room, and this arrangement is flexible enough to be a constant source of interesting change. Here she achieves height with a tall Ficus, and by using a jardinière. Tricia's love of flower and plant forms is established in the upholstery fabric and in the window blinds and curtains.

A QUESTION

Symmetry can mean stability and repose. The two sides of the human figure balance, so we have come to take bilateral symmetry for granted, in clothes, in furniture, in classical architecture – and in arrangement. Because it seems obvious design periodically veers away from equal visual balance in search of the dynamism and shock tactics of the asymmetrical and un-expected; at home we can sometimes take advantage of the loosening of these formal constraints: we can go on making arrangements even when one of a pair is broken.

Balance of shape. The one instance when nature comes nearest to mass-production, in shape if not in markings. A dome increases the importance of a beautiful but simple object like an egg. Repetition reinforces the message.

Nature declines to duplicate: flowers and shells are of a pattern but not from a mould. Hence the excitement of balancing natural objects. Flowers will always go their own way and refuse to be shaped into submission in any arrangement, let alone a matching pair.

Symmetry must be strong. When one half of a composition is the mirror-image of the other, the sum of the parts needs to be something special. You can't get away with an inadequate arrangement simply by duplicating it. If aiming for symmetry, do it really well. Don't reject perfectly balanced arrangements because symmetry seems unfashionable and predictable. Make symmetry exciting, dramatic; dignify it. Find its strength: use half of the elements to make one good grouping – and then redouble its impact by making another.

Balance in even numbers. Two is a pair, two heads are better than one, two fine chryselephantine sculptures are twice as good. But when you have a pair, don't separate them so widely that they lose touch with each other.

What has been sought here is not precise geometrical identity but an impression of balanced weight and mass. The central fruit-bowl is symmetrical in shape but not arrangement. The shoes are dramatic shapes bridging the gap between flowers and fruit.

OFF-CENTRE

Arrangements by David Hicks always have a deliberate, considered air. There is plenty of space and the positioning of objects in relation to each other is important. The combination of shapes is interesting, and has an element of the unpredictable. Imagine removing any item: the balance would be upset, and some things would have to be moved around to compensate.

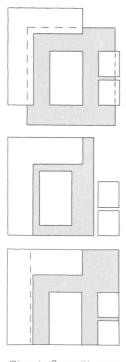

Giorgio Saporiti uses the rug to cut through the line of the chairs and sofa and thus hold the different elements together. Arrangements where the rug simply follows the shape of the furniture are far less interesting.

Within an asymmetrical grouping, individual components can be symmetrical. In Tricia Guild's mantelpiece arrangement, two candlesticks are symmetrical in relation to one of the two mirrors, and a pot is centred on the other. Although essentially four small balanced groups add up to one main asymmetric group, Tricia arranges quickly and instinctively and would not have paused to divide the arrangement into four parts deliberately.

In my view, asymmetrical arrangements are the hardest to make work really well. In room settings, Giorgio Saporiti of Milan is the master: his schemes take both the human factor and the space available into full consideration, producing an effect that is always original and never uncomfortable. The master of the still life is David Hicks, who arranges objects with consummate skill, making seemingly incongruous combinations work well together and using spacing beautifully.

There is no 'right' answer. Give six people the same ingredients and they will come up with six quite different groupings. What these would all have in common, if they were pleasing, is balance.

Balance is a matter of recognition: you know when you have achieved it. Literally, it is a question of equal weight; visually it is one of equivalent value. A mass of flowers has less 'weight' than a pottery vase of the same dimensions.

Adjust balance with space: two light objects close together to balance a single heavier one. Assess spacing constantly: leave too much between objects and they sprawl, so that table-top arrangements look like a jumble sale; too little space, and a group becomes a confused heap. Some objects need to overlap to show their relationship, others to be spaced out. Depth and height in objects gives the group dimension.

SAFETY IN NUMBERS

One thing requires careful positioning; a number of things must be arranged. Quantity is not always desirable, but there are cases where it works.

Quantity can elevate insignificant objects into a display. Objects enrich each other: they don't have to be identical – in fact the group may be more interesting if things are similar rather than exact replicas.

Objects in mass make pattern. Identical things placed regularly make all-over pattern: impressive, like the windows in the World Trade Center, but in danger of

Number benefits second-time-around gas lampshades in both function and appearance. One alone would not only be lost, but would not give sufficient light.

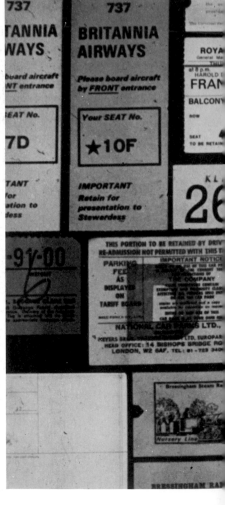

becoming repetitive like wallpaper.

When objects are similar but differing in shape and size, they need arranging. Should all tops or bottoms be lined up? Should they be centred? Should they look as if scattered at random? There are no rules: these pictures show some ways.

How to make the truly ephemeral into a display: make a mosaic. The close-fitting rectangles (right) have unity of shape and material, subtle variety in colour – and sufficiently intriguing printed content to sustain interest when examined closely.

A few objects that are similar but not identical need to be arranged to look interesting. Good shapes make a graphic display on a white wall. They either form a group of their own or fill out a space with overall pattern.

Three flying ducks are a cliché; fill up the wall with them.

ECHOES

Echoes of colour and shape bridge the cultural gap between the chinoiserie table and the abstract impressionism of the painting. Surface decoration on the Gallé glass links the group with the decorated table. And both the elements in the painting and the glass objects on the table-top are arranged in a correspondingly 'random' relationship to one another.

Echoes of a flower theme tie the different ingredients together.

Still-life arrangements are at their best when they have more to them than meets the eye. The richest arrangements don't simply make formal patterns, however perfect, but reverberate, echo and tease.

Arrangement means, literally, to 'put into a proper order, a correct or suitable sequence, relationship or adjustment.' With objects it is entirely subjective: you choose the things, and decide where to place them.

Choice is fundamental: objects that have nothing in common to relate them to each other, however admirably they are positioned, are not an arrangement: they are chaotic. Objects that are *too* uniform, on the other hand, are in danger of becoming documentary, like a museum showcase.

Formal arrangements make patterns with shape, colour and texture: the five on these pages contain an added ingredient that is almost intellectual or literary rather than purely visual. They relate form in two-D paintings to the form of the objects arranged in three dimensions, or the subjects of the paintings to the objects near by. They find relationships of time or period, not just form. They take an aspect of an

*Echoes of a classical theme. It is a cliché
to position a table against a wall: here it
is moved out strategically to give
importance to the objects on it, and not
to detract from the painting. This is
balanced by the terracotta pots in the
space below.*

Echoes of ancient Rome – and of shape.

object, like surface decoration, that is
almost incidental, and give it emphasis by
putting it into a context where this will be
amplified and enriched. But at the same
time they are not as explicit or literal as the
'Double Take' examples.

There is no prescription for the arrangements on these pages: they felt right to the
people who made them. Their success is
dependent equally on the individual's
vision and on the choice of materials
available.

*Echoes of form,
texture, source and
material. The
arrangement contains
themes of glass, of
scale patterns, of
flowers, of
chinoiserie, of shape,
of shine – and the
painting summarizes
the colours and
ingredients of the
group.*

CRYSTAL CONES

Once there was a set of crystal cones in an Art Deco chandelier: now there are seven cones and no chandelier. Few modern houses could accommodate the original in true Busby Berkeley style, but the cones find a decorative place in all sorts of situations.

The message here is to look in your attic, cellar or shed. Don't reject things that are

Seven identical cones regularly spaced in a straight line would make a powerful but monotonous statement. On a window sill changing light might impart interest, but the overall shape is unsubtle.

Seven calls for asymmetrical arrangement. Overlap cones in a casual grouping. Group three and four, two and five, with space between. Add a flower arrangement (incorporating frosted glass, or a relevant colour), or make a dramatic contrast of shape and pattern.

Cones recede into infinity, multiplied by mirrors. Frosted glass contrasts with the clarity of the mirror, and the arrangement changes excitingly as it is seen from different angles.

incomplete or broken; if they are beautiful in themselves, use them in display – and to their intrinsic qualities you add the element of the original and unexpected. In a very different setting, the crystal cones can still reflect and filter light – and be enjoyed.

It does not need to be crystal cones: arrange candlesticks, vases, even interesting bottles for the same kind of effect.

The cones in my office: monolithic shapes against the Venetian blinds, where they take full advantage of the changing daylight.

DOUBLE TAKE

It is a question of using the right ingredients: a geranium would be far less effective than the suitably exotic Codiaeum *used in the pot opposite.*

First came the chair, which the artist incorporated into the picture; later the painting was hung in a Homeworks room, and the matching chair – and some flowers – had to be found to make the statement.

When arrangements are done in such a way as to mix real objects with representations of them, you go beyond living with things into the realms of pure display.

The people who created these rooms or displays were visually aware enough to see the exciting relationship between 3-D objects and representations of them in pictures. It takes boldness to carry the idea through, and humour to make the message strong but not overwhelming: an absolutely perfect double take would impress initially but quickly become boring.

Look for different situations where you can exercise dour humour. See the possibility of making an allusion to something external in an everyday object – for example using the colour of a carpet or ceiling to suggest green grass or a clear blue sky.

Copy (or paraphrase) an object in art: paint a representation of it on the wall. With photographic realism this is *trompe l'oeil*; a more impressionistic effect can act like a

A grass-green carpet invites a golf theme (or tennis, croquet or bowls). The visual pun plays a small, witty part, without dominating the room. Colour and shape work beautifully in the stylized natural objects (imagine the table painted an unrelated colour, or a picture in a radically different style). But then the giant red strawberry introduces an improbable colour contrast into the harmony: if it is taken away does the room lose or gain?

shadow-image. Or start with the painting and recreate it, particularly with still-life and floral subjects. Success here demands a combination of accuracy (the identical chair for the painting below left, for example), and freedom so that it is not all done for you.

The Ficus benjamina *stencilled on the wall echoes the original, giving it a context as well as a shadow.*

A pretty, but not over-literal, reminder of a picture. Here is one instance where artifice would be justified to hold the flowers in the position that would make them imitate the portrait exactly.

SHOWCASE

Proprietary clips and angles of plastic or metal mean that cubes and shelves can be assembled from glass or acrylic – and altered easily.

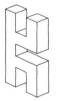

Cut dado grooves into sheet acrylic squares or rectangles to use as connectors for lightweight cubes and shelves.

Interlocking shelves make cubes within cubes; the slightly smoky colour of the acrylic adds to the air of inscrutability of these objects.

Tailor-made cubes (like little blocks of ice) give a selection of gnomes more dignity than they would find in most gardens. Each has its own minute 'lawn' of artificial grass.

An 'invisible' shelf made up from leftovers of thick acrylic sheet makes a subtle contrast of shape against the panelling and the mouldings of the unused door. The ornaments suit the shelves: the ceramics like frozen plant forms sustain the cool feeling of the shelving material.

A museum puts an object into a glass case to protect it from dust and interfering fingers. When the same thing is done at home, it is a signal that the object is to be accorded special attention: it is a sign of pure display. The object need not be especially valuable or delicate, but just important to its owner. The display case means that it is not to be taken for granted. It invites a closer look, maybe a detailed examination – a response of some sort from the casual observer.

I set this old carpenter's table and tools in a vast case because it seemed almost a sculptural still-life – an 'art object'. The sun's low rays illuminate the scarred table-top and the curly wood shavings, and the tool shapes throw dark shadows.

UNDER GLASS

The thimble, buttons and cowrie shells give away the minute scale of these antique domes.

In the arrangement I did (below) at Homeworks, the two domes on the left contain plastic fruit and flowers; the others, genuine old sweets. I used glass jars on a glass shelf, and candy stripes with the candy colours, to tie the ingredients together. This is a conscious arrangement; the jars are in carefully positioned pairs, a bowl of real sweets stands ready for the tasting, and a Warhol print balances the objects.

Ordinary things are dignified by domes of glass, which also keep them dust-free. Like sweet-jars, the domes look best when filled right up with trivia like shells or witch-balls. But they maintain an old-world dignity when used as traditional cover-ups for garlands and figurines.

When searching, go to antique dealers and junk stores, kitchen departments for spaghetti jars and also to the makers of laboratory equipment. (The thick, slightly distorting glass of bell-jars makes them attractive in a different way.) The Victorian domes have handsome bases: when using modern bell-jars, add wooden or marble bases possibly cheese- or bread-boards for the finishing touch.

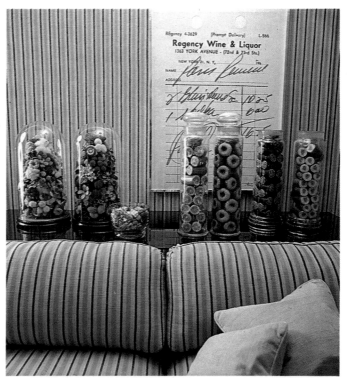

A glass cover decorated with flowers makes even wrapped-up cheeses look as interesting as a display. At other times it could cover a low posy of flowers or magnify something trivial.

These items are not arranged, but hold together because of their nostalgic associations and their flower and colour theme, which has a period flavour.

PRIVATE VIEW

Isolated objects command attention (and so does a group put together as a unit). Making objects look important is a matter of composing space, height and lighting.

Surrounding space shows that an object is valued and enables it to be viewed from all angles. Irrelevant things should not be allowed to intrude on the space.

Some things stand out – if other things keep a low profile. Putting a three-D object on a plinth adds height physically and, more subtly, adds status.

Lighting must be good enough to show off the piece, especially with dark materials like bronzes. A light background shows profile, and may help with reflected light, but too great a contrast dazzles. Specific lighting not only illuminates – it calls attention to an object.

Use these techniques to show off, and to show your enjoyment of, simple things: a doll, a bunch of flowers, a piece of driftwood, or even a pebble.

The brick floor and the plant-filled courtyard of the top photograph are the background to part of a collection of African and Oriental art. Seating areas for relaxing in, and the whole paraphernalia of the home, are kept quite separate, so that the objects and the architecture have nothing to detract from their clean lines.

Plinths, glass cases, framed displays and, in particular, the ceiling lighting, give the study in the lower photograph the calm atmosphere of a museum gallery.

Space is found
vertically to display a
collection of statues
and figurines; clear
acrylic shelves keep
the display
lightweight, but
accord full
importance to the
figures – as well as
enabling them to be
seen clearly.

Paintings, pottery and
sculpture are fully
integrated into a
sitting room, but are
given importance by
the low levels of the
seating and 'living'
impedimenta.

REFLECTIONS

Use mirrors to give an illusion of extra space and to make visible the side of an object that is turned away from you. But mirrors confuse: they make surfaces look as though there is nothing there.

Two mirrors are better than one. Conventionally, a mirror covers the back wall of an elevator. To give the illusion of increased space mirrors on the two side walls would be more efficient: it is when mirror reflects mirror that space really begins to seem infinite.

Because mirrors are light-reflecting, they also seem lightweight. Plinths and tables of mirror seem insubstantial; make a virtue of this confusing property to show off fine objects like plants and flowers, making them seem more numerous than they really are. (But do arrangements in the round when they are to be reflected and the back needs to look as good as the front.)

As long as confusion is fairly explicit, I think it works; for instance when a mirror is many-faceted, you make allowances for distortions of perception. When mirror is plain and functional, it is another story. Sometimes, when a wall pretends to be a mirror it is downright dangerous: you can walk into it. At other times it can be uncomfortable. I seldom, for example, perform the optical illusion of filling an entire wall with mirror: it is hard to imagine relaxing facing a full-size reflection.

The fireplace is a focal point for relaxation: you want to stare at burning logs, not at yourself. Although this mirrored chimney breast gives the mantelpiece an interesting freestanding quality, it is not something I would recommend. But the room is rich in textural contrasts, and the chrome shelves harmonize with the mirror.

Homeworks' mirrored room literally reflects the room's furnishings; decorative detail like the gilt tramlines picks up curves and borders in the room's furnishings. The different levels of Philip Geraghty's design break up what would otherwise be a straightforward reflection. Handle mirrored ceilings in this way: make them interesting as well as reflecting.

The mirror-based coffee table (this has a smoked glass top) is a marvellous background for these Art Deco dancers. Mirror comes into its own with sculpture: showing more different angles than you can normally see. A combination of mirror and glass is exciting.

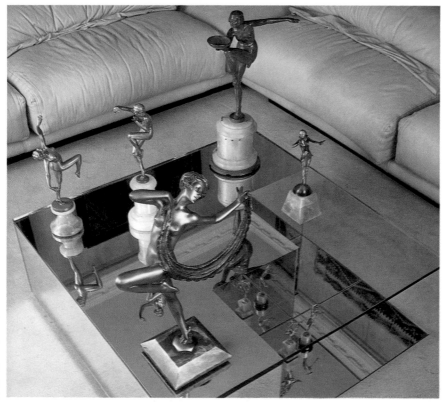

HANG IT

The walls represent overwhelmingly the largest
proportion of surface space in each room, yet as a
display area their function has been extremely
limited. Walls were for pictures – perhaps Great-
Uncle's shotgun and a stuffed fish – and that was that.

But now we've broadened our definition of the
things that merit display. Hang decorative things,
certainly, but also hang useful things as long as they
look good and make interesting shapes.

The kitchen is an area where this makes special
sense. Try continuing the theme into the bedroom:
hang out your clothes so that you can see them and
enjoy them. In the playroom, hang up toys rather
than pile them all into a box.

And when you do hang it, hang it where you can
see it. That means never higher than eye level, and,
if it's a room where you spend time sitting or lying
down, that means letting it hang low.

USE YOUR WALLS

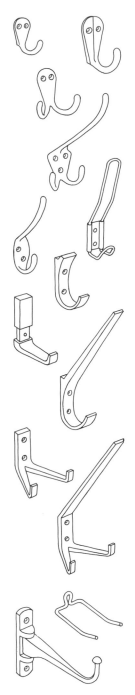

Hang it – on the wall. Because it's visible. Because it's decorative. Because you need it often. Because it's for sale.

With walls of raw wood, use nails. Pin it up, hang it, anywhere on the wall you fancy. There's scope for changing minds, and changing displays.

In most homes, the walls demand gentler treatment. Drilling holes takes effort; plaster wounds gape as reminders of mistakes. Solution: fix softwood studs at intervals floor-to-ceiling, and nail planking to them. Choose the texture that suits the environment: smooth and varnished or planed but unfinished. The horizontal lines between the boards create a pattern like a musical stave on which to compose an arrangement of nail-hung objects.

Or compromise: mount onto the wall,

with relatively few fixings, a panel into which you can bang nails, screw hooks or stick tacks and pins. It can be fibreboard to use as pinboard, or perforated pegboard. It can be good-looking hardwood to take a row of hangers. Using a panel of any sort as an intermediary cuts down the work and gives more flexibility.

In a wall any substantial hanging needs, say, two drilled holes per hook, and then plugging or anchoring, depending on the type of wall. Six hooks mean twelve holes. You could mount all these on a single batten or board with regular screws – and secure this to the wall with only four of the appropriate fixings.

For the more energetic, and particularly where there are children, pattern and play-space could be made by erecting gymnasium rails all along the wall. Things can hang on these rails when they are not being climbed.

Chairs for sale: but the Shakers hung up chairs that were not being used, and anyone can do the same at home, especially with spare folding dining chairs.

Coat-hooks are not just for coats. Hang umbrellas, ladders, chairs, canes, pots, tools, bags, bicycles.

Going all the way, with gym bars instead of boards: exercise the principle of hanging 'on the rails'.

The farmhouse above inspired me to cover one Homeworks wall with white-painted rough wood. Wood-stain streaking detracts from the black gaps between the boards. I arranged objects from right to left, enjoying the freedom of banging in nails anywhere. While this is a show-room wall where everything is for sale apart from my raincoat and my daughter Lisa's painting (left), exciting arrangements could be done at home.

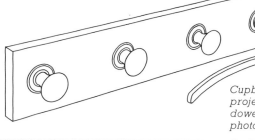

Cupboard doorknobs project less than the dowelling pegs in the photograph.

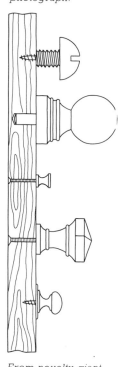

From novelty giant screws, newel-post knobs to a range of cupboard and door handles, the hanging potential is as wide as the imagination can stretch.

TRAVELLING LIGHT

The only time when pendent lights are justified is when they're flexible. The traditional light hanging limply from the centre of a ceiling casts only gloom and should be eradicated, replaced or adapted.

Three aspects of the flexibility essential to good lighting are important in the place where you eat, whether it's a fixed-purpose dining room, part of the kitchen, or a room for all seasons. Vertical adjustment: it's useful to push the pendant up out of the way out of mealtimes or so that candles can replace it. It's even more important to be able to adapt the height of the lamp to the comfort of guests of different stature, though this is often a question of taste.

Horizontal adjustment: you may use different parts of the room at different times. A long cord with a loop, hooks at appropriate places in the ceiling, and a certain amount of climbing on chairs is one way of achieving this flexibility. A track-lighting variation provides a single-axis movement that is easier to manage.

Intensity adjustment: it's nice to be able to dim the light right down for the mellow stage at the end of the meal.

Pulley lights, often in brass or porcelain, are attractive period pieces, but need back-up from functional lighting for work areas. Recessed eyeball fittings in the ceiling are neat enough not to obtrude.

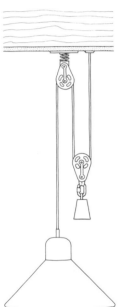

For a home-made pulley light, use blocks from a ship's chandler and choose a medium-weight shade of aluminium, enamel or acrylic.

Counterbalance with an equal weight: literally, from an old set of scales, or use an attractive pebble. Attach securely with a screw-threaded chain connector link.

Modern adjustable pendants with curly cable and rise-and-fall units rise neatly to any occasion.

Coloured glass shades are good for dining areas: they give a less concentrated downward light than an opaque reflecting shade, but also diffuse soft light more generally.

Fix curtain fittings to the ceiling for two-way movement of a pendant from a central ceiling plate.

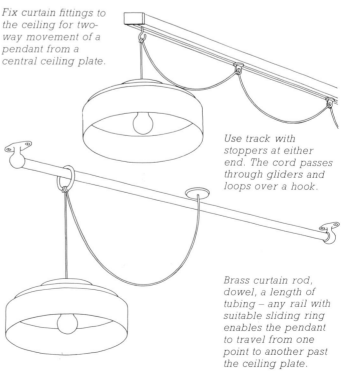

Use track with stoppers at either end. The cord passes through gliders and loops over a hook.

Brass curtain rod, dowel, a length of tubing – any rail with suitable sliding ring enables the pendant to travel from one point to another past the ceiling plate.

BEADS AND BAUBLES

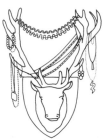

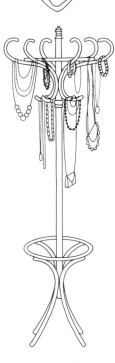

Use baubles, bangles and bright shiny beads to adorn your environment as well as yourself. The same goes for artificial flowers, little purses, amulets, belts and other bits and pieces. It's good to have them visible when choosing what to wear, as well as to enjoy their shape and sparkle.

There are two ways of going about it: the *objet trouvé*, and the purpose-built. When you hung your satchel on the newel post at home on arrival from school you may have been starting the lifelong habit of the hanging opportunist. Pieces of furniture are meant to stand on their own: hanging impedimenta is incidental, like creeper on a tree. People who like clean lines eradicate parasitical growth; those who go in for decoration encourage it – but train the creeper to go where it is wanted, and not to smother the parent plant.

The alternative is to contrive a shape to hang the jewellery: it could be a series of hooks, or an anthropomorphic shape like a shop-counter or window-display dummy. This will make a stronger statement, and need its adornment of baubles and beads.

Hang necklaces and things on furniture with knobs on, or on objets trouvés: a gnarled branch of driftwood, a set of antlers, or hands from a shop-display dummy.

Tricia Guild's bedposts (above) wear embroidered pouches, hats, and the chunkier bead necklaces – nothing too fine on this substantial base. The bamboo shelves in the same room (right) are only partly being used for their conventional purpose; they are also festooned with finer necklaces and with silk flowers.

A fringe of necklaces clasped or looped around the fretwork gives this ornate Liberty screen a useful role.

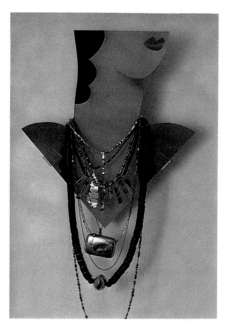

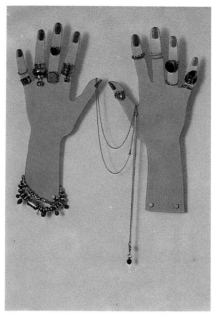

Head and hands are cut out of acrylic plastic, and painted. Attached to the wall at the base, they become slightly three-dimensional when wearing their jewels. Imitations are simple to make out of stiff card, plastic, plywood or découpage.

HANG TOGETHER

How would you arrange this? It has contrived a balance (if you took away any element it would fall apart), but the white background and the lack of context is an invitation to try out other shapes and groupings.

The principle of protective plating: to cover up and shield from sight. Also the display of a collection on the lines of the more the merrier. When you can't attain overall uniformity with matching sets, the more variety the better: even the oddments find a place here.

Someone had the eye to match up an existing space with a collection of keys to make a repeating pattern with a suggestion of perspective.

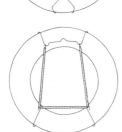

Sprung plate hangers come in different sizes and shapes, but can be made up to suit odd shapes with bought springs and stiff wire.

Up in the air is the logical place for kites and model aircraft, even in storage. Their lightness defies their size so that they don't seem to clutter the space excessively. Use easily detachable hooks of light wire and loops of nylon fishing twine if they're working models.

A pair of nails serves a dual purpose: Calman uses them to hang a drawing.

What's the plot? In the case of these hangings, it's not a question of whodunnit, but what was the motive? Or *was* there one?

Making a pattern. When you have a collection of similar objects, make use of the repetition of shapes, especially when there's an appropriate space to take them. With a relatively small number, concentrate them. Define an area with them or use some ready-made frame.

Making a picture. Faced with the temptation of the virgin wall, be bold. In the absence of a frame to hold them together, things must declare themselves an independent group – be tightly packed, and balanced by surrounding space.

Three-D wallpaper. Friends of mine covered their walls with objects, because they weren't happy with the appearance of the walls. When they had decorated they appreciated the wall colour so much that they couldn't bear to deface it, and were left with boxfuls of things with nowhere to go. Think: do you really need to hang anything? What's wrong with bare walls?

Filling a space. Don't do this halfheartedly: the lack of an overall plan of campaign will show in the bitty result. If empty space is offensive, perhaps it needs painting or lighting – rather than covering up.

An informal combination of conventional and unusual hanging material creeps upwards like a hedge. But its base line is firmly established on the pair of shelves that run the length of the room: ragged growth at top and bottom of the group would be too confusing.

IN THE PICTURE

A block of six pictures form into one. Portraits are best looking towards each other, or into the centre of the group. Similarity of colours, subject and style, and frames that don't distract, marry these together.

Safety in numbers – and a strong reference to the structural elements in the room as a whole. Photographs – even full-page enlargements – are usually too trivial to hang in the average room; giving them each a sizeable frame and grouping them together makes a positive statement.

Hanging pictures, think big. Unless it's special and in a prime position, a single small picture is too often a nonentity. Rooms can often take a far bigger canvas than anyone dares to hang in a normal house. And a number of pictures hung together add up to a large one.

When they are to be regarded as a unit, put pictures in matching frames and keep internal spacing within the group to a minimum. Or tie them together with the techniques graphic designers use: linking lines; framing devices; telling a story with the pictures' contents, strip-cartoon style. Choose to group pictures that have something in common: colour, shape, medium. Put photographs together, or mix them with other black/white/grey subjects – etchings, pencil and charcoal drawings. See pictures forming groups together with any objects near to them. The impact of potentially striking arrangements of objects can be diminished by a picture that is hanging too close; conversely, a good picture that needs isolation sometimes has attention-drawing objects infringing its space. Furniture has the same sort of relationship with pictures: in the first picture the sofa and picture group balance perfectly.

All the groups here were conceived as a whole; add any new element, and the composition needs rethinking, and maybe complete rearrangement.

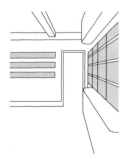

Tramlines drawn on the wall reflect the thickness of the shelves.

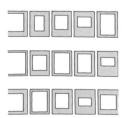

Uniform frames impose order on a sequence of photographs of different sizes.

A symmetrical group of asymmetrical things, plus textural contrast of the smooth wooden frames with the rustic wall. The frames are the raison d'être of the group. Their contents are pleasant and consistent in style and subject, but remain incidental.

Bathing scene. Surprisingly, the odd picture out doesn't unbalance the impression of symmetry. A vertical column of pictures like these is often a useful device to define an area used differently to the rest of the room.

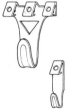

Picture hooks with steel pins that enter the wall at an angle.

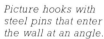

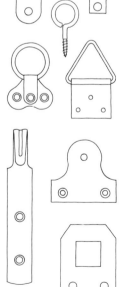

Use screw eyes for frames thicker than 15mm. Use D-rings or eyelets fixed to backing for lightweight pictures. Use back hooks or mirror plates screwed into frame back for heavier pictures.

123

MOST IRREGULAR

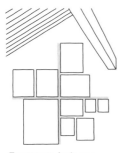

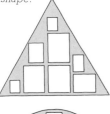

Four-way balance around a cross shape is more successful than fitting these reluctant pictures into a preconceived shape.

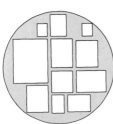

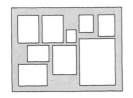

Balance from the inside. This effective grouping depends on the cross of space that makes it four quarters. The hero at the top happily fits into the ceiling's angle – but the group would work without him.

Balance from nowhere. The birds' take-over of the room on the right might have begun with a small group of strongly framed pictures – the principle of packing. Gradually the wall was filled, and birds and birdcages made for the ceiling. The arrangement may seem haphazard, but the theme makes it cohesive.

Balance from the outside. It is not possible to beat the visual dominance of these structural beams. The pleasant artefacts know their place.

Rectangular items grouped don't have to add up to rectangles. Work with them in a kind of controlled irregularity. Seek out some form of balance – not necessarily the symmetrical balance of a pair of scales.

Play one of three games with the pictures: work from the inside, from the outside, from nowhere at all. Pack the ingredients into a cohesive block, maybe in a geometric shape which makes sense within the space available, and is balanced by surrounding emptiness.

Work from the outside, starting with the idea of a frame. The entire wall could be your canvas. But when the sum might be greater than the parts, don't spread them too thin. Convince the eye that the ingredients form a whole by avoiding awkward gaps.

An old trick I learned from an art collector friend is to check that you like what you are going to do by making your arrangements on the floor before you make holes in the wall. Tape out an area corresponding in size and shape to the wall and work out positioning in that.

IN PASSING

There are places in every home with purposes so clear-cut that we overlook their potential as galleries. A hallway is where we shake the snow off boots; a stairway only leads to somewhere else. In fact such unconsidered spaces can be made interesting in their own right. It is even possible to turn to a positive advantage the fact that people are in passing, and constantly seeing things at new angles.

These places are ideal for collections: the witty, succinct ones that need to be isolated, and those that are too extensive – and sometimes, maybe, not special enough – to occupy pride of place. (Favourite things tend to hang where they are seen most often – where we spend most time.) Height available in stairwells gives scope for a massive picture display; the length of wall area in a hallway may be just the place to build up a collection of collections.

When natural lighting in places of passage is too poor to suffice, one solution is to go for a dark scheme and make adventurous use of artificial lighting. Collections profit doubly here. Dark walls make cohesive backgrounds for hanging things. And lighting systems that have to be set up anyway can be designed with maximum benefit to the hanging collection.

But simply because room is available in these places, don't feel you inevitably have to fill it up. Hang things that are worth looking at, and balance them with empty space.

Fickle fingers. One would not be insignificant, but the more there are, the better.

A single painting on a landing is never in the right place from all viewpoints. Here there is always something in view, whether looking upwards or looking down.

Certainly the bottom line of pictures has had to come to terms with the line of the stairs. But thereafter it is a group uninfluenced by that shape. There are flat pictures on a curved wall.

Making a virtue out of old-fashioned plumbing: the vital downpipe becomes the backbone of a display of signs and advertisements.

Maybe the decoration of this hallway began with the piece of furniture. Then there was a squared-up display of nice things above it. And then it just spread, like ivy, towards the doorway. Once again, evidence that a compact start gives further opportunities for addition.

ON THE RAILS

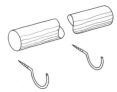

The simplest rail: dowel, bamboo or metal slung on hooks.

Bathroom towel rail for short distances.

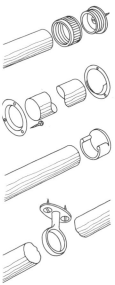

Wardrobe hardware: tube sockets for short rails, a centre bracket for mid-way support.

Sliding wardrobe hanger, more stable than ess-hooks or butcher's hooks, which can be knocked off.

Time was when every self-respecting room had its encircling picture rail – often a wooden moulding, sometimes a brass rail attached by brackets or hooks. A continuous rail looks good and gives an infinite variety of positions for picture hanging. But it's not just for pretty faces. When putting a new one up in a room try to make it serve as many purposes as possible: the principle of streamlining. Position it just above the top of the window so the curtains hang from it as well as the pictures. Conceal lighting flex in or behind the rail and run it down the supporting chains to light paintings individually. Run wiring through it so audio speakers can hang from it.

For a room without an existing all-round rail, be inventive with the whole range of wardrobe and bathroom rail fittings – in brass, chrome, stainless steel, wood, plastics – and colours. Any of these fittings hung high on a wall are potential picture rails in brief – and places to display anything from bottles to bathrobes.

When one single rail will not serve every purpose in the room, make sure the different ones match up in materials, in weight and in fittings wherever possible.

A touch of brass in my 'antique' room
supports two pictures loaned me by
Anouska Hempel, whose broad,
discriminating taste I admire.

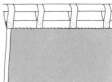

Self fabric loops.

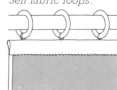

Sewn-on rings.

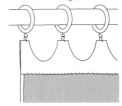

Eyelet rings to use
with drapery hooks.

Paired rails for café
curtains hung on loops
of fabric or on any
kind of curtain ring.

THE BUTCHER'S HOOK

Tricia Guild cooks and collects baskets: her hanging basket collection is both decoration and a place to store fruit and vegetables.

Butchers and grocers have been hanging their wares from rails for generations – simultaneously creating display and efficient storage. In the kitchen of a fast-working cook, it's good to have things at eye level and within hand's reach.

Some items in the *batterie de cuisine* obviously get used more than others. Hang the most frequently needed utensils nearest the cooker – the area likely to be dirtiest – so that they are constantly being cleaned in the normal course of events.

Some things call for being hung away from the heat – onions, garlic, herbs and fruit for example. Others need to be within easy reach. But work at making kitchen rails a living display. Don't hang things simply for the sake of it: do so because they're used, or useful.

And keep reappraising what is hanging: move things sometimes to make them look better, or be more accessible.

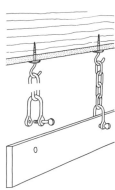

Steel bar is supported by shackles threaded through chains. Hooks are screwed firmly into the ceiling joists.

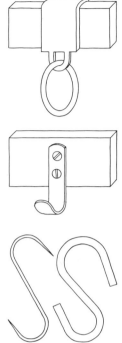

Sliding ring and hook to bolt onto flat steel butcher's bars. Ess-hooks work on flat bars and tubular rails, but you may need to develop the knack of using them without knocking them off. And it's safest to file the sharp points off butcher's hooks.

The space between the working surface and the eye-level cupboards (left) is always an awkward one to know what to do with: here the view presents an enviable solution. To reflect light and make the kitchen seem bigger, try mirror in this space. It may need frequent cleaning, but the effect is well worth while.

It's fine to be able to show off immaculate pans in gleaming copper (above), but you should not feel that without matching sets you can't hang and display your kitchenware. If you use it, hang it. Although carefully chosen matching items do look good together, there's a lot to be said for collections of random things that achieve effect through sheer mass and diversity.

Many old-fashioned ranges are still in loving use. Modern alternatives are more convenient, but keep an old one if space permits; it is an attractive display area and a useful parking place for pots.

131

THE HANG OF IT

Tricia Guild's cushions are a patchwork of recycled lace, which also decorates her gathered blinds. Don't be afraid to mix scraps of different design.

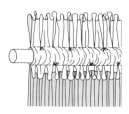

The fabric in the white curtains and on Tricia's walls hangs on rods.

A kelim supported by battens becomes a picture. Kelims of finer weave look good in less formal display – thrown over a sofa, or on a table protected by a glass top. Such casual treatment sometimes conceals wear or flaws.

Fine fabrics ruffle and ruche, but need to be sturdy to withstand the rigours of use as curtains. Hang new fabrics at windows and keep crochet and lace heirlooms – or remnants of them – for places where they will have less handling. But unless they are very precious, enjoy old textiles while you can; they won't last indefinitely in any case. Give lace a fabric backing and use it as a hanging. The good parts of badly torn lace can be incorporated second-time-round into cushions or curtain trimmings – or perhaps will throw over a table, carefully draped so that holes won't show.

On the whole I prefer to be able to see the lines of good furniture, but covering tables – especially round ones – with lace, embroideries or cloth is fine if you're looking for a pretty, soft effect.

A coloured fabric backing and brass rail exhibit an old lace curtain. The lampshades and china cake-stand echo the crisp ruffles of curtains and tablecloth.

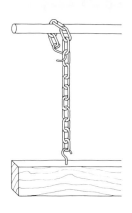

Velcro attaches back of kelim to framework of battens. Ess-hook on suspending chain permits height to be adjusted.

HOOK HANG-UPS

Far better to reach than to search, so in a really active kitchen, equipment is likely to ready to hand – as in a professional kitchen – and not behind shiny sterile doors. Thus an appealing display of useful equipment hung on hooks or slotted into racks is a natural reflection of the room's function.

Outlining the shapes of pots, pans and tools on the wall indicates their rightful positions. But before committing to that idea, establish which are the most often used things, and settle their places at mid-height, which doesn't require constant stretching up on tip-toe or low bending down.

Hook-hanging makes for its own precision of placing. And it's easier to screw hooks into wood than into the average wall. Take advantage of wooden shelves (and utilize the hanging space beneath them). Or put rows of hooks or nails on battens, doubling some of these to make knife racks.

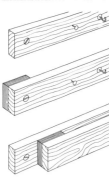

Flush battens take nails or screw-in hooks. Set away from the wall with spacers, they take the lipped handles of utensils. A knife rack is simply a double batten with spacers screwed in from behind.

This kitchen misses an in-character storage opportunity: a shelf supported by the central table's cross-beam could be the stage for an attractive show. Painted shadows on the wall locate each piece of equipment.

Tricia Guild's tiles doing what they are supposed to do – providing clean-looking, easy-to-care-for surfaces. And it doesn't matter that they are all different; the exotic background rescues a dull picture. The shelves and the supports are there anyway, so the hooks for cups and pans become a finishing touch.

Cuphooks to screw into wood; flanges make them look neater.

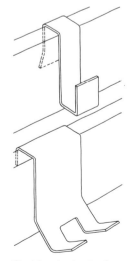

Coat hooks in steel or aluminium which hook over battens can also have a place in the kitchen.

TOOL UP

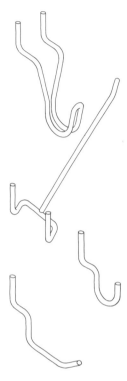

Whether the tools of your trade are pliers or pans, it is vital to know where they are when the pace gets fast. Some workshop and toolshed walls can take nails driven directly into them; hammer heads rest on pairs of nails and screwdriver handles fit between spaced nails. Indoors where wall finishes are less rough-and-ready, these tricks have to be translated into clips, to screw into woodwork, or the wall has to be covered with an intermediate surface such as pegboard.

Some people complain that the pegs fall out and that it is all more trouble than it's worth, but choosing fittings that suit the things you're hanging answers that problem.

A grid of steel wire takes hooks for pans and visually holds the shapes together as if on graph paper. While this panel is purpose-made, the effect could be achieved with all sorts of wire frames – like those used in reinforced concrete, for example.

A pegboard panel (far right) is today's way of hanging tools: good when it fills up a space like this.

By the look of it, the workshop below has had several generations of tools nailed up on its walls and beams. The car mechanic's light has a place here – as well as indoors.

Hooks for pegboard vary in size, style and strength: shop-fitting suppliers can be a good source for the more unusual shapes.

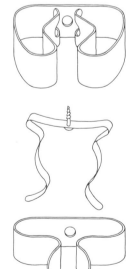

Screw-in spring clips hold tools and cans securely, so are useful to hold things on the backs of doors.

Pegboard needs a
furring strip of wood
or a spacer behind it.

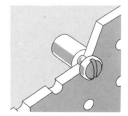

Tool silhouettes on
the wall make panels
above two sections of
the storage and work
surfaces below. While
the hieroglyphic
shapes of the tools
'read' well at a
distance, the widely
spaced pictures
would be easier to
see if they were more
tightly grouped and
lower down.

PIN-UP

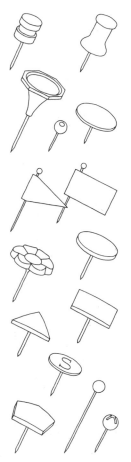

A free shape for freewheeling ideas. The design could be figurative: an apple, a leaf – anything that suits the environment. Curves are a relief from the rectangles that make up the majority of people's pin-ups.

A pinboard with a sense of permanence. It's well colour-coordinated, and many of the items are not strictly ephemeral. But elements can change, and a complete revamp is only half an hour of enjoyable work.

If you've coloured your pinboard, use map pins in good colours, too, or choose from a variety of novelty pins.

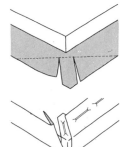

Covering with fabric: allow about 2cm surplus all round, plus depth of board. Slash into the fabric at corners to mitre. Turn fabric to back and staple or tack.

The lights here are strong enough to illuminate Lisa Guild's desk properly, but diffused for the pretty contents of the pinboard. Fabric from a room's soft furnishings is an alternative to the felt covering.

The image not quite worth a frame or preservation in an album – pictures and posters, letters and recipes – can serve a bright decorative function in an informal area. Pinboard is the secret – fibreboard painted or covered in fabric: felt comes in an astonishing range of colours.

A pinboard can be the front page of the family newspaper but, as every newsman knows, there's nothing quite so stale as yesterday's headlines. So discard an item as soon as it's out of date. As with a front page, a pinboard needs light relief even when it's a communications centre. But edit it regularly – a principle office managers would do well to remember when dealing with staff notice boards.

A project centre can almost always use a pinboard, to take the trifles that would get lost if they were put away, and the reminders of tomorrow's needs.

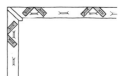

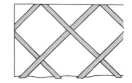

A trellis of elastic slightly stretched over the front of a board and stapled in place at the back, holds items instead of pins.

IN YOUR POCKET

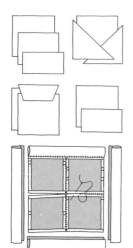

Wall tidies are crutches for untidy people; at least they can help to keep flat surfaces clear. The bolder they are, the more they are likely to be used.

When a wall tidy is not designating an office area or being a functional display in the kitchen or bathroom, it can hang on the back of a door and make use of space inside a cupboard without projecting too far into the storage area.

Treat hanging pockets like those in an overcoat: turn them out from time to time to get rid of the odds and ends.

Patchwork pocket squares will work in a variety of shapes, sizes and materials. Pattern on pattern looks good even when the pockets are empty.

Individual pocket squares are made up of separate pieces with exposed edges bound. Raw edges are turned to the wrong side and pressed; squares are then oversewn together within plain fabric border.

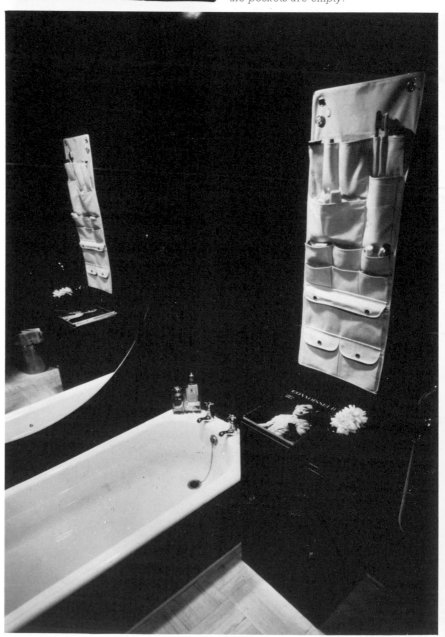

This canvas holdall derived from the principles of camping gear could be rolled up and packed away in a suitcase.

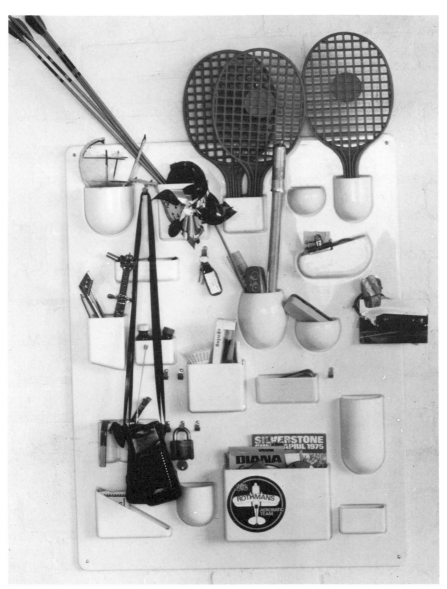

The plastic wall tidy – tempting the disorganized to be systematic.

Storage second time around: fix interesting tin cans to a board for a wall tidy. Turn under or file down any rough edges and lacquer cans to protect them. Secure each can to the board through a drilled hole using a nut and bolt, countersunk at back; then fix whole board to the wall with screws at each corner.

CLIP IT

Washing is pegged out on the clothes line only for as long as it takes to dry: it isn't kept there longer than is necessary. Use this time-scale as a model for the things you peg up in the kitchen or the office area at home. Even more than with pinboard, keep pegs and clips for the real ephemera – the bills that need paying, the recipe you're actually following, the photos of the children you mean to send on to Aunt Sophie. The decision to have nothing out-of-date on display could be the visual evidence of a new efficiency all round.

Ephemera here includes greetings cards and summer postcards from friends on holiday. An alternative to wall space is the screen principle, maybe with its every-day place in the children's room as a gallery.

Clip-up areas can be informal without being messy, but they never have the graphic discipline of pin-board. A painted board contains the changing display: the principle of defining an office area in a room by framing it. The board's colour, and the way it runs the entire length of the room with its accompanying shelf, makes the whole dignified and well integrated.

There's a variety of decorative novelty clips in plastic and metal as well as the plain, functional ones. Or why not use old brooches or odd earrings?

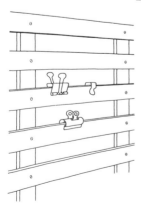

Battens nailed or screwed to uprights anchored to the wall make a good clipping ground; gardening suppliers provide fencing panels ready-made to save a lot of do-it-yourself work. Use these if you're not looking for too smooth a finish, and if they are the right size.

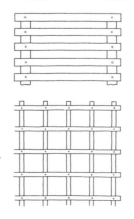

Fill in a hinged screen with battens instead of wire to stand alone or to take clipped-up items.

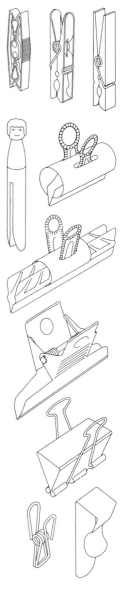

The screen principle, hinged wooden frames here threaded at regular intervals with wire, bids for the sort of clippings that are not quite so transient – or it would lack its screening properties. Hence its attraction for children's rooms: its overall shape is good for defining play areas, and it also serves as a pin-up area for displaying paintings, for games, and even a learning aid.

Borrow it from the children on feast days, when there are Christmas or birthday cards to show off.

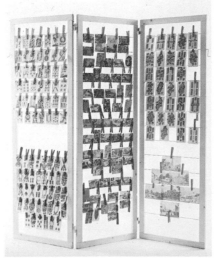

Clothes pegs from the hardware store, clips of all sorts from the stationers' – if they don't come in the right colours, paint them with modellers' enamels.

143

ON THE SHELF

Shelves are for storage and display – although traditionally the storage function has been the dominant one in most homes.

Reverse that assumption and use your shelves as miniature stages where your things – books, flowers, toys – can be made to perform. Remember to change the production from time to time: an arrangement left on the shelf too long loses its impact and begins to bore the audience.

Move the shelves themselves around: we now have all these wonderful, flexible systems, but when did you last alter the position of a shelf?

I like thick shelves – the thicker the better – and shallow shelves; I'm also fond of covering shelves with fabric to match the walls.

Don't feel you must always fill up every shelf: occasionally, leave space for space.

NATURAL SHELVES

Shelves are everywhere. Mantelpieces, windowsills, ledges, steps, the floor – any flat surface can be a shelf for display. There are almost as many different kinds of shelf as there are objects to combine on them.

But any flat surface can also become a dumping ground. Exercise some shelf-discipline: resist the temptation to fill. Sympathetic objects make an arrangement; unsympathetic objects make clutter.

Sometimes the right object for a particular place is incontrovertible: anything different is unimaginable. But keep testing

this out. Change the contents of these shelves around once in a while; even if you revert to the original plan, experimenting will have confirmed it, and refreshed your appreciation. Flowers help; as they change with the seasons, so the balance of any display including them alters, and everything needs adjusting.

The low-hung lights, almost camouflaged by the window uprights, become crucial to this casual display's success at night.

The panel of changing light from a skylight gives added emphasis to a mellow natural arrangement in a place which hasn't enough headroom to be useful.

Steps – though these were obviously built with rising display in mind, and the materials suit. Small objects that might be missed are given a soft backdrop.

The elements of the old kitchen have been retained, the temptation to remove the cooker and turn the recess into a cupboard resisted, and the whole area becomes a display of favourite china, its common elements being pattern and period. Interest is sustained at all levels, with upright plates bridging a potentially bleak gap.

WALLS OF SHELVES

The most effective built-in shelving occupies the whole area available; it goes all the way from floor to ceiling and from wall to wall. In this way the shelving system is not so much an added element, like a piece of furniture, but part of the room itself, like a wall.

Architectural features – beams, alcoves or studs, for example – may suggest or even dictate the positioning of the shelves and their design. Modern houses often have simple box-like rooms where these factors don't apply and 'architectural' elements can be created artificially. In the same way, the fabric of the room should indicate the choice of materials; a preponderance of wood makes wood the natural medium; a high-tech style can take industrial-style shelving; in a bland, modern room the shelves can be covered with paint or fabric like the wall behind to integrate with the structure. Shelves should seem an organic part of a room.

While built-in shelves may become part of a wall, freestanding shelves can act as walls, dividing the different areas of a large room or bedsit with a screening bank of shelves. These can be purpose-built units, modular systems built up of individual elements or even of 'second-time-around' items like beercrates or boxes (locked together for stability). Again the shelves' location should be prompted by some architectural feature of the room – positioned under a beam, for example.

The silver-and-black theme is sustained in both the furniture and the shelving system with cupboards that occupies the whole of one wall, and then turns the corner. Mirror-covered uprights make strong vertical lines and reflect light (which matt black absorbs).

Shelves make a monumental room divider. It is good to see some shelves widely spaced for the display of tall objects. The uprights are the parallel lines holding the pattern together: the horizontals are staggered. My only objection is to the hanging speaker, which interrupts the shelves' line.

These shelves are wall-to-wall and floor-to-ceiling, with a break for a display. A full wall in such a tall room could be overpowering in spite of the informal way books and objects intermingle in the shelf compartments. It is surprising in a flexible system giving variable heights between shelves that some books still lie flat or tip at angles. The sliding ladder is necessary for safe access to the higher shelves.

The books make a natural, functional pattern in my Ditchling house: I arranged bowls and wig-stands (both rounded and wooden) in contrasting pure display. The window makes a break in the shelves, like the picture gallery in the photograph above.

FILL THAT SPACE

When regular cubes don't fit the space exactly, build elongated boxes to size and fit them with adjustable shelves.

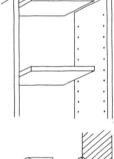

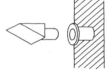

Uniform cubes fill an entire end wall and frame the door. Continuing the line of the skirting board as well as that of the cornice would improve the appearance further.

Shelf-adjusting though not shelf-evident: a discreet flexible system matching the rest of the room. The shelves are supported on studs plugged into the holes in the bookcase sides. The face of the shelves is flush with that of the staircase wall – a professional tip for anyone setting shelving into a wall.

The finish on the filing drawers sets the mood of the room. When colour and shape are right, it's good to see storage used boldly instead of being hidden away apologetically.

Facing white-painted shelves and uprights with wood-stained moulding emphasizes a trapezoid shape and aims to suit the objects rather than blend into the background.

When filling an entire wall with shelves is not possible, or not wanted, the next best thing is to fill out an architectural space. To tailor shelves to fit an alcove, end wall or under-stairs triangle, for example, makes them look an integral part of the scheme of things, rather than the afterthought they may in fact be.

Choose material that will either blend shelves into the walls (see Skin Deep, page 170) or marry them up with the room's structural woodwork. Take clues as to thickness, finish and height from architectural details like skirting, windowsill or mantelpiece. And if there is no existing space to fill, you may be able to create one by careful imitation of the existing mouldings and style.

With the unobtrusive hardware available to make shelves adjustable, flexibility is not incompatible with a really tailormade appearance. Pegs fit into holes drilled into the uprights (or into the perforated metal strips rebated into the uprights), and these slot into grooves made on the undersides of the shelves so that they are hardly visible. The choice is as wide as the types of timber available, not restricted to the ready-made adjustable systems.

The alcove as office: storage shelves of good thickness on a bracket-and-standard system. (In most situations thin shelves look mean.) The desk shelf, of consistent thickness, is additionally supported by battens.

BELOW STAIRS

The diagonal line of an open staircase breaks away from the ubiquitous horizontals and verticals of most rooms. It makes an interesting shape to work with and the space beneath is a challenge: turn it into something more positive than the usual dumping ground or built-in cupboard disguising the architectural elements. Here are three ways of working.

Instead of being boxed off behind a blank wall, the space is filled with a bed, striped like the banisters. The mattress sits on the line of the first riser; to have taken the top of the skirting would mean losing precious toe room.

Open stairs permit the room to go on as if they weren't there. The table has the same painted finish; had the design been done as a whole, one tread might be at table height – and the opportunity taken to run shelves from the treads to the convenient pillar.

This total design sees the potential of steps as shelves and extends them along the wall. It widens some treads into desk/table and platform/seat/bedside table. The theme of black stripes continues on the bedspread. Chrome handrails go with the geometrical black shelves in one of the classical marriages of modern furniture design. Evidence of integrated design is the curved shelves with built-in lighting.

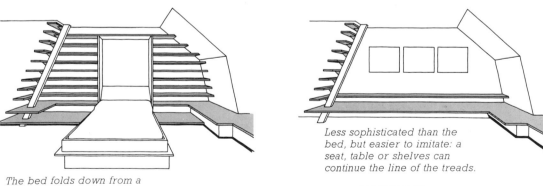

The bed folds down from a recess in the shelves.

Less sophisticated than the bed, but easier to imitate: a seat, table or shelves can continue the line of the treads.

The shelves' line could be continued on the bed base when closed in strips of batten of matching thickness.

CONTINENTAL SHELF

It's very rare that shelves cope happily with the curves of the washbasin when they try to incorporate it at waist level. Here the shelf steers clear of the basin – but continues the line of the bath top.

The single shelf needs to make a bold line. Look for some strong architectural feature in the room – the windowsill, the top of the door or window opening – that can be extended in a unifying line. Alternatively infill a complete window bay or alcove to make a low platform. Match the height of the skirting board, and run this along the front of the platform.

A high-level shelf running right round a room counteracts the impression of a lofty ceiling in the same way as a picture rail does. Obviously the things you display at this height should be fairly bold, graphic shapes, since you will neither be able to see detail nor pick up objects to examine them more closely. Don't make a high shelf too wide, and also make use of it to conceal light fittings: build in lighting to wash the ceiling, as well as spot fittings to illuminate specific objects.

At seating height, a shelf fills out the no-man's-land between chair-backs and wall. Depending on the space available and the

I like to run a shelf along the length of a wall behind a sofa – this shelf is fabric-covered to match the walls. You lose a few centimetres of room space, but gain a matter of metres of display shelves.

Overlapping shelves enfold the sitting area in Saporiti's design providing an abundance of display space and table room. The horizontal lines of the very wide shelves exaggerate the feeling of breadth and space. Low-hung pictures are at sitting height. Consider wide shelves if you are seeking to give a loft or large room a greater intimacy – when space shortage is not a problem.

room's style, this shelf can be no wider than a book – or so wide as to be virtually a table.

Although its thickness should relate in the first place to other woodwork in the room, when a shelf is of strategic importance it needs to look substantial. And the wider the shelf, the thicker it should look. Flush hollow-core doors can provide a ready-made solution that is far lighter in weight than nominal timber or chipboard. You can saw a door lengthwise to make two narrower shelves, but you may have to reinforce each shelf with blocks of wood inside the sawn edge – which, naturally, goes against the wall.

Continuity is always important: take single shelves right into the corner to make them look an intrinsic part of the room. If they work round a corner, so much the better. It's sometimes possible to overlap shelves at corners, as Giorgio Saporiti does: in fact his use of interleaved shelves in the room below is a study in what can be done with shelves and space.

TO SEE OR NOT TO SEE

Sliding shelves run on castors and are steadied by overlapping bevelled strips attached both to wall and to back of unit at top. Incorporate the lines of the skirting and window moulding in designs like this one.

Size shelves according to window size and to space available at each side – and build trays big enough to take bought plastic plant troughs, or flower-pots. Horizontal dowelling rods allow plants to trail and some pots to be hung.

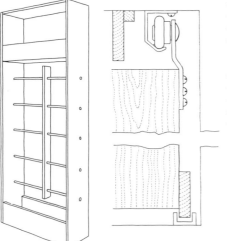

An alternative sliding mechanism is to suspend the shelves from above using a wardrobe track (hide this with a fascia board) and have a locating channel running along the floor beneath the back edge of the unit.

Supplement the windowsill by adding a shelf at the window's crosspiece, without interfering with the architectural lines. Clear glass objects let light through but give privacy as frosted glass does.

Plant curtains and a filtering screen of glass bottles afford less apologetic protection from passers-by than conventional lace. Most plants like light; in the absence of outlook to enjoy, give the window over to beings who can enjoy the situation. I personally dislike hanging plants in the usual macramé efforts – they get messy, watering them is a problem and they can be a bother to move about. I prefer to stand plants on the floor in a low window, or on shelves or furniture: if some flexibility is built in, so much the better.

But even given a room with a view, at night the window becomes a black hole. Screening and curtaining devices assume a new decorative role. They may just pick up and reflect the room's lighting – or be specifically washed with light themselves. Here too something more positive than net curtains gives better value. Shiny, shapely things – plants, glassware or decorative objects – can have their place on narrow, unobtrusive shelves lining the window.

By all means consider whether it matters more to you to see or to be seen – there's an infinity of ways of solving the latter question, at least. But think, too, how best to use daylight – and what to do in the absence of it.

Sympathetic objects and minimal shelves do nothing to impede the view – but make a dramatic show at night: they pick up some light from the room but would benefit from specific spotlighting.

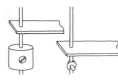

A metal bar threaded on a pair of wires or cords rests on a grub-screwed bush or a knot, and supports the end of a shelf. Use eyelets when the wire ends cannot be concealed behind floor or ceiling of shelf area.

MADE TO MEASURE

Tailor-made shelving for the mature album collection that is not growing too fast. If you constantly renew equipment or add to your collection you will need more flexibility than a built-in system can give. Either way, make shelves strong enough to take the considerable weight of an album collection.

Tailor your shelves to your belongings – albums or anchovies, pie-dishes or Proust. Tightly packed storage shelves make maximum use of space and look good. Don't build before you're ready with things to fill out your shelves – they have no justification in themselves, and don't look nearly as effective half-empty as when jam-packed. Consider resorting to vertically adjustable systems that expand as collections grow or change as taste does. Or cheating: groceries on display can be attractive organized supermarket-style, but then buy to keep up appearances rather than nutrition.

Know yourself. Build in permanent shelves for things you are going to need in steady supply, and for the cream of a collection whose overspill can be accommodated elsewhere. Otherwise, build in flexibility.

Adjustable commercial shelving fitted wall-to-wall and floor-to-ceiling is ideal for a well-equipped kitchen. Sectioned wine boxes fit snugly between shelves and serve as makeshift wine racks.

Shelves built to size by someone who is sure enough of their culinary tastes to know what they are going to need. Since few homes have larders nowadays, narrow shelves could line kitchen walls, for example between work surfaces and eye-level cupboards.

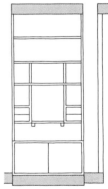

It improves the look of built-in cupboards and shelves to incorporate the room's architectural features and carry through the line of an architrave or skirting. And infill the dust-trap space under a bottom shelf.

A 'bespoke' shelving system, with an efficiently classified library. The serious collector needs adjustable shelves for different sizes of book; plenty of space shows the intention of systematic expansion.

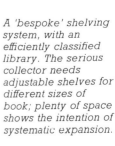

SHELF-CONTAINED

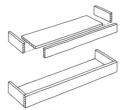

Battens fixed around shelves in situ make lipped containers.

Cut a dado groove at the back of a shelf for plates.

Fix a strip of wood as a plate stop.

Plates, trays and shiny lids lean outwards against a strap, and hence are easier to lift out and use. Round shapes make a decorative pattern without shelves taking up space in the room: reminiscent of storage aboard ship. This is a good example of simple, functional storage making unselfconscious display.

When the shelves of dressers are deep they look best packed with crockery: plates kept upright by plate stops, cuphooks holding jugs and cups. Built-in shelves can have the dresser treatment: add hooks and plate stops (or cut grooves), or maybe fix straps flush with the shelf fronts so plates lean outwards.

The simple and agreeable kitchen shelving designed to display plates tends to be shallow and widely spaced. Few other objects look so well in this situation.

So make patterns of circles to contrast with the horizontal lines of the shelves, on the understanding that the display then becomes more decorative than functional. Or arrange seldom-used dishes at the back and more everyday things in front (or interspersed in piles), so that using and displaying can amount to the same thing.

The present day is not the first renaissance of the dresser. They have been in and out of fashion since they were devised in the 17th century as the taste for 'farmhouse furniture' has had its sporadic highs. Derelict pieces of oak and pine were used to make fine specimens at the turn of this century, when the dresser was an inevitable kitchen fixture.

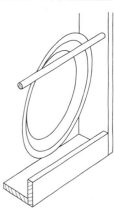

On a narrow shelf plates lean outwards against a strap of wood or dowelling.

SHELF-ADJUSTING

Some steel-shelving manufacturers tailor their units to the customer's design, and do brighter colours than the conventional stove-enamel grey. Or use a metal primer and two thin coats of enamel on industrial units – after assembling, and after filing cut edges smooth. Protect jagged corners with plastic ferrules.

A room divider by Interlübke: its classic regularity gives strength, style and convenience. The uprights can be tailored to fit the height of the room, and the cubes infilled with a variety of fittings, including drawers and dividers.

Combination of squares with triangles and hexagons makes this system rigid and surprisingly stable. Metal rings fit into rebates in the corners of each plywood square.

It's likely that the more flexible a shelving system is the more expensive it will be. 'More flexible' means easier to dismantle and re-erect, less likelihood of showing scars when set up differently, greater potential for fitting into differently proportioned spaces.

But it's a waste to pay for flexibility and then not use it – and most people leave their systems in the same place for years. So choose a modular system if you know you are going to re-arrange it, or if frequent removals make you reluctant to put money into built-in shelving – into the fabric of a home you are likely to leave.

Styles range from heavy-duty industrial and commercial shelving through manufacturers' interchangeable systems: these offer so wide a choice of forms and materials that it takes someone dedicated to go to the lengths of do-it-yourself to create 'something different'. It is the lightweight individual designs that are more decorative than functional whose design and erection needs precision and patience: like the examples here made of dowelling and of plywood.

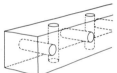

The dowels are set into holes bored in the square timbers.

For effect and light-weight display rather than heavy-duty storage – and a design for someone who likes to play with dowelling. Gluing the rods in place in some of the cubes increases stability without restricting flexibility too much. Fewer dowels might make a more open system. Or a scaled-up version with dowels of broom-handle dimensions could become a climbing frame.

FURNITURE SHELVES

Neither dramatic nor special, but pretty and nostalgic: the bamboo shelves and their contents (including the parasol) have an indeterminate period quality. The variations on the jug theme are informally arranged, but work because they are a good size and weight for the shelves.

Shelves can be used for storage, or display, or both. Sometimes when shelves are part of a piece of furniture, filling them can destroy the horizontal elements that are an integral part of the design (the carelessly placed television set being the main offender). Consider carefully, therefore, what to put on them.

Suit things to their context: go for period accuracy, for harmonies of colour, material, shape, or for the surprise tactics of putting things together with conviction and creating a style.

The objects have to work together, and with the shelves. You don't have to go along with their original intended use, but it could be a useful guideline. A dresser that was designed (at whatever period) to hold crockery is more likely to look 'right' with cups and plates on it than a collection of African carvings. Or is it? Follow the prescribed course, or break new ground – but be convinced.

You can do nothing but play up to a period piece like this jazz-age bureau: exaggerate its symmetry with two plants, two pictures, two busts; underline its vintage with contemporary light fittings, china and sculptures – and either decorate the whole room to suit, or allow plenty of space around it to make the transition to other times gentle.

The clean lines of this revolving bookcase make it almost a sacrilege to confuse by adding anything at all, but the odd book, period piece and plant prevent it from being stark.

Strictly speaking there is a discrepancy of style and period between the 'thirties and 'forties china and the old pine dresser. But quantity helps: Tricia Guild has conviction and packs the dresser with things that work well together; pieces are arranged carefully in groups and patterns.

Objects stand out in silhouette on this dresser which has no back: the spoons make a lovely and unusual display. It might be better to reposition the pots and plates on the lower shelves to make true symmetry or more solid groups.

SHOW-OFF SHELVES

Cross-halving joints subsequently glued make firm compartment shelves on any scale, although imitating the small size of the type-case would be a fiddly job. Screw the grid to a back panel of plywood or chipboard of the same thickness; add an all-round frame if you like.

The shelving on these pages shows a sense of scale. Tiny things easily get lost on the expanses of the average shelf: printers had the right idea when they subdivided their type-cases into minute compartments. With the demise of hot metal a lot of these find their way into homes as second-time-around shelving units in miniature.

Existing shelves can sometimes be sub-divided to take small things. Do this horiz-ontally if the shelves are not very deep; consider putting in a false backing if their proportions get out of balance. For in-stance, a collection of shaving mugs might well look lost on 25cm shelves – too deep. Insert a vertical backing sheet half-way back between each shelf so that the mugs seem to be on shelves only just wider than they are themselves. This will also avoid the temptation to mar the display with the storage clutter you get on shelves that are bigger than necessary.

The printer's type-case is just right for displaying collections of tiny objects like thimbles. If the wood is in good condition clean it up and varnish it; use sprayed-on paint only if you don't like the ink-stains.

A simple idea to show off objects that need to be seen in three dimensions: cubes reversed to form boxes. These have been proportioned to the figurines.

More brackets than shelves, these are perfectly proportioned to their contents. You could imitate this idea by sawing vertically in half suitably flat pieces of turned wooden profiles.

A rough crate has been divided by a grid of uprights and horizontals whose smooth finish makes a subtle contrast. An emphasis on treen – wooden (and rounded) objects – makes a harmonious display.

Crazy slatted plastic cubes with adjustable shelves for a Mickey Mouse collection. Cloud shapes and blue 'sky' sustain the mood.

Lisa Guild's own arrangement of her collection of tiny objects on the bamboo shelves in her room. Using three shelving units (asymmetrically placed) makes an interesting group: shelves this small could easily get lost on their own.

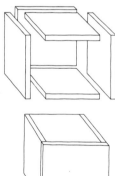

The cube: used as an open shelf, a thin plywood or hardboard backing suffices. To reverse and use as a plinth, make all sides of the same board, and finish well to conceal joins. Support cubes like this on split battens.

SEE-THROUGH SHELVES

Plant shapes show up in silhouette in a window like specimens in a catalogue. Curtains of trailing plants (which need tending so they don't straggle) give a different effect: these have the relative neatness of a blind.

In those places where a wooden table or shelves would be too heavy and solid, but nothing at all would leave an undesirable vacuum, something transparent is the answer. A glass or clear acrylic shelf can have solid supports, or solid objects on it, but it serves its purpose in not looking too heavy, and not blocking any light.

Glass shelves have an obvious affinity for windows and look good with glass and metal objects, delicate displays, and plants.

Giant metallic insects are trapped inside a tiered table/display-case of clear acrylic plastic with a plate-glass top. The room's textures range from the corded upholstery through fur cushions and throws, and fine wood graining on the floor, to the pattern made by the book bindings.

There's not really much difference in the appearance of acrylic and glass shelves; the latter are sometimes a bluish-green in colour, and since glass is stronger it can be used thinner and thus be less noticeable. On the whole it's better to use plastic for verticals, and glass (which is tougher and scratches less easily) for the horizontals. Often the sheer weight of a plate-glass table-top is enough to hold it in place. Where it could be a danger, as over the stairwell in the photograph (right), it can be bolted to its supports.

Where glass is being used on adjustable shelving, choose supports with lips or suckers to hold the glass securely in place.

An unusual shelf arrangement (right) sandwiches two sheets of plate glass to make a desk. The stool, also 'invisible', is a column of acrylic sheet.

For the stairwell cover below, spacers help locate the glass horizontally. But the mounting must allow for even the slightest movement of the base.

Plain bottle shapes in clear and coloured glass make a simple, effective distraction from an unprepossessing outlook.

An arched opening between two rooms is segmented by glass shelves to give display space proportionate to a collection of glassware.

A slab of plate glass makes a shelf of the space over the stairwell – but does not cut out light. The smooth thickness of the glass is well proportioned to the rough-hewn white-painted wood.

SKIN DEEP

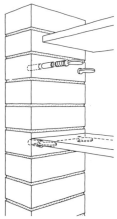

Shelves in mortared bricks: use pegs as for adjustable shelves. The most secure have threaded sleeves which you bang into holes drilled in the brick. Spade-shaped pins are then screwed in.

Bricks come close to earthenware flowerpots in their natural mellowness: often to paint them would be to diminish them. Here, though, there is justification for painting modern bricks to make a dark background for a collection of all-white china.

The colour choice is obvious in its relation to the wallpaper. Less obviously, it is tonally just the right complement to the bright, sometimes brash bindings of a paperback collection. The system works very well as an example of interwoven book and display shelving. Things fit their spaces comfortably, and there is a bookstore idea here: displaying some of the dust jackets head-on.

Designing shelves to marry objects with their environment may mean using a 'skin' of fabric or paint instead of using the natural, or man-made, surface. But if this means covering good wood, think again.

Change the colour of shelves to make the room's scheme work. Change it to one of the colours in the displayed objects themselves to make a display look perfectly at home. Or make a dramatic contrast between the shelves and the objects. Consider texture.

With paint, aim for a perfect finish: filling, sanding, sealing, and sanding down again between coats. Try to get a plastic smoothness, or a lacquer-like finish.

Fabric to stick on shelves should be of medium weight, substantial enough not to stretch when handled. Choosing patterns involves the same decisions as wallpaper – in fact the fabric used to cover shelves may well be that on the walls: an overall pattern that will not be too confused by the lines of the shelves themselves, or by the colour and shape of their contents.

Interlübke's modular shelving is immaculate, satin-finish: a modern surface whose colour and quality make it the match for the finest pieces. Successive coats of silk-finish paint could achieve the equivalent effect on good quality shelving units.

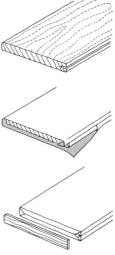

Covering loose shelves with fabric: Make a 2cm kerf cut in back edge of shelf; sand front corners to rounded contour to prevent wear.

Cut fabric to overlap shelf by about half its depth at each end, and to measure about 3cm longer than distance all round. Tuck ends of fabric into kerf cut.

Make envelope folds of fabric at short ends of shelf; if these show (as in some adjustable systems), hide folds with battens of wood, or fabric-cover.

A Designer's Guild fabric demonstrates shelf- and wall-covering. The pattern is of soft, subtle, organic shapes that don't jar with lines of the shelves, and meanwhile make a harmonious background for the objects Tricia displays.

171

SHELF-EVIDENT

I am often asked what is the best way to light shelves, when it is not the shelves themselves that we want lit but the objects on them. It is important to make the distinction, since badly placed lights may not only fail to show up the significant objects, but may also cast deep shadows.

The choice between the classic solutions – glass shelves, filament or fluorescent tubes, and individual spotlights – must depend on the nature of the objects to be lit. A downward light over a succession of glass shelves will not be effective with a

A combination of glass shelves, shiny metal supports and background mirrors always works; recessed lights above the two units keep the design streamlined and illuminated.

wide plate on the top shelf; this system works best for small, fine objects like figurines, or things made of glass.

Shelves for display that are to do justice to their contents need to be widely spaced apart; this spacing usually gives enough scope for extra-thick shelf material into which lighting can be incorporated, or a fascia or baffle behind which a lighting tube can be fixed (without causing glare). An intermediate shelf can be built like a light box, lighting tubes sandwiched between glass sheets. Individual spotlights need to be carefully placed to illuminate what is needed; tiny track-mounted ones especially suitable for shelves are now marketed.

As far as possible plan shelves and their lighting in one unit, so that all wiring can be incorporated in the structure. Never plan display shelving without taking its illumination into account.

Lighting bookshelves is a different problem. Provide occasional light to read titles (ceiling spotlights directed at the shelves are best), and the rest of the time just enough diffused light to show up the books as background pattern and texture.

A downward-directed light recessed into a drop ceiling above a set of glass shelves gives a streamlined effect.

Almost a Chinese puzzle of glass shelves and mirrored walls: the recessed ceiling light just shows as a reflection. Figurines like these suit the glass shelves and overhead lighting, and their whiteness looks good in a white-fitted bathroom.

A fluorescent tube incorporated into the curving fascia above adjustable bookshelves gives adequate light for reading titles.

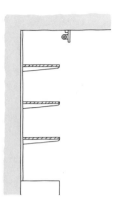

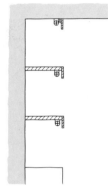

Small-diameter fluorescent or filament tubes can be positioned on the ceiling in front of the shelves (top), or below each shelf.

An intermediate shelf can be made like a light box, from tubular light fittings sandwiched between two layers of glass – either clear or opaque – thus transmitting light upwards and downwards. Carry the thickness of the light-box shelf through other parts of the design, such as skirtings and fascias.

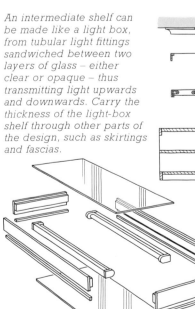

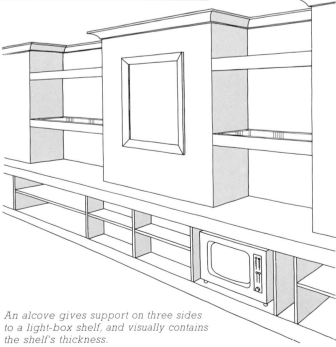

An alcove gives support on three sides to a light-box shelf, and visually contains the shelf's thickness.

GIANT SHELVES

The clean lines of this massive shelf break a medium-sized room into two cosy areas, each with sufficient head-room. In the sitting area giant pencil-cushions and an outsize light-bulb continue the joke of destroying the scale.

A shelf can be big enough to display people on. All it takes is a ceiling high enough to give the necessary headroom. Sleeping platforms create space in crowded quarters, making them ideal for one-room living. And there is the bonus that the warmest air in the room, otherwise wasted, is right where you need it – in the bedroom.

The space underneath can sit people comfortably at a table for dining or a desk for working. They help in large buildings too (lofts, studios, converted chapels) reducing a vast height to more human proportions without all-over loss of spaciousness. The area beneath seems more intimate –

after all, people sometimes use the device of dropped ceilings to counteract an excess of space.

As always, tailor the proportions to the space available and the style and materials to those in the building. A giant shelf does not have to be clumsy. When there's a three-D shelf to be built and a 'high-tech' style suits (for example, in a loft), consider scaffolding: but it's not cheap or easy.

A bed on a shelf of its own is always interesting, often inviting. Provide good lighting for reading by and for seeing the steps, and keep enough room for bits and pieces.

The sleeping platform is not immediately noticeable in this spacious studio – life goes on around it, demonstrating that it is possible to use a light touch when doing things on a large scale. Beneath the shelf/platform is a dining area screened by well-proportioned shelves.

An interestingly shaped block of wooden storage boxes bridges the gap between the floor and the relatively high sleeping shelf. Neat brass locker handles give the finishing touch to a well-proportioned design in a room where the wood, wool, plaster and plants make a balanced mixture of textures.

OUT OF SIGHT

This book is meant to encourage you to be proud of your things, make interesting arrangements out of them, and put them on display.

From the nursery onwards, we have been far too conditioned into putting things away. As a designer, I am always being asked to suggest ways of hiding the television set; the real answer is to find a well-designed set – or else to put the thing on a trolley and wheel it away when not in use. Nothing needs hiding if it looks good.

Obviously there are some things that need tidying up, if not tidying away. I hope the next few pages will make the business of putting things away less of a secretive chore, and more of an interesting design exercise in its own right.

BOX NUMBER

What starts as an emergency measure usually stays in situ for years, so it should look as nice as possible. Cardboard crates have been painted in favourite colours in photographer JayJay Lichauco's apartment.

Better than an amorphous heap of things is a pile of boxes. When people are in a state of change – waiting for a new office or piece of furniture or larger apartment – or even constitutionally untidy, the answer is boxes: containers which can be moved aside for cleaning and easily shaped into a semblance of order, if not actually stacked up. Things can still be a mess within the boxes, but the mess is out of sight, which is a step on the road to order.

Wooden ones are good if they don't have sharp edges or splinters (although some can be sanded smoother, and others lined). Strong cardboard boxes are fine for things that need to be held together in fixed positions; they won't stand up to being humped around or manhandled by children.

Bright plastic crates, either second-time-around bottle crates with divisions, or purpose-bought, have their place as explicit displayed storage or inside closets and under beds. And even if the contents get tipped out to free the crates for play, at the end of the day they can be righted again and the contents piled back in, ready for the *real* clean-up.

Castors can be fitted to the more substantial plastic crates – turning them into carts and containers for small people as well as their belongings.

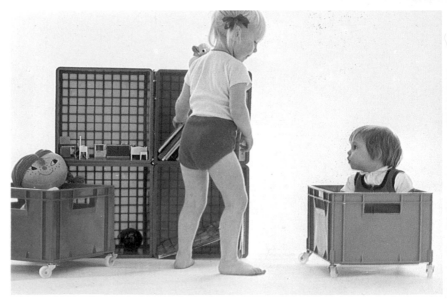

The bottle crate at three angles and being used in three ways: divisions add to the strength, but some can be cut out to store books and things bigger than bottles and children's shoes.

BASKET WORK

Square basket trays hold working books and papers; filing trays and cabinets, desk and lamp are all there in the efficient-looking study below: but only the typewriter and phone have not been specially chosen to suit the mellow style of the woven rug, patchwork cloth and comfortable, natural environment.

There must be a basket for every occasion. They can be strong, fine, open-weave, skin-tight, soft, hard, with handles, with lids, deep, shallow, rounded, rectangular, spherical. It is the intricacies of the woven texture in every case that makes a basket something special: the pattern of light and shade, and the blending colours of the materials. You can use a basket in any room: the simplest weave adds textural contrast and interest in a plain, almost abstract room, and is an obvious element to put with the plants, patchwork, loose-weave fabrics, stripped wood and stone in the homes of people who like natural things.

Cane and wickerwork have their own mellow colours, sometimes enhanced by polishing, staining or lacquering. It is always a shame to cover up natural materials, but there could be a case for varnishing, and even painting, the cheaper raw-cane baskets to give a deeper texture to their rather flat finish.

I collect old baskets from South-east Asia. These need to be protected and polished with plain wax.

Rectangular baskets like bicycle baskets hang in a hallway corner: use them for plants anywhere, or for implements and impedimenta in kitchen, bathroom or office.

Two different basketweaves introduce textural pattern into a stark modern environment. There is an appropriate weight and scale of basket for every situation: a large size does not necessarily mean a chunky, rustic style.

The obvious containers for toys so they can be moved from playroom to garden, and can be quickly put away again. The picnic basket could be taken on journeys like a suitcase, too; it is one of the more ordinary baskets you could paint or varnish.

TRUNK CALL

There's a mysterious appeal about trunks. One wonders on what romantic shipboard journeys they have been. 'Not wanted on voyage', maybe – but people are delighted to find the old trunks and suitcases that are too heavy to take on airplanes in their attics, and to put them to new use.

Since there are more modern and convenient forms of storage, the chances are a trunk is on display because it looks good. Their proportions make super out-of-the-ordinary coffee tables. The mass of a trunk seems to be broken by its handles, studs or corner pieces.

Old trunks in good condition need to be polished and preserved. Less-than-perfect trunks of wood or tin can be given disguise treatment: paint, stencilling, or *découpage*. Being stood against a wall can help disguise a damaged back or side.

The stencilling on the trunk does not obliterate the lovely grain of the wood. The colours of the stencilled design on the floor, the rough wall texture, and the bay tree in the doorway give this corner a Mediterranean feel.

The coordinating cotton prints, picture frames, trunks and even the ferns, all contribute to a style that is fresh and lightweight, but not over-feminine. Cushions give important height to the long horizontal line of the trunks and bed, and the positioning of the pictures over to one side counteracts the symmetry of the arrangement.

The stripped pine trunk goes well with the bare boards; the bamboo print of the cushions relates to both the spiky plant forms and the bamboo table. A trunk this simple could be given cushions or objects that would make it fit in anywhere, but resist the temptation to paint it.

In my composition of shiny objects in silver, black and glass, the studded leather trunk acts as visual counterweight to the large lamps and picture, and its texture contrasts with the reflective surfaces. A traditional Indonesian print makes a cohesive backcloth to the objects – a combination of the antique (the trunk), the ultra modern (the painting) and Art Deco style (the table and glasses).

BELOW BOARD

The sleeping platform with storage underneath can be based on modular units or can be entirely do-it-yourself.

Purpose-built storage for young children's rooms follows the principle of using boxes and crates – containers into which things can be thrown without too much fuss. A box may be quite small, perhaps fitted with castors, and used as a drawer to slide away out of sight – or can grow into a platform. As a less permanent alternative to built-in fittings, furniture such as beds can be designed or modified to incorporate storage boxes. For an older child who can manage a ladder and use the discipline of shelves, bed time becomes an adventure on a high-rise bed over storage drawers and cupboards. When installing such a bed, never disregard the safety rail.

The three elements of the platform can easily be modified for different situations. Stout drawers on castors are worth having on their own. Holes are used for opening, rather than protruding handles.

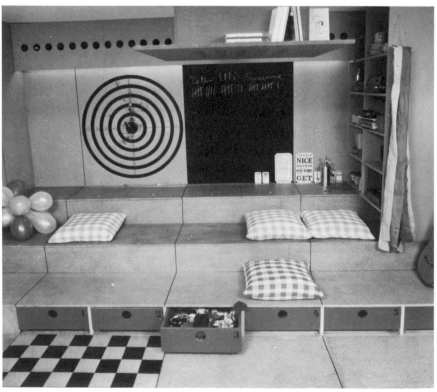

In a more constricted space – where play-room doubles as bedroom – it is important not to waste the space under the bed. A conventional drawer unit could hold toys or clothes, but this bed is purpose-built to take a model train layout.

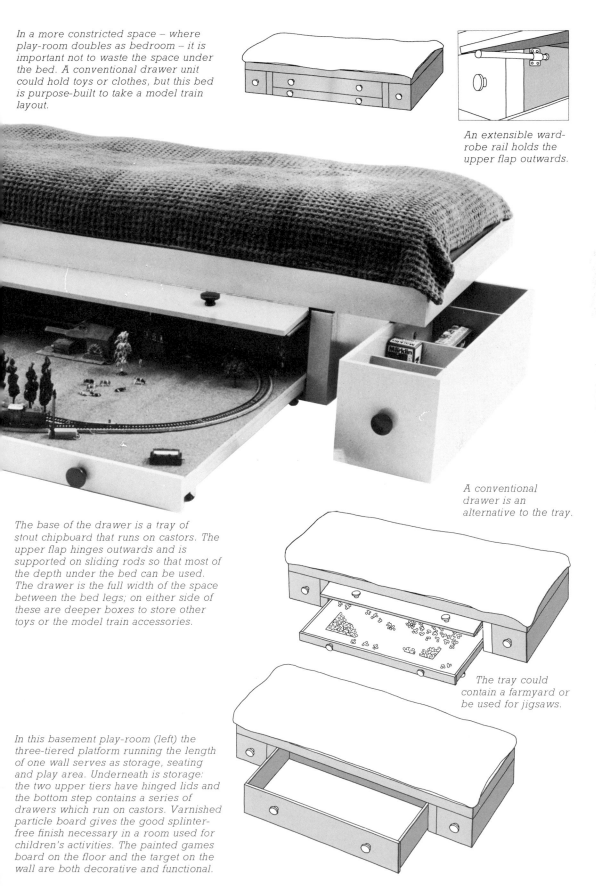

An extensible wardrobe rail holds the upper flap outwards.

The base of the drawer is a tray of stout chipboard that runs on castors. The upper flap hinges outwards and is supported on sliding rods so that most of the depth under the bed can be used. The drawer is the full width of the space between the bed legs; on either side of these are deeper boxes to store other toys or the model train accessories.

A conventional drawer is an alternative to the tray.

The tray could contain a farmyard or be used for jigsaws.

In this basement play-room (left) the three-tiered platform running the length of one wall serves as storage, seating and play area. Underneath is storage: the two upper tiers have hinged lids and the bottom step contains a series of drawers which run on castors. Varnished particle board gives the good splinter-free finish necessary in a room used for children's activities. The painted games board on the floor and the target on the wall are both decorative and functional.

STOW AWAY

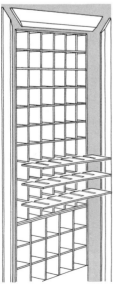

The space under the stairs is often wasted – and in old houses with stone floors it's often cool, making it a good place for storage. Quite often this can accommodate the everyday wine storage. Here the divisions at the bottom take larger bottles. For the sake of visual continuity, the grid is carried all the way up, although at the top left-hand corner the winders of the stairs leave no room for bottles.

The clean lines of the wine-rack seem to interrupt the carved banister, but this is not an original part of the house, and the combination of old and modern innovations is part of the style.

The first time I was involved in designing the interior of a yacht, I learned about 'a place for everything and everything in its place'. It *is* pleasing to see things stowed away all shipshape and Bristol fashion. There can be something satisfying about using tight corners and oddly shaped spaces, and filling them up with things of appropriate size and shape. It's the jigsaw-puzzle principle of interlocking pieces. And it's perfectly possible to create something that is visually satisfying at the same time.

The principle of good-looking storage works both when space is short and when it is in abundance. Well-designed storage can make more living space available in a small home, and, conversely, can divide up large rooms without making the separate areas feel enclosed, like a series of rooms. If the scale of the storage fitments is boldly designed, it should not conflict with the architectural proportions of the room – but enhance them.

Bizarre units are honeycombed with hinged doors and segments – 'storage' of an unorthodox kind. Their space-age shapes are contradicted by the mellow natural wood of which they are constructed.

Large slabs of storage dissect this room without destroying its volume. The low cupboards under the bank that separates the living from the dining area make a distinct barrier but don't obstruct the eye. Above the table – but also out of the way – hang useful shelves. The proportions of the two large storage units and the table balance, and the plant and chimney hood sustain the sense of scale.

A low divider contains the kitchen functions, bringing a human scale to the lofty, barn-like interior, but not dividing it up into completely separate spaces. The clean lines of the simple table and the bench that tucks away beneath it make a stable, restful contrast to the soaring pillars beyond.

INSIDE STORY

Layered compartments and trays that lift out contain bits and pieces. Spools of thread fit onto pegs – screws would achieve the same end.

Spice-jar shelves on the back of a door need to be lipped so the contents don't fall out if the door is jerked open. Inside the cupboard the shelves are narrower, preventing things from being pushed to the back out of reach.

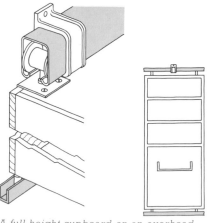

A full-height cupboard on an overhead rail slides out sideways and makes use of a narrow space on the right of the picture between the cooker and the wall.

Explore the possibilities shop fittings offer for making full use of the space inside cupboards. Don't be afraid to use kitchen or office fittings in clothes cupboards: wire baskets mean contents are visible. Shops and stores closing down can be a source of useful second-time-around storage containers, which can be painted to suit the surroundings.

If you don't pack a freezer tightly, you waste energy. If you don't pack drawers and cupboards tightly, you waste space. But packing things in often makes some of them hard to find, and damages the fragile ones.

One answer is to use the inner surfaces of storage spaces: the sides of drawers, the backs of doors. A system of drawers-within-cupboards (the freezer principle) and lipped shelves, boxes, clips or hooks inside every vertical surface keeps most things in order. When everything has its own place, it reduces the space available for muddle.

If you hang things on the back of a door, you lose shelf space within the cupboard: make sure the gain in order is worth the loss of space. (The majority of kitchen units and many cupboards have interior shelves so deep you find it hard to reach the back of them anyway – they benefit from shallower shelves on which everything can be seen and reached easily.)

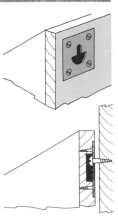

This breadbin hangs on mirror plates so that it can be taken off and the crumbs shaken out.

INNER SPACE

The division and arrangement of the inner space of a room is dictated too often by two factors: symmetry and positioning against the perimeter walls of the room.

How often do you start from the middle of the room and work outwards? It is worth experimenting with furniture (and without preconceptions) to see if an unconventional approach suits.

In the bedroom the bed must project into the room, but not necessarily with its head against the wall. The perimeters of the room are broken up into small pockets of space that can't be used for anything anyway, so something more positive might as well be done with the arrangement. Try a long shelf above and behind the bedhead, or a table or desk at the head or foot. Or even make bed and closet an island, using the back of the closet as a display area for pictures or textiles. Use lighting and mirrors to compensate for any dark patches in the room.

Or arrange storage and audio-visual equipment in a mass that challenges with its complex shape the box-like interiors of many living rooms. Use it to define different areas; it can change as you do.

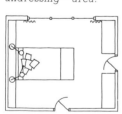

Mirrored sliding doors save space, and closet can be centrally placed.

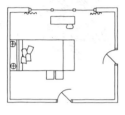

Closet against bedhead creating a discreet dressing – or undressing – area.

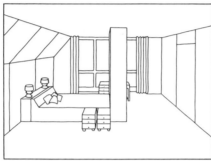

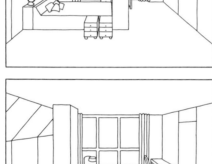

Full-length shelf behind bedhead holds lights and frees bedside cabinets.

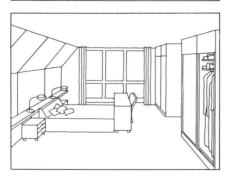

Closets are against the wall, and the desk at bedhead holds reading and working lights.

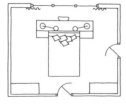

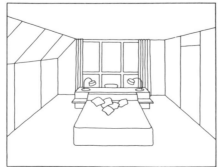

Modular cubes chosen in almost any permutation can be fixed together into a larger unit, used individually, or built up and dismantled like building blocks.

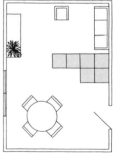

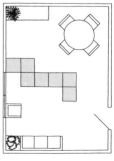

Since you are free to arrange them in any position, they work very well in three dimensions as room dividers, piled as high or as low as you want.

SOUND SYSTEMS

I believe that audio equipment should be heard *and* be seen. But the people whose ancestors concealed piano legs in modest frills are now hiding the latest electronic equipment in Louis Quinze *armoires*, stripped pine linen presses, walnut cabinets – or whatever piece suits the surroundings. I belong to the school that lets function dictate style – that allows audio equipment to make its own patterns and shapes, just as pots and tools hanging in the kitchen can combine usefulness and decoration.

Certainly it is possible to some extent to choose equipment that looks good in context, although sound and function should be the first criteria in choosing. When bridging the gap between what looks good and what sounds good, bear in mind that the reason ormolu speakers and Chippendale tuners aren't right is that they are inappropriate – they are the wrong sort of compromise. It is flexibility that provides the answer, and a good look at the way equipment is used gives useful guidelines. In the short term flexibility applies to day-to-day listening and viewing: where you sit at different times, what other uses the room has, where else you may want music relayed to. In the longer term, planning has to take into account whether you redecorate every other year, or are a hi-fi buff always catching up on the latest technology (in which case tailor-made housing for equipment is continually being outmoded, but appearance is likely to be secondary to function anyway).

The solutions here seek to compromise between equipment and surroundings in different ways – by containment, or by camouflage. And one by-product of designing a purpose-built container for the different pieces of equipment is that the usual tangle of wires is controlled.

Plinths that actually rotate (the vast heads are wall-mounted on shelves) house both speakers and shelves for general storage. The scale of the San Francisco fire house is indicated by the piano – and by the presence of John Dickinson himself. Castors on the bottom of a cabinet or plinth that is neither too tall nor too heavy are an alternative to the turntable (opposite).

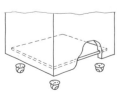

Two designs (far left) that recognize the angularity and hard lines and textures of the equipment, and house it accordingly, creating something that is compact in style and even of sculptural interest.

A superb finish on the wood is necessary for this notion to work – to make the cabinets appropriate bases for a pair of oriental vases.

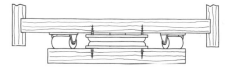

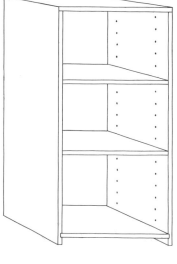

I had these cabinets built at Homeworks to house audio equipment and records and tapes. The shelves are adjustable so that different-sized equipment can be accommodated as it comes along. And the cabinets revolve to become plinths.

Each cabinet swivels on a turning plate and a set of four rollers – like a television turntable – set on a smaller board which is completely concealed.

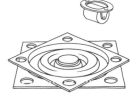

BEHIND THE CURTAIN

A fragile-looking lace curtain hung on brass fittings maintains the mood set by a brass bedstead and a converted gas wall lamp. But behind are the functional lines of a fitted shelving system, complete with pull-out trays. The curtain doesn't aim to hide this structure, but it softens it.

The curtaining in Tricia Guild's spare bedroom matches the wall fabric; the plainness of the curtains covering the built-in wallful of shelves and hanging space contrasts with the gathered blinds at the window. The shelves are also fabric-covered.

*The lines of this long, narrow hallway
are softened by the curtaining, the curve
of the stairs, the furniture and the plants,
and a touch of humour is added with the
begging, outstretched hand.*

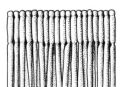

Pencil pleats

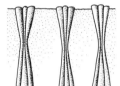

Pinch pleats

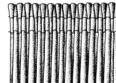

Regular gathers

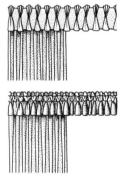

*Gathered headings
make curtaining
decorative, not just
softening.*

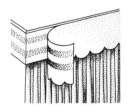

*Fabric-covered
pelmets can be
tailored and plain, or
decorative.*

*The choice not only
of fabric but also of
heading helps
curtaining to suit
the style of a
room.*

Between the curtains are glimpses of things stored – usually clothes, but not necessarily in bedrooms and dressing rooms. Curtains hide but don't disguise. Behind them you know there's a window or a series of shelves.

It's their softness, their design and the pattern of their folds that appeals. This need not be flamboyant or over-feminine: but see what a discreet softening touch the two fabric curtains here lend to their rooms – maintaining the wall covering (matching fabric or paper), but relieving it without harsh contrast.

Or curtaining can introduce a new element, be a new surface that makes a contrast with the rest of the room, or maybe echoes the window treatment.

How it is hung depends on the general style. A brass rod, rings, and a lace curtain become ornamental; a fabric matching the

wall pattern hung in what is no more than an opening in the wall itself, without special pelmet or heading treatment, influences the look and the feeling of the room much more subtly.

Scale is the guideline for good-looking storage curtaining: make the storage area the size of a good-sized window for the room. Remember the holiday-cottage 'wardrobe' screening-off of one corner behind a skimpy curtain hanging askew? It is a reminder of the need to be generous with fabric. Make long, dignified folds with lots of fabric, and make it as wide as possible.

And, just as with curtains, there are times and places when storage spaces and shelves can be hidden behind blinds instead: slatted ones, roller blinds, Roman blinds – whatever type suits the character of the surroundings.

ROOM FOR A CHANGE

Interlübke's cupboards like little rooms line the fireplace wall; they can make the room into a study or a place to relax in. Only comfortable seating and coffee tables are needed as additional furniture. The panel doors open and slide away into the wall or project and act as screens.

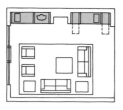

You don't have to give up half the garden: building an extension to the house is not the only way of solving space-shortage problems. Storage is something else for the magpie-collector type, but since one aspect of the problem is the need to use each room for several different purposes, astute planning can produce multi-purpose rooms which look good and use space well. The Upstairs Downstairs days of separate rooms for shoecleaning, ironing, and every different task are gone – and so have the people to do them; now we not only have to do it all ourselves, but all too frequently have to do it in a home that is too small.

Often it's the hobbies done at home that need extra space (so unfinished projects don't weigh on the conscience when relaxing); leisure equipment like audio centres and televisions is usually allowed to stay on view as part of the fittings, although it is good to be able to shut away the unblinking eye of the blank television

The multi-purpose wall acts as a complete room divider; its thickness takes up space in a barn-like room or loft, and divides it up into a more intimate scale. Matching spacers fill up the gap between Interlübke's units and the high ceiling, and the textured panels don't present a blank face even when none of the sections is open.

screen at times. And every home has its office space, larger or smaller, where the accounts are worked out.

One answer is to apportion a wall or corner to these activities, and fit it with flush touch-close door panels, sliding or bi-fold doors, or as the German company Interlübke now use, doors that open and push away. Inside, efficiently laid-out pull-out units, drawers and shelves provide a place for everything. Closed, everything functional is out of sight. You open up the office section or the drinks cabinet or the audio section as it is needed.

Whatever doors you choose, avoid making them a 'feature'. Decorate them the same way as the walls of the room or paint the walls to suit the doors.

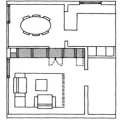

The corner of a room is closed away behind concertina doors to make a sewing area: good overhead lighting is an essential element. The blank doors could have some decorative treatment or covering to add interest, and pull-out drawer units on castors could make more use of the space below the counter.

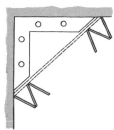

SCREEN PLAY

A see-through screen may seem to be a contradiction in terms, but it's a reminder that screens have more than one purpose. Of course, they provide protection: from sight, and from draughts. (Instead of spending a fortune on gadgets to conceal the television set, screen it attractively.)

But even the flimsiest demarcation line can define different areas, and open-mesh screens, like garden trellis, can let through all the light and air needed, but still contribute a feeling of relative security to those on a sofa who like to have their backs to the wall. Screens give a feeling of privacy and closeness without losing the spaciousness of a room as a full-height wall divider would. It's not in physical strength or solidity that the value of a screen lies, but in its role as a boundary between one area and another. Hence a row of plants stacked sufficiently high, or some open shelves, or even a clothes-horse arrangement like that on page 143 serves a purpose that belies its flimsiness.

But then there are the screens that are beautiful in themselves, the Victorian *découpage* ones, the painted ones, or the Art Deco mirrored ones. Some are too fragile to stand where they could be harmed (and they seldom have equally interesting backs and fronts): why not treat them like pictures? Support a screen carefully and hang it on the wall – the effect could be that of a giant triptych.

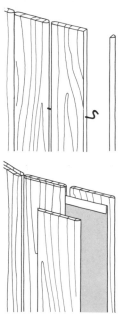

A screen that actually screens (right) is laths of wood threaded onto cord, with a half-dowel stuck to the end. Alternatively thin laths could be sandwiched (and stuck) around fabric.

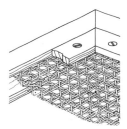

Sheets of bought woven cane are anchored into a rebated frame by beading: round-head brass screws would give an attractive finish.

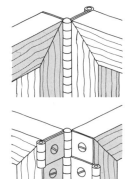

Two-way hinges are best to give full flexibility to framed screens.

The screen that pretends to be shelves: the perspective is a challenge but it fascinates. It works well in the context of a room full of surprising still lives and interesting bits and pieces.

199

BACK-UP

Design is a marriage of taste and technique. Now
that you know what you want to do, here is some
information about how to do it. And now that you
have found things that you want to show off, here is
how to deal with them to make them look their best –
and to keep them looking that way. There are
practical reminders and tricks of the trade.

The information comes in the form of specialist
articles by people who, over the years, have taught
me how to appreciate things and look after them,
and by people who know their subject inside out. I
commend their advice to you, because it comes from
some of the best teachers I know.

METALS

Copper, brass and pewter
Copper and brass (an alloy of copper and zinc) and pewter (alloy of tin, lead, antimony, copper and bismuth) may be repaired at home depending on the value of the piece and the severity of the fault. Brazing, hard-soldering and welding, and replacement of rivets, are best left to experts, but soft-soldering can be done by one who knows how.

Repairing brass Cast brass should be hard-soldered by an expert, but brass hollow-ware can be soft-soldered with silver solder – coloured to match the brass with a metallic coloured regilding wax – and holes and cracks can be filled with acrylic resin mixed with brass filings.

Cleaning brass Remove furniture fittings, if possible, to prevent chemicals from harming the wood. Wash first with an ammonia solution, using a toothbrush to lift dirt from chased areas, then in detergent, and rinse thoroughly. Next clean in a solution of 1 tablespoon salt and 2 tablespoons vinegar to half a litre of water. Rinse in distilled water, then polish with a proprietary metal polish, or a little vegetable oil.

Deep engraving can be cleaned by applying metal polish on a toothbrush and then rubbing away the polish with a soft brush wrapped in a duster.

If the brass is badly corroded, wash it in a solution of washing soda and warm water. For really persistent stains, rub (in one direction only) with an emery cloth or fine steel wool, polishing out any scratches with jeweller's rouge.

Lacquering brass and copper Regular polishing gives the best finish, but a less laborious way to preserve the shine is to apply a thin coat of cellulose lacquer. Clean all traces of grease and polish by washing in water and household soda, then rinse thoroughly and dry. Use a new watercolour brush and work quickly in a warm, dust-free place. Lacquer will perish after a year or so; before replacing it, clean off the old layer with acetone.

Repairing copper The low melting point of copper means brazing and welding should be done by an expert; but copper can also be soft-soldered, after first cleaning the joints of all grease. Epoxy resin adhesive is also suitable.

Cleaning copper Damp atmospheres tarnish copper, and water spots mark it. Clean the bluish-green tarnish with a paste of French chalk and methylated spirit rubbed in with a soft cloth. Finish by polishing with a proprietary polish or crocus powder. Remove water spots with a paste of turpentine and French chalk, or rub with a piece of lemon dipped in salt. Remove small spots of corrosion with a 5 per cent solution of citric acid. Never use harsh abrasives on copper, since it scratches very easily and the scratches are impossible to remove.

Repairing pewter Soft-soldering should only be done by the experienced, since pewter is easily damaged by heat. Some breaks can be repaired with an epoxy resin adhesive in the usual way.

Cleaning pewter People have different ideas as to how much pewter should shine – it can gleam like silver or have a dark patina. Keep dusted; wash occasionally in hot soapy water, rinse and dry with a soft cloth. Alternatively, remove grease with acetone or methylated spirit and then apply a thin coat of microcrystalline wax.

Removing corrosion Light stains can be removed by rubbing with a mild abrasive such as jeweller's rouge applied with a rag moistened with vegetable oil. More severe corrosion can be removed with either a dilute solution of hydrochloric acid (taking care to protect your eyes and skin from splashes), or a thorough soaking in liquid paraffin followed by polishing with the very finest abrasive and a soft cloth.

Storing pewter The acidic organic vapours given off by some wood – notably oak – attack pewter, so you should avoid keeping it in drawers or cupboards of unseasoned timber.

Bronze
This is an alloy of copper and tin; although it is very susceptible to corrosion and turns blue-green or brown when exposed outdoors, this patina is usually accepted as one of the attractions of bronze.

Removing corrosion Scrape the patina off carefully with a knife or with a brass wire brush. Remove difficult patches with a 10 per cent solution of acetic acid in water, rinsing and then rubbing off any resulting red discoloration.

Cleaning Normal methods of cleaning consist of washing in distilled water, drying and then polishing with microcrystalline wax.

Removing dents
The following technique is suitable for brass and pewter hollow-ware (as opposed to cast pieces). But undertake it only if you have had previous metalwork experience, as it can produce more dents than it removes.

Don't obliterate any hammer marks that are planishing marks introduced in the original manufacture. Nor should you hammer if there is corrosion, since the pounding could create a hole.

Ideally, cushion the object on leather and hammer from above with a good rubber-headed or leather-topped hammer. Otherwise, for curved objects like kettles and saucepans, shape the end of a piece of hardwood to a suitable curve or angle

with a rasp or file, and secure the wood firmly in a vice with the shaped end facing upwards. Place the dented area of the hollow object over the wood and press and rub the object over the shape until the surface is as smooth as you can get it.

If dents remain, protect the wood with leather or cloth. Return the object to its position on top and very gently hammer out the remaining dents with the hammer. Move the item constantly so that it is not being pounded more than once in the same spot.

The dent will be less noticeable than it was, but do not expect to restore the surface to perfection. Once damaged, metal stretches and never again returns to its original shape.

Silver

Repairs to silver should be carried out by a craftsman, since silver is both delicate and valuable.

Cleaning and care A commercial silver dip is useful for ornate or badly tarnished pieces. Alternatively, lay the piece of silver in a bowl on a piece of aluminium foil and cover with a 5 per cent solution of washing soda or caustic soda. Electrochemical reaction will cause bubbling; as soon as the tarnish has gone, wash in warm running water, and dry. Remove small persistent areas of tarnish by applying a paste made of French chalk, methylated spirit (denatured alcohol) and a few drops of ammonia.

When in contact with certain substances and gases, silver can seriously corrode. Rubber bands, even those wrapped around tissue paper, cause permanent scars. Other things to watch out for include vinegar, egg, salt, fruit juice, perfumes, olives, and the gases from decaying fruit and flowers.

Polishing Remove scratches first by rubbing with jeweller's rouge or fine crocus powder, or by burnishing; use a longterm brand of silver polish to give lasting protection. Items that are not on display are best wrapped in polythene bags or tissue paper after thorough cleaning and polishing; pieces on display tarnish more slowly when kept behind glass.

Lacquering Jewellers can supply a lacquer suitable for silver. Pieces should be cleaned first.

Gold

Because gold is so valuable, repairs and restoration should be left to an expert.

Cleaning Wash gold in a warm mild soap solution. Use jeweller's rouge and crocus powder on a chamois leather to restore the shine (and to remove scratches). Small items that are not engraved can be burnished.

Electroplate

This term describes the groups of metals such as brass, bronze or German silver which have had thin layers of more valuable metals (e.g. gold, silver, copper, nickel) electrolytically deposited onto their surface. Silver-plated objects which have been made in Britain frequently contain the engraved initials E.P.N.S. (electroplated nickel silver) which is the easiest way of recognizing silver-plate, but an acid test can also be performed (most advisedly by an expert).

Cleaning and care To avoid scratching, do not use abrasives, chemicals or cleaning agents containing silica. Clean and polish (very softly) according to the advice given for the relevant plate metal on this page. In the case of silver, use the French chalk solution and not the dip, and to preserve the shine wrap in paper. (Silver-plated articles tarnish even more quickly than sterling.)

Chromium

Also referred to (incorrectly) as chrome, this soft, silver-coloured rust-proof metal is used as a plating for several different base metals.

Removing rust Although chromium itself does not rust, the metal underneath can show signs of it if the plating has worn away. Apart from rubbing the affected area with steel wool, which would only damage the surrounding surface, the only solution is to have the object re-plated by a professional.

Cleaning and care To keep chromium shiny, all that is required is a wipe with a damp cloth and a final buff with a dry one. Should the object be greasy or sticky, wash with a mild soap or detergent, using paraffin (kerosene) on a damp cloth if the film is particularly stubborn. Never use abrasives or metal polishes and try to avoid contact with salt, as this corrodes chromium.

Tin

This silvery-coloured metal, which is yellowish when cast, is used chiefly as an alloy with other metals: with copper or iron on older objects.

Pure tin objects are rare and, unless exposed to prolonged periods of moisture and oxygen, do not corrode. When oxidization has taken place, however, the corrosion will make the surface look grey and granular. Rub with a fine emery cloth and protect the metal with a coat of microcrystalline wax which will also help restore the patina.

Japanned-ware is tin-plated iron or copper which has been covered in lacquer. Only remove the lacquer if it is crazed or if the object is pitted and rusty. Scrape the paint off the affected area down to the base metal; then rub with fine steel wool and paraffin (kerosene) to remove rust (or prod, if pitted, with a paraffin-soaked steel wool swab), wash with soap and water and dry.

Re-touch with artist's antique oil, leave to dry for two weeks and coat with microcrystalline wax.

Restoring printed tin advertisements and toys is described on p204.

Iron

Most 'iron' items are made not of pure iron but from combinations of iron ore and carbon. The three types of iron (cast, wrought and steel) are categorized according to the percentage of carbon in each, with cast iron containing the most and wrought iron the least. Wrought iron is fusible at high temperatures and is softer than cast iron; steel is more variable in its strength and heat-resistance than the other two.

Repairs For minor gluing, use acrylic resin. For larger jobs soft-soldering may be attempted, but bear in mind that the heat can alter the metal's strength. If in doubt, seek specialist advice.

Cleaning and treating for rust Remove rust with steel wool or a fine emery cloth, working in one direction, treating stubborn patches with a chisel or penknife and a proprietary rust remover. After removing all the rust, dust thoroughly; then apply a protective layer of furniture wax to prevent further rust from forming – unless you plan to cover the article with a special metal paint, lacquer, or heat-resistant finish, in which case follow the manufacturer's instructions.

Sandblasting To bring up the finish or remove rust on large cast-iron or steel items (which *must* be in good condition), save yourself a lot of time by using a sandblaster. The people who hire them out usually give full demonstrations on use and safety, but bear in mind that the job will have to be done outside and that for a good shine you will also need an industrial polisher. Both jobs can be done by professionals in the field.

TIN EPHEMERA

Vintage tin containers, pressed-tin toys and enamelled tin advertisements are not pure tin but tin-plated steel. They are popular as collectors' items but they were not designed for posterity, and many now show signs of their age.

Cleaning
In a perverse way, the tell-tale scars add to the appeal of old tin objects and certainly to their authenticity. Cleaning is often all that is needed to restore them. First establish how the objects were printed: by transfer or by offset lithography. The printing looks remarkably similar but you can usually assume that offset lithography was used if the piece is turn-of-the-century and the surface is raised and not flat. If uncertain, treat it as if it has been transfer-printed, since this has the more delicate finish.

On the transfer-printed signs, toys or advertise-

Enamelled signs
These signs, made for outdoor use, had glass baked onto their surface as a safeguard against the elements.

The care is virtually the

Mechanical tin toys
These might have broken components and often all this means is that a spring has gone. You can take the toy to a watch or clock repair shop where a skilled craftsman can replace the spring.

On the other hand, if your toy is simply for show, a broken spring

ments, use a solution of mild soap or washing-up liquid and dry the tin thoroughly to prevent rust. With the other type, which requires less delicate treatment, the best cleaner is a non-abrasive metal polish – though collectors may use anything from car paint-work restoratives to mechanics' cleaning gel. (The latter can leave the tin tacky, so rub it in well.)

Apply the cleanser with a soft cloth and gently rub the surface in small circular movements. Tackle each panel separately and use as many applications as necessary. After each application, wipe away the loosened residue. (For

same as for tin cans or advertisements, but, being more resilient, they can take abrasives such as scouring pastes or powders. The only *caveat* is to go lightly, and not often.

should cause you no concern. The only thing needed will be to clean the toy (see 'Cleaning').

There are beautiful old toys you can buy, dating from as far back as the middle of the last century. Displayed together on a shelf – or wherever – they look stunning, bestowing a room with not only

getting into the nooks and crannies of embossed or novelty tins, use an old toothbrush and absorb the polish with tissue.) Finally, buff the tin lightly with a soft cloth.

Protecting the surface Use a wax polish, but do not varnish; the subtle silk finish of age is preferable to a new-looking shine which would reduce the value of the piece.

Rust Remove with a non-abrasive metal polish or with paraffin and steel wool as described for japanned-ware (p203), but this leaves a bare patch which can look worse than the rust itself. On printed tins, most collectors ignore the rust spots and do what

Damaged paintwork can be put right with enamel paints. Try to get a good colour match – with the old deep blues, the most difficult to match, prime with white enamel.

vibrant colour, but also imaginative shapes.

Tin containers
You can use or display these. Large ones can be made into a table base with a sheet of glass placed on top. Small ones look good just about anywhere, placed in a cluster for impact or on their own.

they can to prevent further rust by keeping the item in a dry place.

Removing dents
The metal will have stretched so that not even the most painstaking attention will completely remove dents. But you may be able to lessen them.

Place the object on a hard flat surface covered with newspaper and, using a wooden spatula, apply even pressure from the inside with firm strokes.

Scratches
These are there to stay. Some you can paint over, but never so that the repair is invisible.

Hanging If the sign has pre-drilled holes, drive nails or screws gently through these. If there are none *do not* drill holes – secure with mirror mounts or angled nails.

STOVES

Old stoves are enjoying a heady revival and the main reason, apart from providing a cheap and efficient form of heating, is their looks. With their hand-crafted detail, the older examples are much more exquisite as collectors' items and every bit as economical to run as the modern ones. But if they have not been used for several years, they will probably need some attention.

Buying an old stove
How do you know you are getting one that will work? The most important thing is to examine the cast-iron structure. If it is cracked, don't buy it; the smoke will leak and mending cast iron is specialized and expensive.

Cracked enamelling also involves specialist attention and even with this it never comes back the same colour. It was the addition of lead which produced the vibrant shades of old and now legislation forbids lead.

Don't worry if you see rust, chipped mica on windows or missing firebricks. All these can be put right, but the teeth on the door and the riddling (shaking) grate, if damaged, will need complete replacement. They are not mendable because, being in direct contact with the coals, they oxidize and thus cannot be welded.

Wood or coal?
Stoves run on coal or wood. Use coal-burners with smokeless fuel in cities where there are strict air pollution regulations and either type in rural areas. Wood stoves are long, to accommodate the shape of the logs, and the wood should be placed on a bed of ash to prevent it from burning too quickly. Coal stoves

Wood-burning stove (above) Coal-burning stove (right)

work on a riddling (shaking) and grate system, for the most part, and give off more heat than wood.

Clearing the air
The two things which put people off most about stoves are the dust and the fumes, but these can be minimized.

In coal stoves, use the best-quality fuel you can buy – and this means the most expensive. A bowl of water placed near by will absorb some of the fumes; if your stove has a humidifier, keep it full of water. Riddle (shake) the coal ashes with the door shut and empty ash pans outside the house.

Wood stoves need their ashes removed about once every two weeks. Fumes are only a problem if the stove is not drawing properly, in which case check seals or have the chimney cleaned by a professional chimney sweep.

Have chimneys swept, in any case, at least twice a year for wood-burners and once a year for coal.

Home repairs
Some, like replacing firebricks, you can do.
Firebricks line the inside of the firebox to protect the cast iron and to stabilize burning temperatures. Without them the stove would get red-hot and not run efficiently, so it is essential to replace them if they are damaged.

Clean away all the broken bits and apply fire (furnace) cement, a compound specially formulated to resist heat. Wet the surface of the cast iron and paste the cement round the inside of the firebox (so that it covers the same areas as the original bricks), aiming for a constant thickness of about 25mm. The cement sets in about 24 hours, and then can be fired by the heat of the fuel.
Mica windows are a common sight on the doors of some old stoves. If the mica is chipped, buy a sheet of mica from a hardware shop. Take the damaged plate off the back of the window by re-

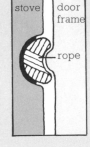

moving the backing frame which holds it in place. Undo the nuts and bolts which secure it and gently ease the plate off. Trace the shape of the missing piece, or of the whole window area, and cut the mica to size. Place the new mica in position on the back of the window, seal it with fire (furnace) cement and then re-screw the backing frame into place.
Ceramic tiles often adorn the external case. Remove cracked ones and stick the pieces together with epoxy resin. The tiles are usually held in place by a metal frame secured from the back by bolts. Apply

the adhesive as you would for mending a china plate (p206) and when it has dried, re-assemble the tile into position.
Asbestos seals around doors and windows must be in good condition for the smoke not to leak. Replace if they are not.

Most hardware stores stock asbestos in rope form; choose it wide enough to fit in the female groove of the door and to the length of its perimeter. Push the rope into place with a screwdriver, using epoxy adhesive if the rope will not stay in place. Then shut the door tight and leave that way for 24 hours.

Cleaning and polishing
Use wire wool or a wire brush to remove rust on cast iron, and polish it with stove blacking which will also retard rust. On nickel, use car-bumper polish; heavy-duty hand cleanser on enamel; liquid bathroom cleanser on tiles.

When the fires stop burning the rust will set in, so it is essential to polish and clean at this time and to empty out all the ash, as this, too, breeds rust. For general up-keep, clean and polish regularly.

Specialist repairs
Cast iron, as has been mentioned, is the outside repair to avoid; if you do opt for it, prepare yourself for the bill. (Also bear in mind that stoves are extremely heavy to lift.)

The smaller, more feasible jobs include most sheet-metal work, such as having a new ash pan made, or new sheet linings on wood stoves.

CERAMICS

All clay-based artefacts – of porcelain, stoneware (china) and earthenware – are fragile. Yet we expect a lot from them, especially when we want to enjoy favourite pieces in use as well as admire them on the display shelf. Damage is commonplace; accidents, sadly, are inevitable.

But take heart: if you have all or most of the bits, repairs are possible. Take a valuable piece to an expert restorer, who will be able to make the joins almost invisible. But satisfactory results can also be achieved by painstaking efforts at home. Holes can be filled, faded areas restored, the soil and stains of misuse can be removed. Armed with the practical guidelines that follow, you can view with greater compassion the battered but interesting pieces you find in junk shops or the attic.

Cleaning china

Start with warm water and washing-up liquid. Very hot water can cause crazing (minute cracks) on the glaze, and sudden changes in the temperature can break delicate china. Non-liquid detergents may cause damage to glazes.

Use a plastic washing-up bowl and put rubber guards on taps to avoid chipping.

Rinse with clean, cold water and dry with a soft lint-free, linen cloth.

Don't immerse porous ceramics like earthenware, but wipe with a soft damp cloth.

Dust terracotta pieces with a soft brush, then clean by brushing with a little ammonium acetate.

Don't immerse any piece with a metal mount, as the metal might rust and stain the ceramic. Clean the ceramic and metal separately.

Stains

Any commercial stain removers, such as those for cleaning teapots and dentures, should only be used on non-porous pieces of no great value, as they can cause discoloration or crazing to set in later.

Normal household stains (fruit, coffee, tea, ink) Cover the affected area with a thick layer of damp salt, or a paste of water and bicarbonate of soda. Leave for a few hours to let the mixture draw out the stain, then rinse with warm water or, in the case of porous surfaces, wipe clean with a damp cloth. If there is significant improvement, but the stain has not been completely removed, repeat the process accordingly.

Rust marks First soak the object for several hours in distilled water. (This is a process common in the renovation of ceramics – both glazed and porous – as it prevents the absorption of impurities into the ceramic and keeps stains from becoming more deeply embedded in the material.) Then cover the stained area with a pad soaked in a rust remover. Leave until the stain has been completely removed. Don't leave longer than necessary as such strong solvent can damage the glaze. Clean off any remaining traces of solvent with acetone.

Brass stains Treat in the same way but instead of rust remover, soak the pad in a 30 per cent ammonia solution.

General stubborn stains On porous surfaces, first soak in distilled water for several hours. Then coat the wet pottery with a centimetre-deep layer of magnesium silicate mixed to a thick paste with distilled water. When the paste has hardened so that its surface cracks, chip it off gently. Repeat if necessary.

For more stubborn stains, try swabbing with acetone, carbon tetrachloride, with methylated spirit (denatured alcohol), surgical or white spirit.

Don't let the first two solvents go near the glue in joins or decorative material – they may dissolve them. Bear in mind that solvents are highly inflammable.

On non-porous surfaces, again, begin with a soak in distilled water. If the piece is of no great value, swabbing with concentrated hydrogen peroxide is quick and effective. Otherwise, cover the stain with a pad soaked in a solution of hydrogen peroxide to which a few drops of ammonia have been added. Remove as soon as the stain has been drawn out. The solution will damage the glaze on prolonged contact.

Cracks

Stains usually form in and around most cracks. Remove before mending. Use the method most suitable for the type of surface and type of stain.

If the crack is closed, it may be necessary to prise it open slightly with a razor blade, but this must be done with the absolute minimum of force to avoid deepening the crack or causing a complete fracture. You need only open it by a hair's breadth to give access to cleaning liquid by capillary action. After the crack has been cleaned and dried thoroughly, apply a thin layer of epoxy resin adhesive along it, using a razor blade or scalpel.

Run the warm blast from a hair dryer up and down the crack to warm the glue and encourage it to seep in. Press the edges of the crack firmly together and secure with strips of self-adhesive tape. Swab off excess adhesive with acetone or methylated spirit. After it has fully hardened (the time depends on the brand of adhesive used and should be stated clearly on the container) remove the securing tape carefully, particularly if it has covered any decoration. Swabbing with white spirit will loosen it without risk of damage to decorative material. Remove any excess hardened adhesive carefully with a blade.

Removing old glue

Many unsightly 'cracks' are actually old repairs in which the glue has discoloured or a poor join has allowed dirt to gather or stains to form. On non-porous objects, try soaking in warm, soapy water to loosen the join. You do run the risk of opening up other good joins in this way. Devise means of suspending the object in the water to keep them clear (for instance, hanging them inside old nylons).

Using a razor blade, prise the join apart as the glue softens. Remove the remnants of the old glue with tweezers or a fine-pointed knife. Every last piece must be removed or the pieces will not fit together properly to form a good new join.

If soaking does not work, use any of the solvents for removing stubborn stains mentioned before. Use paint stripper where epoxy resin adhesives have been used.

Remove all traces of each solvent before applying the next, as they might react with one another.

With porous ceramics, first soak in distilled water for several hours. This will prevent the absorption of any solvent applied and softened glue seeping further in. This is particularly important with shellac resins as they can cause purple stains. Swab freely along the joint.

Repairing simple breaks

Valuable items should go to a professional restorer, but a practised handyperson can achieve good results.

For the least conspicuous join, the pieces need to fit together perfectly and to be scrupulously clean. Even if it is not a break which has been fixed before, scrub the broken surfaces with methylated spirit, or acetone, using an old toothbrush.

Before application of the adhesive, work out how best to clamp the pieces together. Adhesive tape across the join is the easiest method. Clothes pegs, woodworking clamps, weights, thick elastic bands and scaffolding from children's construction kits can all be used to effect. If the object has to be kept upright and cannot stand on its own, embed it in a box full of washing soda crystals or large-grade gravel.

Apply adhesive in a thin, even coat as per the instructions with the glue. Press edges firmly together ensuring they interlock in exactly the correct way, then clamp in position. Remove excess smears of adhesive with a swab soaked in alcohol or acetone. If the hardening process needs to be hastened, focus a spotlight or desk lamp on to the join. When dry, remove the clamp and take off any excess hardened glue with a scalpel. Smooth join with wet-and-dry sandpaper used wet.

Repairing multiple breaks

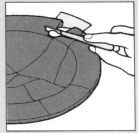

Basically the same technique is used. First check that you have all the pieces and make a dry run, joining them together with adhesive tape. This gives you the opportunity to judge how best they might be assembled and understand the complex relationships fractured edges have with each other. Number the pieces in the order of assembly. Try to work from the inside out.

When gluing, work on one join at a time where possible. With broken appendages, like handles, glue these together as a unit first.

Filling chips and holes

The most common filler is epoxy putty. This can be modelled to fill small areas where the piece is incomplete or has splintered beyond repair.

For translucent objects use an acrylic (clear) resin.

Clean the surface to which filler is to be applied. On a flat surface back the crater with masking tape; use modelling wax behind a rounded surface.

Wet all surfaces with which the filler will come into contact and apply a very thin layer of adhesive to the edge of the fracture. Apply the filler with a wet instrument; a spatula is best for large holes, and a dentist's probe for small (a fingertip or kitchen knife will also do). Squeeze the filler well into the hole and press down as firmly as the strength of the backing will allow. Ensure elimination of all air pockets. Over-fill rather than the reverse. When the filler has dried, remove backing and clean off excess filler by swabbing with methylated spirit. Fill deep cavities in several stages one layer at a time, letting each harden and cleaning off excess before applying the next. When thoroughly dry, rub the surface with wet-and-dry paper, used wet, until the surface matches the original shape and blends smoothly with the edges of the repair.

Painting

When painting repairs or retouching faded pieces, the two most important points are the matching of the original colour and making the merger of the old and new as little noticeable as possible.

Careful thinning of the paint or lacquer and repeated applications can help. Try to reproduce any tonal variations or imperfections in the original or their absence will draw attention to the repair.

The best paints for ceramic are French colours – transparent or opaque, as appropriate. Use watercolours or tempera, as oils fade in time. Finish with a coat of cold-setting varnish. Enamel or cellulose lacquer (car) paints obviate the need for varnishing, but they dry too quickly to give time for any delicate or subtle mixing of colours.

GLASS AND MIRRORS

Clear glass ought to be almost invisible, except where its curved surface or cut facets refract light, or when it is decorated, or silvered like a mirror. There are ways of removing most of the superficial stains that mar its clarity and of bringing back the sparkle, but sometimes years of lying in the ground or being slowly affected by moisture have left their mark – which becomes part of the history of the piece. Although you can't always restore a piece to its former glory, it is possible to preserve it from further harm.

Glass

Glass is unusual in that it is not truly a solid, but a 'super-cooled' liquid made from a fusion of silica (sand), alkali and lime which hardens on cooling without crystallizing and thus remains transparent. Various other substances are added to the mixture nowadays to make the glass stronger and clearer.

Perhaps the best known additive is lead. Leaded glass, used since the 17th century for cut glass, has superior light-refracting qualities which resemble those of natural rock crystal. This explains why the term 'crystal glass' is often confused with real crystal, which is still carved directly from the ice-like mineral.

Although everyone is aware of the fragile nature of glass, it is a common misconception that the substance itself is incorruptible. Damp, heat, strong sunlight and accumulated grime can all have deleterious effects on the chemical composition of glass. So can sudden, extreme changes of temperature.

Decomposition The carbon dioxide present in the air dissolves in moisture to form a dilute acid (carbonic) which can react with glass to form a cloudy film. The iridescent sheen much sought after by collectors of ancient glass is actually an advanced form of this type of chemical deterioration.

Modern glass, although less susceptible, can still exhibit 'white stains', particularly on the insides of decanters. To prevent them, wine and spirits should not be left inside containers for too long.

If you wish to fill a vessel for long-term display purposes, use distilled water, as this is relatively free of the damaging carbon dioxide; to colour it use food dyes.

Storage and display Glassware should be kept in well-ventilated conditions, so storing it is not advisable. Certainly it should never be packed in any wrapping that might attract damp – tissue paper, for instance.

Cleaning Even if not used, glass should be cleaned at least two or three times a year. Wash, separately from anything else, in clean, warm water (never hot) with a mild liquid detergent (non-liquid detergents can scratch). Use a plastic basin and put rubber guards on the taps to avoid chipping. Handle so that no undue pressure is applied, particularly on stemmed glasses.

If the glass is decorated with enamel or gilt, it is safer not to immerse it, but to use a soft cloth dipped in the water-and-detergent mixture. In the case of old, valuable pieces, cotton swabs soaked in plain warm water are safer still (and as far as it is wise for the non-professional to go).

If glass is very dirty a few drops of ammonia in the water can remove most ingrained grime: but don't use ammonia on glass which has applied decoration. A soapy toothbrush with soft bristles can be used to clean the crevices of cut glass.

Let all glass cool naturally and then rinse thoroughly in cold water. Polish it dry with a soft linen cloth: cotton cloths usually leave fluff.

Mending Superficial scratches can be removed by polishing with jeweller's rouge, but extensive areas are best left to the professional, as are most repairs. Many of the larger, quality department stores operate a glass-mending service. Chips can be removed by re-cutting and grinding; broken glass put together; and even missing pieces replaced.

No matter how well glass is mended, though, the fractures will always show.

To repair a simple break at home, first clean the pieces in warm water (this also helps prevent the heat generated by the glue-hardening process from cracking the glass). Assemble the pieces with adhesive tape, keeping the tape clear of applied decoration. Then apply a good epoxy resin glue (which will not discolour) along the fractures. The glue will be absorbed into the joins by capillary action. After the glue has hardened, remove the excess with a sharp scalpel blade.

If the adhesive tape has covered decorative material, a little white spirit helps the tape to come away easily without any decoration peeling off.

If the pieces cannot be assembled first with tape, they can be stuck together with an ultra-fast glue – but only by someone with a steady hand.

Repairing ornamentation The average handyperson can repair and retouch damaged ornamentation as long as the piece is not valuable and frail with age. Use stove or modelling enamel for retouching faded or damaged enamelling; for extra sheen and protection coat with clear polyurethane or nail varnish when dry. To match an existing paint or to give an artificially aged look, mix different pigments or thin the paint with white spirit. Talcum powder sprinkled in the paint gives a matt finish.

Decanters Unlike the thick old bottles which have been buried in the ground (see 'Bottle collections'), decanters should never have their insides scrubbed with a bottle brush, as this could cause scratching and even breakage. Swirl warm soapy water around and if this fails, add some ammonia, or try soaking with a denture cleaner overnight.

Stains On persistent wine stains, use a dilute solution of 5 per cent nitric acid or sulphuric acid or a commercial stain remover (always follow instructions carefully and use rubber gloves when handling such materials). Then rinse thoroughly (at least ten times). This technique can also be used on badly stained drinking glasses, bottles or vases.

If the stain is still there, it is probably one of the 'white stains' mentioned earlier, which cannot be cleaned. To *avoid* such damage, decanters and vases should be drained and dried carefully, possibly using a hair dryer.

Mild staining can be removed by polishing with jeweller's rouge or a fine metal polish applied with a soft rag, but if the stains show an advanced state of decomposition, hand the article over to a professional who will treat it with concentrated hydrofluoric acid. This is far too toxic and volatile to use at home.

Removing glass stoppers Stoppers must be completely dry before they are replaced in decanters, otherwise they can get stuck fast.

If this should happen, on no account try to wrest the stopper out by force; pour a mixture of glycerine, alcohol and common salt or methylated spirit (denatured alcohol) and cooking oil around the join, and leave it to soak in for a day. Ease out the stopper with a gentle side-to-side movement.

Mirrors

Glass mirrors have been used for over 2,000 years but only since the 17th century have they become commonplace. Indications of antiquity are the thinness of the glass, softly bevelled edges and slight imperfections of the reflecting image. But the backing is the best clue.

Backing Mirrors of 17th-century plate glass were given backings of tin and mercury amalgam; they look grainy and metallic. Silver with a protective coating of red lead or brown paint followed in the mid-nineteenth century, a refined version of which is used today.

Old mirrors tend to go grey with exposure to damp with spots and patches appearing where the metal has corroded and come away from the glass. Silver will even flake away in patches and tarnish, a more dramatic example of what happens to modern mirrors when kept in a very damp atmosphere. This can be avoided by ensuring that the frame forms an effective seal around the mirror's edge. Better still is to have the mirror totally sealed in a damp-proof mounting (as with many mirrors for bathroom use.

Re-silvering Modern mirrors can be re-silvered professionally, but it is unwise to have old mirrors re-silvered or the mirror itself replaced, as they are more valuable as they are. Indeed, mirror manufacturers now produce artificially faded and aged mirrors for reproduction furniture.

Cleaning Window cleaner, followed by buffing with a soft linen cloth, is the simple way to clean modern mirrors, but older mirrors should be wiped with a soft cloth impregnated with a mixture of equal parts water, methylated spirit (denatured alcohol) and paraffin (kerosene). This cleans and polishes in the same operation.

Never use too wet a cloth, as excess moisture could seep under the frame and corrode the backing.

Ornamentation Mirrors are often etched or painted like glassware, and this decoration should be cared for and cleaned in the same way as described for glassware.

Frames Mirror frames should be cared for in the way most suitable for the material in question – be it plain wood or tortoiseshell (see pp210 and 212).

Bottle collections

Old bottles can make spectacular displays – torpedo-shaped or marble stoppered, fluted ink bottles and embossed beers. The colours can range from blues and pale aqua greens to ruby reds (coloured by the addition of real gold) to the sun-tinted amethysts favoured by American collectors.

There is a collectors' market in bottles, but there are still many to be found where they were dumped a century ago. In rural areas, clumps of nettles are often a clue to an old disposal site at the edge of a farmyard; on cultivated land, the undergrowth around trees which the plough can't reach may reveal the now valuable litter of generations of thirsty farm workers. In cities the bulldozers on regeneration sites may well unearth ancient household treasures.

Bottles found in such places are fragile when they first see the light of day, so leave them for 24 hours or so to adjust to pressure and temperature changes, having gently wiped off any loose dirt.

Washing The best approach is the three-bath method: one bucket of cold water containing half a kilo of washing soda, a bucket of clean water, a bucket of half-strength soda solution. Wash each bottle individually in the clean water, then in the strong solution. Then submerge it upright (to get rid of trapped air bubbles) in the weaker soda solution. Leave to soak until really stubborn stains have gone; that may be a day or a week. If, after a final cold rinse, there are still stains, determine whether they are inside or outside.

External stains Fill a bucket with soft sand, burrow the bottle into it and turn it to and fro. This loosens many stains so that they can be washed off – and it doesn't scratch the glass. If any remaining stains are the brown residues caused by iron, try a dab of rust remover. Carbon tetrachloride – clothes cleaning fluid – acts on chemical stains.

Internal stains Quarter-fill the bottle with water and add a handful of fine gravel. With your thumb over the end, shake it vigorously. If that fails, fill the bottle with lemon juice, vinegar or household bleach and leave it to work overnight. Or try the rust remover or carbon tetrachloride treatments.

Old toothbrushes or the round brushes used for cleaning babies' bottles can help the solvents reach the right spots. Or make a brush by attaching strips cut from a nylon hair roller to a piece of dowelling or the bendable (plastic-covered) wire of a coat hanger.

Polishing Shine bottles with a damp cloth and cerium oxide, a reddish-brown powder available at craft shops and lapidary stores. If you cannot get cerium oxide, use light machine oil; but avoid commercial window cleaners as they streak.

FURNITURE SURFACES

Furniture responds to the atmospheric conditions around it. Extremes in temperature or humidity can warp or shrink joints, so keep furniture, indeed any wooden objects, away from fires and radiators. Central heating, however distant the furniture is from the source, can be harmful; keep temperatures moderate. The other safeguard is to hide a bowl of water underneath furniture during the winter months to prevent the wood from drying out.

At the beginning and end of winter treat your furniture to a wipe with water and vinegar and a good polish with beeswax. This seasons the wood at the times it needs it most.

Otherwise, polish at regular intervals throughout the year and protect against stains by using mats or blotting pads.

Routine checks Inspect from time to time for loose veneer or moulding. With luck you will find the bits before the vacuum cleaner sucks them up; store them somewhere safe for the next time you do any repairs.

Recognizing finishes
Rub a small, inconspicuous area with pure turpentine. If the wood has no applied finish, but only wax and oil, a rub or two will take the spot down to bare wood. If it retains a sheen, rub it with a tiny amount of methylated spirit (denatured alcohol); the surface will be sticky if it has been French polished, in which case rub no more.

Another test is to scrape a small area with your thumb nail or a razor blade. French polish produces very thin shavings; oil varnish, thick curls.

Stains and blemishes
Most can be treated. For an unnoticeable repair, strip the top surface at least and then re-finish. (See 'Stripping'.)
Ink stains should disappear with bleaching. After stripping, apply domestic or wood bleach (see 'Bleaching'). Re-stain the area to match the rest, and finish as appropriate.
Alcohol marks take the polish away with them; even so, strip the remaining polish for best results. Colour in the spill marks with a matching stain, working a fine brush carefully back and forth along the grain. When dry, re-finish to suit.
Water marks usually go away with equal parts of linseed oil and turpentine, or with camphorated oil. (You shouldn't need to strip first.) Wipe four or five times with a rubber (see 'French polishing') and then with a cloth moistened with water and vinegar. Repeat this process until the mark disappears; otherwise strip the finish.

Professional restorers have a quicker method – simply two brisk wipes over the marks with a tiny amount of methylated spirit. This is fine for the experienced, but too much spirit can seriously damage the wood.
Dents and scratches vary in their depth. If they do not penetrate the polish, ease them down with fine sandpaper dipped in linseed oil and then polish with beeswax.

Fill deeper scratches with liquid coloured beeswax (see 'Beeswax') and then smooth the surface with a cloth or with the paper side of sandpaper.
Bruises can be removed in one of two ways. Either fill the hole with molten beeswax and rub it smooth when hard as described for deeper scratches, or strip and then apply water and heat. For the latter, fill the bruise with water, keeping it topped up for about half an hour; then apply a moderate iron with cloth and sandpaper (smooth side down) between. Position the iron so that only the bruise is affected by the heat.

Soldering irons are more accurate than domestic ones, for small blemishes. An alternative is a cooking salamander, the utensil used for caramelizing *crème brûlée*.
Cigarette burns should be scraped with a pen knife or small chisel to remove charred areas. Then simply fill with molten beeswax, and rub smooth; colour the beeswax if necessary.
Spilt paint can be on the surface or firmly entrenched in the grain. Scrape away carefully for the former. Otherwise, strip and rub with beeswax-smeared wire wool.

Woodworm
Areas badly affected should be replaced but this will reduce the value of the furniture. Here is a trick the professionals use.

In a large bucket mix up a runny plaster of Paris solution, adding 1/10 part glue. Stand the affected member in the solution for half an hour; then remove it and wipe all the residue with a damp cloth. When dry, stain to match the rest of the wood and finish to suit. Your furniture will be heavier than when you began, but it will no longer have any holes.

Treat smaller outbreaks with insecticides and fill the holes with coloured beeswax (or glue and sawdust if the part does not show).

Spring is the best time to apply insecticides since the wood-boring beetles come to the wood's surface at this time.

Chipped veneer
On corners or edges this is a common fault. Cut away jagged pieces to make as straight an edge as possible for the veneer that will replace it. Try to match the grain of the veneer you have just cut by taking a pattern of it with tracing paper. When you buy your replacement (there are usually specialist veneer shops in larger cities), take the old veneer and the tracing with you and slide the tracing over the new veneer until you get the closest match to the old one.

Mark the area and cut it with a sharp, thin knife.

Glue it into position, and rub down gently with the smooth part of a hammer and sand when dry.
Bubbles in veneer Cut along one edge with a thin knife to make an opening for glue to be inserted; or if necessary, soften the old glue with a hot iron placed over a cloth and sandpaper, smooth side down.

Carefully scrape away the old glue with a scalpel; then apply new glue, using the nozzle of the adhesive container. Press the bubble down with the top of a small hammer, clean off excess glue with a damp cloth and let the new glue dry.

Stripping wood

Bare wood looks good and is also the best base for refinishing, but choose your stripping agent carefully. Furniture strippers and caustic soda are the strongest chemicals; but these can permanently discolour the wood. Turpentine or methylated spirit is safer, since neither penetrates very deeply with each application, but methylated spirit can dissolve some glues.

Wax-polished and oil-varnished surfaces Rub with fine wire wool dipped in turpentine. Then mop up immediately with an absorbent rag. Repeat this procedure until the wood is bared; the colour will probably change. Bleach if it does.

French-polished surfaces Do not go down to the bare wood if you plan to French-polish again. Rub with fine sandpaper dipped in linseed oil to take off the top surface and wipe clean with a cloth. Otherwise, remove the whole thing with a generous cloth application of methylated spirit and a rub with wire wool. Repeat if necessary and finish always with the cloth and spirit to remove all polish. Remember to go sparingly on the spirit if there's veneer or inlay to prevent either of these from lifting.

Cellulose-based varnishes and lacquers Use a commercial stripper or cellulose thinner. For a stronger treatment, strip with ammonia or caustic soda, but since these can burn you and darken the wood or turn it red, exercise caution. Wipe with water after use; wear protective clothing and work in a well-ventilated place, away from children and pets.

Veneer Strip the polish on this according to the type of finish as previously described, but see that water or other solvents do not loosen the glue.

To remove veneer, apply an iron and a damp cloth to soften the glue and then gently prise it away. If the glue is not heat-sensitive, or you want to re-use the veneer, dab the edges with methylated spirit continuously until it penetrates enough glue for you to remove the veneer intact.

Bleaching

Apart from fading the overall colour, bleaching is used to remove stubborn stains. Bleach only if you are experienced or you may do more harm than good. If in doubt, consult a professional restorer or an antique dealer.

For small jobs domestic bleach is suitable, but where greater strength is required a wood bleach is preferable. Use 1 part bleach to 2 parts water.

Timing is crucial, so follow the manufacturer's instructions for this exactly. Wear rubber gloves and apply with a brush or cloth. Always wipe afterwards with water to stabilize the acid. Should the wood turn white after rinsing, wipe the surface with camphorated oil.

Staining

Water stain, spirit stain and oil stain cope with most needs. Oil stain, available under many brand names, is the easiest to use and the most lasting of the three. It should not be used, though, on pine, spruce or hardwoods such as beech or birch; on these resinous woods it gives a patchy finish.

Spirit stains do not sink well into wood but are suitable on small areas.

Of the water stains, the most effective (and least expensive) are those containing aniline dyes. Water stains can, however, raise the grain, particularly on pine. Unless you seek this effect, counteract it by rubbing the grain with fine sandpaper to bring it more into line with the rest of the surface. If the stain causes the grain to become darker, which can also happen, apply a pigment solution of Vandyke crystals and hot water (wait for it to cool); this will cause the colours to merge. The Vandyke crystals produce a darkish oak colour; dilute according to the intensity desired and then add a small amount of turpentine to provide a sealer.

Wax or French-polish stained wood.

Varnishing

Varnish on old furniture is usually shellac- or cellulose-based – and to touch it up can be difficult, because the joins will be obvious. If the cracks are tiny, you can try to touch them up using a pencil brush, but it is usually better to remove old varnish and varnish again.

Apply varnish with a brush. Let it dry and finish by polishing with a cloth.

Beeswax

This is the base of good furniture polish; it is also used as a wood filler. Pure beeswax is rock hard and needs to be melted before use, but exercise extreme caution because it is highly flammable. Use an old saucepan with a handle; spoon in as much as you need and melt it over a low heat. Never let it splatter over the flame. Turn off the heat the moment it liquefies and stir in dry pigment to colour if necessary. Let it cool slightly before using.

French polishing

You might prefer to have this done by a professional, but there is no reason why the amateur should not attempt it on less costly objects.

To revive jaded French polish, dust the surface and clean it off with vinegar and water. Then polish with beeswax.

The rubber The most economical way to apply French polish is to use a rubber made from wadding or cotton wool wrapped in a cotton or muslin cloth. When applying polish to the rubber, wring out the drips to avoid patchiness.

Application Apply the first coat of polish with the rubber as described below. Then rub the surface, still along the grain, with fine sandpaper and linseed oil. Begin to build up the polish; rub first along the grain and then in circular movements. As the amount of polish on the rubber is used up, increase the pressure. At the same time, work in gradually diminishing circles and make sure that the rubber is dry before you recharge it. If the rubber becomes sticky, apply a tiny amount of linseed oil to it.

Satin finish When the final coat has been applied and the polish is dry, the finish will be glossy. Pumice powder will reduce the sheen.

Sprinkle some on the dry surface and rub it in with a fine, soft shoe- or clothes-brush; work in the direction of the grain each way, two or three times, and the glare will disappear. Wipe off the excess powder with a rag and then rub the surface with beeswax.

MISCELLANEOUS

The collectors' items on these pages are likely candidates for professional restoration. But there are simple cosmetic techniques to halt decay and to fit objects for display.

Once restored, objects last longer if handled as little as possible, and kept away from heat, bright sunlight and damp.

Ivory

As it shrinks and swells in response to changes in atmospheric conditions, an ivory item can warp and crack; keep it in a fairly humid, even temperature and away from direct light. Store in tissue paper, away from metal or rubber objects.

Old ivory has a fine yellowy patina; don't try to remove this or the object will lose its value and beauty. For those objects which look better white, like piano keys and knife handles, make a stiff paste of whiting (chalk) and 20 volume hydrogen peroxide. Coat the piece and leave to dry, then wash off and dry the object thoroughly. Apply some almond oil on a soft cloth to give the ivory a protective coating.

Use a woodworking adhesive for repairs (remove excess glue with a damp rag). Keep ivory clean by dusting regularly or by wiping, if grimy, with a damp soapy cloth or a soft toothbrush.

Leather

Leather is found on all sorts of old objects – on trunks, dressing cases, sword grips and scabbards, bottles, desk tops, furniture and books. If the leather has been well looked after and is still supple, wipe it clean with a damp cloth, adding a drop of liquid soap if necessary; then coat it with hide food. Leave that to soak in for a while, then buff with a soft cloth or brush.

Soft, delicate leather of the kind used for book covers and desk tops can be treated with the following recipe, which is similar to the leather dressing used by the British Museum. The beeswax in it produces a high shine, so for a matt finish omit this ingredient.

Dissolve 15g of white beeswax in 300ml hexane (no heat is required), then add 200ml of anhydrous lanolin. Stir well. Finally add 30ml cedarwood oil.

Apply the mixture with a soft cloth and leave the coating to soak in for several days, then polish with a cloth or brush. The dressing lasts many years.

Dry saddlewear, such as harnesses, bags and boots that are worn or cracked, should be cleaned with saddle soap first. (The leather will improve with further applications.) Then apply a coat of oily preservative.

Tougher leather items, such as furniture and trunks, can be treated with tallow if they are worn.

Rub the paste in with a cloth over your fingers. When dry buff with leather polish. Alternatively, refurbish the leather with a mixture of 3 parts castor oil to 2 parts alcohol.

Tortoiseshell and horn

Both are tough and deteriorate little with age. Repair horn with cellulose adhesive and tortoiseshell with epoxy adhesive.

Remove dirt and grease with soapy water and dry immediately. Using a circular motion, rub in linseed oil with the thumb. Leave the oil to soak, then clean off with a dry cloth. Repeat the process over several days and finish with a microcrystalline wax. Display away from direct heat and harsh light; or wrap in tissue paper and store in a dry place.

Marble

Though hard, marble is neither tough nor resilient. It is porous and suffers damage from atmospheric pollution, frost, rain and excessive heat. Marble figures are best kept indoors away from open fires; but if they are outside they should be covered in black polythene in the winter months.

Crystallization of salts often occurs in marble (the salts present in the stone move to the surface with the retained moisture as it dries, leaving a white flaky deposit). Treat this condition with a papier-mâché pulp made from plain blotting paper and distilled water which draws out the salts as it dries. Apply a coat 10mm thick around the salting and remove it carefully when dry. Repeat if necessary.

To seal the marble and prevent further damage, paint it with a syrupy mixture of polyvinyl alcohol powder and warm distilled water, or use a sealer from a marble merchant.

Clean polished marble and treat any stains with soapy water. Stubborn stains should be treated by an expert.

Remove grit with the brush attachment of a cleaner, and then clean the marble with a solution of half white spirit, half water and 1 teaspoon of mild liquid detergent to each 600ml of the mixture. Apply sparingly with damp cotton swabs, changing them frequently.

Marble should be repolished with a succession of coarse, medium and fine carborundum stones, and finished with fine emery paper. Use a circular motion while polishing and keep the surface lubricated with water. Apply powdered oxalic acid on a damp rag to bring up a shine and when dry polish with beeswax.

Cane and wicker

Badly torn wicker and cane furniture should be taken to an expert for repairing or recaning, but cleaning can be done at home.

Remove surface grime with warm soapy water on a rag, cleaning both sides of the object if possible. If the object is left in the sun to dry, the sun will bleach the cane; cold salt water scrubbed on will have much the same effect.

Take the old polish off cane chairs with methylated spirit (denatured alcohol); old paint or varnish will need a coating of paint stripper and a lot of patience since the strands will need individual scraping.

If any parts need sticking together, do this with wood glue after cleaning. When the glue is dry, polish the object with a silicone furniture polish to bring up a sheen. The various shades of French polish can be used to produce different effects; experiment on a part that won't show. White polish produces a milky effect; transparent enhances the natural tone; button polish gives a yellow tint, and so on. Apply one thin coat only, protecting non-cane areas with newspaper if necessary.

To protect wickerwork from dirt, give it a coating of clear polyurethane glaze; a non-glossy preservative can be made from 56g of white beeswax and benzene. Flake the beeswax into the benzene and stir until it dissolves. Apply with a brush or cloth.

To paint wicker, use acrylic paint: it won't flake off the glossy surface. The best method of applying the paint, since wickerwork is so intricate, is an aerosol spray (see p242).

Musical instruments

Valuable old instruments should be restored by a specialist. Temporary repairs can be performed on less valuable ones, particularly those for display.

Missing strings can be replaced on stringed instruments (under enough tension to keep them straight) as long as the soundpost is secure. (A collapsed soundpost can be heard rattling around inside. Expert attention will be required to replace both it and the strings, since the instrument could snap in two if tension were applied over a collapsed soundpost.)

Obtaining new strings for lutes and harps can be difficult – try lengths of nylon fishing line instead.

Wooden casings on stringed and woodwind instruments can be rubbed with linseed oil. Leave to soak in, remove excess with a rag, and then polish with a soft cloth. Take any gilded instruments that need new gilt to an expert.

Woodwinds On woodwind instruments the waxed thread that binds cork at the joints may disintegrate. Scrub the joints clean and re-bind with waxed dental floss. Joints should be airtight, but if they are so tight that dismantling is difficult coat the cork with a grease available from music shops.

Clean the keys with the appropriate metal polish and never remove them.

Books

If you have an old book that is badly damaged, ask an expert whether it is worth the cost of professional restoration. Preserve any loose fragments for the restorer.

When old books have been over-handled, their spines break and their covers become worn; when under-handled, the leather dries out. (In moderation, the oiliness of our skin is good for bindings and helps preserve them.)

General care To prolong a book's life, take it down from the shelf properly. Use two hands, top and bottom, rather than one finger hooked into the top of the spine, which can tear it. Rest the spine on a tabletop and open the front board out flat. Opening the book in the middle may break the spine.

Books should be kept in cold, dry, dust-free conditions. Books must be able to breathe, so airtight cases are not a good idea, and damp airless conditions cause fungus. Never keep books near a gas fire as the acid fumes eat into the leather; equally, an over-warm room dries books out.

Keep cleaning to a minimum. It is best simply to wipe books with a dry duster.

Covers As most leather book bindings are fragile, avoid cleaning them with water. If treatment is necessary, use either the special preservative dressing (see 'Leather') or a colourless polish.

Stained cloth bindings can be cleaned with dry-cleaning fluid on a rag.

Pages Clean blemishes on pages with an art eraser or with a ball of soft breadcrumbs from the doughy centre of a loaf rolled over the spot (remove all the crumbs afterwards). Treat red 'fox marks' with a mild solution of domestic bleach, applied on the tip of a brush. Repeat until the stain disappears, then wipe the area with distilled water. Benzine on a cotton wool pad can be used to remove greasy spots. You can clean the page edges (dust them first) by clamping the book together firmly and rubbing gently with an art eraser, a ball of breadcrumbs or with cotton dipped in white spirit.

Insects Get rid of silverfish and bookworms by placing the book into an airtight box, and then surrounding it with cotton wool soaked in vermifuge. Seal the box and leave for a day. Repeat the treatment a few weeks later in case any eggs have hatched.

Clocks

Leave mechanical repairs to an expert; let him restore the face and casing too if the clock is valuable. Once the clock is running, set it level and firm, until a plumb-line aligns with the 12 and the 6. If the tick is uneven gently bend the crutch piece, which moves the pendulum or rod, to right or left. Sometimes a coin placed under a mantelpiece clock will correct this fault.

When fixing a clock to a wall that has a skirting or baseboard, take up the gap with a block of wood of the same thickness and screw the clock through casing and wood.

Casings Clock casings come in all shapes, sizes and materials. Clean wood with either soap or white spirit on a damp cloth; then finish with a good furniture polish. Ormolu can be cleaned with ammonia, but wear rubber gloves and wash it off immediately with clean water. Porcelain can simply be wiped with a soapy cloth. Clean a plain glass face with damp newspaper, and buff it with a chamois. Leave painted glass and brass faces to experts who can also fit new hands if these are needed.

Guns

First make sure the gun is unloaded! To test for this, first measure the outside of the barrel, and then put a wooden rod or dowel down the muzzle and mark the point at which it stops. If the difference in length is 25mm or more the gun is probably loaded. Remove the ball and scrape off old powder.

To clean, dismantle the gun first. A good selection of screwdrivers and pin punches is needed to avoid damaging screws, pins or wood. Cover the jaws of a vice with leather or wood, and place the gun inside with lock uppermost. Loosen screws of the lock with penetrating oil, and remove the lock carefully, noting exactly where each screw and pin came from. Soak the lock in penetrating oil to loosen the screw, then clean gently. Be sure to preserve all makers' marks on butt, side, lock and barrel. Remove textiles and leather and clean these separately.

Clean the barrel with paint stripper or white spirit on fine wire wool or a toothbrush, but remove none of the original paint or blueing. Scrape spots with the end of a copper scraper, but do not go beyond the spot itself. Further rusting can be prevented with preserving oil, and if re-blueing is necessary use commercial blueing, following the makers' instructions for application exactly.

Clean the stock (the wooden part of the gun) with white spirit on a damp cloth, followed immediately by a coat of linseed oil. Let this soak in, then remove any stickiness and polish with a good furniture polish. Treat any steel that is out of sight with a minute quantity of anhydrous lanolin.

When handling the restored gun, wear cloth gloves to prevent corrosion. Display guns in a clean, dry, dust-free place; store them in a well-ventilated plastic sheath.

PICTURES / Care

How many paintings, prints and photographs are you reluctant to display because they are no longer perfect? If they are valuable, take them to a professional restorer: if you are not sure, ask an expert for an opinion. If professional restoration is not worth while but you would like to be able to show them off again, some simple remedies can be attempted.

Even if a piece is partially damaged (the edges are torn, for example) at least part of it may be salvaged. If the main subject is in good condition, cut it out and glue it to a piece of toning background paper, discarding the damaged parts. Or use it for *découpage* with a mass of several different subjects.

Picture restoration
Picture restoration is a highly skilled craft. The homemaker can postpone the day when such help is needed by attending to the effects of ageing and by preventing accidental damage. Most pictures are made up of organic materials which deteriorate with age. Light, atmospheric conditions and dirt are the most damaging agents.

Light Among the more sensitive types of art are watercolours, prints, drawings and pastels. Less sensitive but still liable to damage are oils, egg tempera and acrylics.

Pictures should not be hung in direct sunlight or near a fire, heater or electric light. Picture lights are not recommended for valuable pieces. Pictures made up of the more sensitive materials should be placed in shaded corners or alcoves so that they get a minimum of exposure.

Atmospheric conditions These refer in the main to the Relative Humidity (RH) and to the temperature. Conditions which we find comfortable (around 20°C, 68°F, and 55 per cent RH) are the best for pictures too. Unvarying conditions are vital: fluctuations in temperature and RH caused by turning heating on and off are among the most destructive factors. Avoid hanging pictures on an outside wall likely to be damp or on a chimney breast where the fire is in use.

Low RH causes drying out of the paint materials; wood shrinks, causing panels to warp and split, and paper is weakened. High RH encourages the growth of mould.

Dirt The grime carried in the atmosphere not only reduces a picture's clarity, but also can contribute to the decomposition of paper and canvas.

Handling and hanging
Paintings are vulnerable to accidents. Make sure they are securely hung or attached to the wall. Don't put them where they can be damaged by children, pets, moveable furniture or swinging doors.

Pictures are most vulnerable when they are being moved. It takes two people to carry a big, cumbersome frame and the path to the new site should be cleared of possible hazards. Support the whole frame; don't get a finger grip between the stretcher and the canvas as this is a sensitive area.

Professional restoration
A restorer can line weakened or torn canvas by attaching a new canvas to the back of the original or by replacing an old lining canvas.

Panels that have split can be rejoined and, if necessary, treated to reduce damage caused by atmospheric changes.

Loose paint can be secured and paint loss filled and then repainted.

Old restorations which have deteriorated or discoloured can be removed and redone. Sometimes there are later alterations which may have to be removed to reveal the original.

The removal of varnish is another job for the restorer; this is not a simple process as the paint may be more soluble than the varnish, which is the case when the same resins have been used in both. Even when the paint is not resinous, it may still be at risk in operations involving prolonged solvent contact.

Works on paper mounted on old acidic board can be lifted off and remounted; dirt, staining and foxing can be removed or reduced; tears can be mended, and buckled paper smoothed.

Every one of these processes demands not only technical skill but a scientific understanding of the materials used – in both the painting and restoration. But even with this knowledge, the restorer can only mend a painting as far as its condition will allow. Once paint has been over-cleaned, flattened or permanently damaged there is nothing anyone can do to revive it.

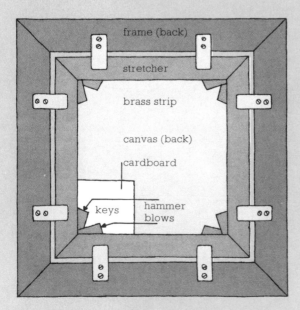

frame (back)

stretcher

brass strip

canvas (back)

cardboard

keys   hammer
        blows

Construction and repairs
To solve the problems it is important to understand fully a painting's components.

Support This can be rigid (artist's board, wooden panels or copper), but the most standard is canvas sized with glue and secured to a wooden stretcher with tacks. Debris and dust accumulate between the stretcher and canvas.

To clear these, remove the picture from its frame and turn the canvas upside down, angling it so that the dirt falls to the floor (and not down the back of the canvas). Insert a blunt, round-ended knife between the stretcher and canvas. Taking great care not to pierce the canvas, gently dislodge the dust by stroking the blade against the stretcher (not the canvas).

Ideally, the stretcher should be adjustable, with keys in each corner. The canvas should be taut and flat, but not too tight. If there are bulges, tap the keys gently into the corners with a small hammer, angling the blows as illustrated. Take care not to hit the canvas. (A piece of card placed between the canvas and the keys is a good precaution against this.) Continue stretching, working around the keys in turn, until the canvas is taut and evenly tensioned.

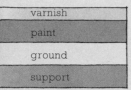

Structure of painting

Chipping

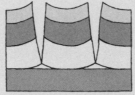

Cleavage

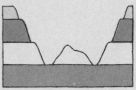

Paint and ground loss

Ground This is the medium applied to the canvas before the painting begins; it primes the canvas and establishes the background tone.

Paint This is pigment ground in a medium such as oil, egg tempera or acrylic resin. Mixed-medium paintings are quite common. Paint layers are structurally very similar to grounds. Deterioration resulting from poor technique or ageing is common to both.

Craquelure is the term applied to the pattern of cracks in the paint, or in the paint and ground. It is caused by age and encouraged by poor atmos-

pheric conditions and accidental knocks. When the edges of the craquelure lift, this is called chipping. Paint and ground layers can lift more substantially in blistering or tenting (cleavage).

All these conditions result in paint loss, subsequent drop in value and expensive repairs. If you detect any loss of adhesion, consult a restorer.

Varnish This is the surface film applied to protect the paint and to bring out its colours. Today, it is usually a synthetic resin, but oils, waxes and natural resins have all been used in the past. If the painting is sound and has a thick,

even layer of varnish, you can remove surface dust with a dry cloth.

More stubborn dirt can be shifted with saliva on a cotton swab. Remove the picture from the frame first, and roll, or gently rub, the swab over the surface. Clean a small patch at a time, changing the swab frequently. Beware of breaking impasto (thick paint). Should the surface turn milky (blanch) or should colour appear on the swab, stop immediately and consult a restorer. Take care no saliva gets on a gilt frame, since this is not protected by varnish and, like some paints, may dissolve.

Restoring varnish An old varnish can be revived by polishing with a synthetic wax emulsion.

If the surface is very dull you can re-varnish, but since it is a risky business it is unwise to practise on a painting of value. Work in a warm, dust-free, well-lit room. Remove the painting from its frame and lay it flat on a table so that it can be worked on from all sides.

Dust the picture, then, using a good-quality brush, apply the new oil-paint varnish a little at a time with even strokes. Leave the picture for at least a day to dry.

Prints, drawings and water-colours
The pencil, charcoal and washes of drawings and water-colours and the inks of old prints are frail; renovation is best left to a professional restorer. But new mounts and frames can do wonders for their contents.

Mounting For mounting techniques, see p217, but bear in mind the following points for valuable pieces.

Use only the best-quality rag-fibre mounting board, preferably of a grade known to be acid-free. One of the chief purposes of a mount is to hold the picture away from the glass; make sure it is thick enough to do this.

Never paste the whole picture to the backing; instead, attach the two top corners with gummed stamp-collectors' hinges or pasted tissue paper.

Framing Glass and backboard are essential as protections against dirt and atmospheric change. For framing techniques, see p216, but the following points for valuable prints and drawings should be observed. To give an airtight seal, edge the glass with tape (making sure it is not visible from the front). When placing the mounted picture into the frame, double-check that

no part of the picture touches the glass. Use hardboard (not pasteboard, plywood or chipboard, as these contain substances which are harmful to the paper) for the backing, and cut this to fit closely to the inner edge of the frame. Hammer good-quality steel panel pins into the inside edge of the frame, parallel with the backing. Seal the back with adhesive tape.

Photographs
Stains Carbon tetrachloride removes most marks. Heavier stains, such as fox marks, mould or mildew need professional treatment.

Photographic shops will copy and enlarge old (or new) prints. Have this done before you do any repairs: the colour contrast with black and whites will be stronger and the surface will be smoother.

Retouching If there are dog-ears or creases on the original, touch out their 'scars' on the enlargement, applying the ink as described in 'Hand-colouring'. Use a sable brush and work with a magnifying glass so that you can reproduce the image dot-for-dot. A line would show up.

Overall colouring Use commercial fabric dyes in a weak solution to give overall colour to a black and white photograph. The print must be wet when you work on it, so soak it in water first.

Dilute the dye, put it in a tray and dip the print in and out repeatedly until the colour builds up to the right intensity. (The black areas will stay black, but this is quite normal.) Let the print dry naturally.

Hand-painting This can be done on a black and white photograph to pick out details or to give colour to the whole thing.

To treat a multicoloured subject, first apply water with a sable brush to every outline of the subject where there is colour change. (This lifts

the emulsion and prevents the colour running into adjacent areas.)

Using water-soluble ink in the colours needed, mix up a solution of this, mild liquid detergent (to make the application smoother) and water. Apply with a cotton bud, and use a sable brush for details. The ink can be used neat for highlights.

Repeat applications for the correct intensity.

Sepia toning This gives a longer life to black and white photographs, is a good way to cover up stains on enlargements or copies, and makes a new black and white print look old-fashioned. But wash a print in sepia only if the tone is light, that is, if the blacks are not dominant.

Sepia kits are available

from pharmacies; they contain toner, bleach and full instructions for use.

Soak the print in water and work on it while it is wet, wearing rubber gloves.

Put the print on a clean sheet of glass (or any other splinter-free surface). Using cotton balls, apply the bleach with straight, even strokes from top to bottom, starting from one side of the picture. The image will disappear. Repeat, this time going from side to side.

Wash the print thoroughly in running water. Clean the glass and return the wet print to it.

Now apply the sepia toner in the same way as the bleach (in one direction only). Rinse in water after applications.

'Pictures' can be paintings, photographs and prints – or letters, stamps, diplomas, labels, postcards, leaves, menus, tickets, bills . . . anything you like.

A picture can be framed with or without glass; it can be sandwiched without a frame between glass and a board, or simply stuck onto a board. Choose a frame that suits the image and the context; if a ready-made moulding seems too formal, make one from simple beading.

Here traditional framing is discussed

Picture-frame mouldings

Since carved and gilded mouldings available from artist's materials suppliers are often fragile and expensive, it is worth having the supplier make the frame, or at least cut the mitres (the 45° angled cuts at the corners).

Simpler picture-frame mouldings are available from do-it-yourself stores and timber merchants.

Jumble and garage sales and antique shops are likely sources for old frames. They can be dismantled and cut to size to make smaller frames, or

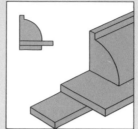
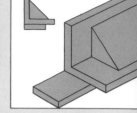

Simple mouldings and cabinet beadings can be stuck together and used to make more elaborate picture-frame mouldings.

renovated and re-used as they are. Damaged mouldings can sometimes be made good using a mould taken from a sound section

of the frame; scratched or chipped frames can be retouched, or given a camouflaging texture (see 'Frame cover-ups' below).

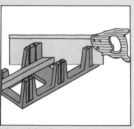

Mitre block

Shooting board

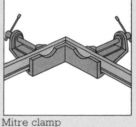

Mitre clamp

Spanish windlass

Cutting mitres

A mitre block is a cheap, simple gadget which ensures accurate 45° saw cuts through a moulding.

Hold the moulding in the mitre box so that it rests against one side of the box, and align the cutting mark on the rebate with the saw blade. Cut carefully to avoid splintering the front of the frame. It is best to cut elaborate frames from the front (using a set square and a pencil to transfer the cutting point on the rebate to

the front) to avoid damaging the moulding. Check that the moulding is angled the correct way before cutting from the outer edge at both ends.

When two mitres have been cut, an angle of precisely 90° should be formed between the pieces. If the fit is not good, trim the mitre: hold the moulding in place by using a shooting board made from a piece of wood fixed at exactly 45° to a board along which a sandpaper block or plane

can pass. Hide remaining imperfections with filler when the frame is finished.

Securing corners Use polyvinyl acetate woodworking glue and veneer pins (driving in from what will become the sides of the picture) to secure wooden mouldings. Use epoxy resin adhesive on aluminium angle. A mitre clamp is the best device for holding the parts while assembling them; otherwise use a vice with its jaws padded and check right angles of moulding

with a set square.

If a cramp or vice is not available, use a Spanish windlass arrangement to hold the corners while the glue sets. Run a loop of string around the frame with corner pieces to protect the mouldings, and twist the ends of the string around a nail to pull it tight, like a tourniquet.

Check that the joints are carefully aligned and that both diagonal measurements are the same. Adjust, if necessary, while the glue is still wet.

Frame cover-ups

Give imperfect frames a textured surface; apply a glaze of thick varnish tinted with oil paint (or a screed of cellulose filler), then dab with a dry brush, steel wool, a sponge or a crumpled rag. 'Distress' a wooden frame by searing its surface with a soldering iron or a kitchen salamander.

Cover the frame with *découpage*, fabric or

string – or glue on small shells, pebbles, sequins or dried flowers.

Glass

Framing without glass is acceptable for most oil paintings (particularly when varnished), cheap prints and other pictures which can be easily dusted. But glass is essential for watercolours, pastel and pencil drawings, good-quality prints,

photographs and any other items that could be damaged by adverse atmospheric conditions and by cleaning. Binding the edges with insulation tape helps seal the glass against the picture, keeping out dust and humidity.

In most cases conventional 2mm-thick picture glass is suitable. Non-reflective picture glass (diffuse reflection glass) can be used for pictures hung

opposite windows, but it is more expensive than ordinary picture glass and tends to dull colours and obscure detail.

Because of its light weight, clear acrylic sheet is sometimes chosen as an alternative to picture glass, but it does tend to attract dust and is more easily scratched.

Buy glass or acrylic about 1.5mm smaller each way than the rebate.

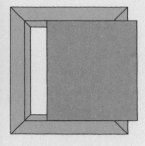
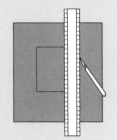
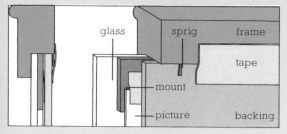

glass

sprig   frame

tape

mount

picture   backing

Construction of a framed picture.

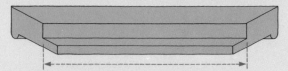

The measurements for a frame are made along the rebate, not the outside edge (i.e. they are the same dimensions as the picture's backing board).

When buying mouldings, allow extra length for the mitres at each corner; the wider the moulding, the greater the overhang.

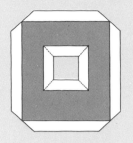

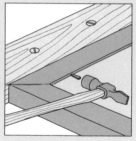

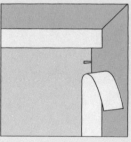

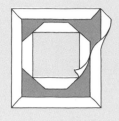

Mounts (mats)

Suit the proportions of the mount to the picture. If the mount is too narrow, a picture can look cramped; if it is too wide, it can dwarf the picture. (But you can dramatize a tiny item by use of a large mount.) For conventional mounting, the margins at top and sides should be of equal width, while the bottom margin should be about 25 per cent wider. Cut the mount to fit the back of the frame.

Window mounts

A separate window mount is useful to hold the picture away from the glass. Otherwise the picture can simply be stuck down onto a card mount.

Make the window slightly smaller than the picture. Cut the opening with a sharp craft knife using a steel rule to guide the blade. Cut the sides straight or at an angle of 45° to give a bevelled edge. (Art suppliers sell knife guides that control the angle of cut.) Practise on scrap card first.

Covered mounts

An appropriate texture can be just the thing to set off pieces of ephemera turning them into 'pictures': a gingham mount for the menu from a favourite restaurant; lamé for the label from a memorable bottle of champagne – or use patterned wrapping paper, tin foil, wallpaper offcuts, black plastic bags, anything that works.

Lay the fabric on a flat surface and cut it 25mm larger all round than the mount. (For a window mount cut a window in the fabric smaller than that in the cardboard.) Spread contact adhesive on the back of the fabric and on the surface of the mount. Allow the glue on both surfaces to become touch-dry. Carefully lay the mount in place on the fabric. Smooth the fabric out on the right side. Cut slits into the inner corners of the fabric, and mitres at the outer corners (see diagram above left). Fold the turnings over onto the back of the mount (see diagram above).

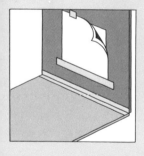

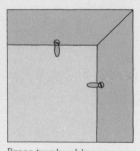

Backing

Position the picture on a backing board of thick cardboard which has been cut to fit the rebate of the frame. Attach the picture to the underside of the mount with two strips of adhesive tape to hold it temporarily in position. Then attach the mount to the backing board with a hinge of adhesive tape along the top inside edge of mount and backing.

Tap sprigs in parallel with the backing board.

Framing the picture

With the frame made, glass cut to size and picture mounted, the next stage is to cut a backing board of hardboard to fit the rebate. If the picture-frame moulding is less than 15mm wide, fit D-rings to the backing board for hanging. Wider mouldings will take screw eyes (see p220).

One centrally placed D-ring is suitable for pictures up to about 300mm wide. Wider pictures (with narrow mouldings) need two rings, set 50mm in from each side. In both cases the rings should be set one-third down from the top edge. Drill the board

Seal the frame back with tape or brown paper.

for the rings and secure them by hammering the split pins flat on the reverse side.

Clean the glass thoroughly with methylated spirit (denatured alcohol) on both sides. Polish dry with a lint-free cloth and then position it over the rebate of the frame, laid face down.

Position the mounted picture, then the backing board and, to hold everything in place, tap glazing sprigs (small headless wedge-like tacks) in to the rear inner edge of the frame. Alternatively, screw brass turnbuckles to the back of the frame; these have the advantage

Brass turnbuckles are an alternative to sprigs.

of allowing easy removal of the picture. The sprigs or turnbuckles should be fixed close to the corners of the frame.

Finally, stick brown gummed paper tape about 30mm wide along the perimeter of the frame's back to seal the gap between the frame and the backing board, or glue brown paper over the entire back of the frame.

Formal frames of wooden moulding with mitred corners are fine for formal subjects, but there are alternatives: aluminium or plastic angle, or frames made up from ordinary deal. Or dispense with a frame altogether; sandwich an image between glass or acrylic sheet, or mount it on a panel. Or stick it straight onto a wall or piece of furniture, and do *découpage*.

Wet mounting

This technique can be used for photographs and inexpensive prints, particularly large ones which might wrinkle under glass.

Size the cardboard backing board with smooth wallpaper paste; when the size is dry, moisten the back of the print with a damp rag and then dry with blotting paper until the print is just limp. Brush a thin coat of

wallpaper paste onto the back of the print. Lift the pasted print carefully by the top edge and align the bottom edge with the edges of the backing. Lower the pasted print onto the board as evenly as possible.

Cover the print with greaseproof (wax) paper and then smooth it with a dry pad, working from the centre outwards to remove air bubbles and

wrinkles. Take off the greaseproof paper and wipe away excess paste.

Cover the print with another sheet of greaseproof paper and of card, and weight it down until dry. Large prints tend to buckle the backing board when they dry: to counteract this, stick some paper of roughly the same weight as the print onto the back of the board in the same way.

Panel mounting

Cheap prints, labels and other paper items can be mounted without glass on chipboard panels. Cut the panels to the size of the print and smooth with abrasive paper. Chamfer the edges with a plane, fill them with a cellulose filler and rub down when dry. Paint the edges with emulsion (black, traditionally) and mount the picture on the panel (see 'Wet mounting', above).

A panel of any size can make the basis for a *découpage* picture.

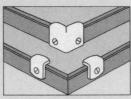

Mirror clips screw into the backing board.

Pictures without frames

Pictures, mounted or not, can be sandwiched between a sheet of glass, or clear acrylic, and a backing board – two sheets of acrylic with clips to hold the layers together can make a two-way picture to hang as a room divider.

Have the 3 or 4mm glass or acrylic cut to size and the edges ground or

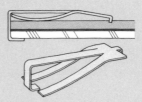

Picture clips are sprung to hold acrylic and board.

polished smooth, and then cut the backing board to fit it exactly; the type of backing depends on the type of clip chosen.

Mirror clips are straight for sides or angled for corners. They screw into the sides of the backing board: use 15mm chipboard or plywood to give the depth necessary to take the screws.

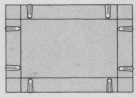

Grooves on the backing anchor the clips.

Picture clips take a 'sandwich' of acrylic and board about 12mm thick. Their advantage is that the display can be changed relatively easily. Use 8mm plywood or hardboard for the backing and, to prevent the clips from slipping out of place, make a groove in the backing board to anchor the pointed ends of the clips.

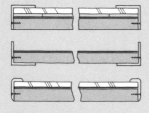

Aluminium frames

Aluminium angle makes simple, modern frames. Do-it-yourself and hardware stores sell it in various sizes; edge lipping for worktops can also be used. Mitre the corners (see p216), but use a fine-tooth hacksaw, and fix the corners with epoxy resin adhesive and no pins. Drill the sides at about 200mm intervals; insert screws to secure the backboard.

Deal frames

A picture that doesn't need to be protected by glass can suit being set deep into a wooden frame: it gives a rustic look instead of the tailored finish of standard frames with glass and mitred corners.

Use deal in a size that suits the proportions of the picture: perhaps 10 × 50mm; if the frame is deeper than 15mm it will overshadow a small picture.

Mitre the corners at 45°

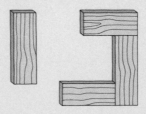

in the traditional way (see previous page), or simply butt them. To secure, pin them from the sides if the deal is not too thick; glue them; or hammer in corrugated fasteners (wiggle nails) from the back – taking care not to split the wood. Make sure the joins are smooth and flush before fixing, and check that the corners make right angles and the diagonals are the same length.

For more secure corners, cut away half the

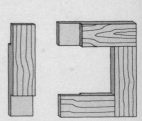

depth of the deal at both ends of each piece to make half-lap joints. The sides of the frame can overlap top and bottom at the corners, or the four corners can interlock as shown.

Mount the picture onto a backing of cardboard, and tape or staple in place on the back of the frame.

Rebates can be made in these frames to turn them into conventional glass-carrying frames.

Découpage

This decorative technique involves pasting paper shapes (usually cut or torn out of printed matter) onto a surface and then applying a thick covering of acrylic glaze so that the cut-outs look like an intrinsic part of the surface. *Découpage* can be done on almost any flat surface of wood, plaster, metal or board: it can look good on table-tops, boxes, trunks, screens, trays, cupboard doors, even walls. It can disguise imperfect surfaces, or just add applied decoration.

In any one room one object with *découpage* decoration will usually be enough; if it is to be used in a number of places, keep the style and content in harmony.

Materials

Any printed matter can be used – labels, tickets, wrapping paper, candy wrappers or materials like foil and tissue paper. It is best to stick to one kind of paper per design so thickness and texture are consistent; choose cuttings by colour or theme.

Wallpaper samples and decorating left-overs are eminently suitable for the process. Choose designs with strong shapes to cut out, and avoid heavily embossed textures.

Magazines and newspapers offer pictures, text and headlines. Use pictures whole or cut around the outlines of detail from different images. Shapes cut out of printed text can make interesting abstract patterns.

Wrapping paper with pronounced designs can provide good cut-out images; plain or all-over patterned paper can be cut into strips to work as frames for images, or into abstract shapes.

Labels from cans, bottles, candy bars and packages often have strong, attractive shapes and colours; individual fruit wrappers are another good source.

Mementoes, ephemera, items like menus, bills, and tickets for travel or entertainment can be arranged in patterns for an effect greater than the sum of the parts.

Posters can sometimes be obtained free from manufacturers – ranging downwards in size from billboard scale ones that could cover an entire wall.

Application Clean the surface, removing traces of polish from furniture. Size the surface if necessary. Use wallpaper paste, latex adhesive or any suitable clear glue applied to the paper. Stick the images onto the surface – pre-cut to fit, or at least so that only two layers overlap at any one point – and smooth out any bubbles.

When the adhesive is thoroughly dry, varnish over the whole surface with at least four coats; acrylic varnish is best because it does not yellow, nor does it make newsprint transparent, as wood varnish does.

Trompe-l'œil is art that imitates reality to the point of 'fooling the eye'. The traditional painted illusion is an expensive form of home decorating, but you can use the techniques of *découpage* to create attractive and amusing visual jokes.

When book jackets tear, save the spines – and the fronts if they are intact.

If you throw paperbacks away after you have read them, first strip the spine off with a craft knife.

If magazine advertisements for book clubs show the books full size, save them.

Paint straight lines suggesting bookshelves. Then paste up the book spines, some at angles, some in disarray. Add the images of houseplants, trinkets, bookends and anything else life-size

in magazine photographs which you would like to see on your shelves. Varnish to finish.

For an easy *trompe-l'œil* effect in the kitchen collect pictures of the items normally stored *inside* a cupboard or refrigerator, and stick them on the outside, on 'shelves' made of strips of paper. Magazine advertisements are a ready source of life-size images of things like table- and glass-ware. Labels from cans and bottles, and pieces of cardboard packaging can be cut off and used directly (stick bottle labels onto full-size bottle shapes cut from pieces of appropriately coloured paper).

To give depth, make shadows with a thick light-grey felt pen on one side of each item. Again, varnish to finish.

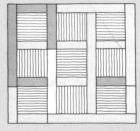

Design Cut-out shapes can make an overall pattern or a design like a border or a garland (see top illustrations). One way to formalize the normal scattering of motifs and give a more subtle effect is to base the design on a grid (bottom illustrations). This technique works especially well on rectangular items, e.g. a trunk used as a coffee table.

Choose a theme and plan an overall layout which sets the images into a regular framework. Cut

the images to a uniform size and shape, e.g. 15cm square. Stick the cut-outs on the surface leaving a regular border around them. Leave the background to show through if it is attractive or painted a suitable colour; otherwise, strips of paper cut to an appropriate width can be used. A three-colour scheme relating to the colours in the cut-outs is one suggestion: e.g. black and two shades of grey strips around cut-outs of newsprint.

If there are old-fashioned picture rails – mouldings or brass tubes on brackets – use them. Visible brass chains and wire or stylish cords can become part of the effect; nylon line is virtually invisible. The great advantage of the system is the scope it offers for changing arrangements without making new holes in the wall.

Fixing directly with hooks or plates means making holes in the wall, but usually allows the hanging hardware to be hidden behind the picture. (If picture plates are used, they can be painted to match the wall.)

Examining walls Before fixing directly, check the wall for pipes and cables. Water pipes will be near radiators. Modern electricity cables run horizontally or vertically to power points and switches. Different types of wall need different fixings: to identify, tap the wall to see if it sounds solid or hollow.

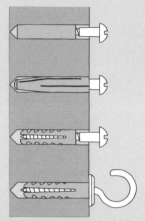

Solid walls should take picture hooks (see below left). These hooks are fixed simply by driving a hardened pin into the wall. If the wall is too hard, it will need drilling (with a masonry bit) for a wall plug and round-head screw (hang the picture directly onto the screw). In a really tough wall, an electric hammer drill may be needed to make the hole.

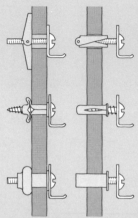

Cavity walls If the wall sounds hollow when tapped try a cavity wall fixing. Use a round-head screw, or thread the picture hook onto the bolt before tightening the head of the bolt into the wall according to the manufacturer's instructions.

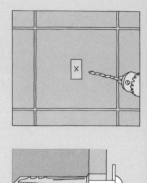

Ceramic tiled walls Drill a hole for a wall plug and fixing screw, using a masonry bit. Prevent the bit from skidding by placing a strip of sticky tape over the tile where you want the hole, and drilling through both tape and tile. Make sure the plug is sunk right into the wall behind the tile: if the plug projects into the hole in the tile itself, the tile will crack when the bolt is tightened.

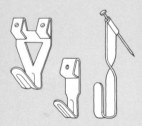

Single or multiple picture hooks, in different sizes, take different weights of picture. The pin enters the wall at an angle.

Hanging hardware
Whatever fixings are used on the back of the picture, they must be perfectly level to make the picture hang straight.

The backing board may be fitted with D-rings; if not, attach eyes or plates to the frame sides about one-third of the way down.

Use small screw eyes for light-weight pictures: like D-rings, these can be joined with picture wire to hang over a single hook, or hung directly onto L-hooks.

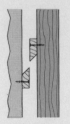

Split battens
If the picture has no frame or is too heavy to hang from two wall fixings, hang it on a split batten, i.e. a batten that has been machine-cut lengthwise at a 45° angle. The batten should run just less than the width of the picture.

Fix one half to the wall, using the appropriate fixings, and nail or screw the other half two thirds up the back of the picture so that the angles of the two will interlock. Slip the picture with its batten over the other half on the wall.

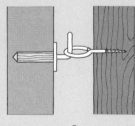
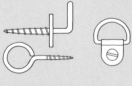

L-hooks Although using L-hooks means making two wall fixings, they make it easier to determine the hanging height and to get the picture level. Heavy, valuable pictures can have back hooks or back rings screwed to the sides of the frame and matched with L-hooks in position on the wall. For lighter pictures use a pair of screw eyes or D-rings.

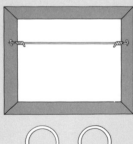

Securing wire The left-hand drawing shows the wrong way to twist picture wire round the eye; the right-hand way is more secure. (Use a bowline to attach nylon line.) String the wire so that it is taut across the back and secured at both sides. Then hold the centre of the wire to let the picture's weight stretch it: the hook goes at the apex of the triangle formed. Tension the wire before positioning the hook; see opposite page.

Accurate positioning
Picture plates Simply hold the picture level and in position on the wall and pencil in the location for the screw holes through the openings on the plates.
L-hooks need to correspond to the positions of the screw eyes or rings on the back of the picture. Measure up from the central line to the height of the eyes and then in from the outer edge to their exact positions. Mark the fixing points and screw them into the wall.

Pictures with wire With the stretched wire held flat against the back of the picture, take the distance between the apex of the wire and the centre top of the picture. Position the picture on the wall; mark a tiny point mid-way across the top of the pic- ture, remove the picture and make another mark below the first to the distance recorded. Drive the picture hook into the wall so that the base of the hook lines up with the mark. (Matching the brad of the hook to the mark may throw the picture above or below centre.)

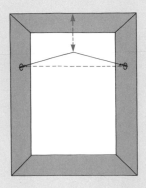

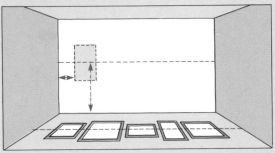
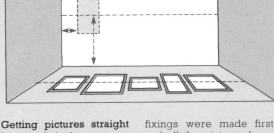

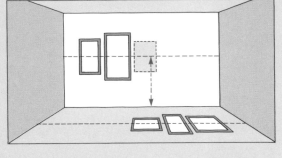

Getting pictures straight
It is relatively easy to position a single picture accurately: making an arrangement of pictures on a wall is more complicated, for example, when you want them to make a specific shape with all their tops or bottoms aligned.

Begin by arranging the pictures on the floor in front of the wall. Decide on their relationship to each other and their position on the wall. Measure the distance between them accurately, but hang them on the wall one at a time so that error doesn't build up – as it could if all the fixings were made first and all the pictures hung subsequently.

Take, for example, a row of pictures that is to be centrally aligned across a wall. First space the pictures out on the floor in their correct relationship to one another. Next decide upon their hanging height and measure the position of the constant line (from floor, ceiling or picture rail for horizontal alignment) that will run through the centre of the pictures – for example, 1.5m up from the floor.

Measure the interval between the first (left-hand) picture and the left-hand wall, the intervals between adjacent pictures, and finally the interval between the last picture and the right-hand wall.

Find the central point between top and bottom of each frame and lightly pencil this onto the left-hand side of the frame as seen from the front.

If the first picture is to hang, say, 30cm from the left-hand wall, lightly pencil in a mark this distance in from the wall and 1.5m up from the floor. Align the central mark of the picture frame with the mark on the wall and then check that the picture is horizontal with a spirit level before making its fixing points on the wall. Hang this first picture before measuring and hanging the second, to ensure that the spacing will be faithful to the intervals allowed for in the dry-run.

For the next picture, measure for the central line again, this time taking the side interval from the picture just hung. Level and hang as before.

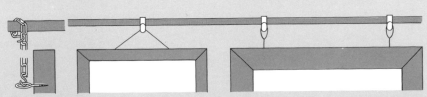
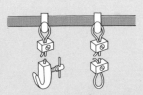

Picture rails
For larger pictures, use brass chain looped over a bracket-supported brass picture rail or hooked onto picture-rail hooks on a fixed moulding rail. Height can be adjusted link by link at the hooks in the back of the frame.

For lighter pictures, use 'invisible' nylon wire: this is sufficiently inconspicuous for pictures to be hung one above the other, and not in the conventional horizontal row. The more old-fashioned arrangement is a single picture-rail hook hung centrally above the picture; an alternative is two hooks, with the wire lines vertical.

You can sometimes obtain the adjustable devices used in art galleries: hooks which slide up and down on rigid wire uprights and lock under the weight of the picture, or toggles which tighten in position on nylon or wire.

Treat pictures not just as two-dimensional objects; imagine them in three dimensions in relation to the room as a whole or as part of a group of objects. Don't regard walls as separate from the rest of the room; they are an integral

part that should work gracefully with it.

Don't hang pictures simply to fill up wall space. A blank wall can be just as interesting as one filled with pictures that seem to be there for the sake of it. Hanging pictures from a

sense of duty gives more pain than pleasure, so one of the most important things is that you like the pictures.

Don't be afraid of empty space; it is not necessary to place a picture centrally on a wall or to space pic-

tures evenly to fill one out. Group some pictures tightly so that they seem to relate to one another or to other objects and balance them with space. Aesthetically, a blank area is just as important as one that is filled.

The single picture

One picture on a wall can be a cliché – usually when it is centrally placed and looks lost because it is too small for the space. To make a single picture work, the key is positioning. Relate it to a piece of furniture or a group of objects, or to an architectural element in the room. Or show conviction and hang it in an odd place – because something in the painting or in the sur-

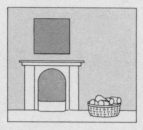

roundings justifies it.

A single picture could be hung very low and in an odd place – next to the fireplace, for example,

and on a level with or even below the mantelpiece. It still has to balance and work with something else – a basket of logs on the

floor, say, and a lamp. Like this it becomes much more noticeable and interesting to the eye.

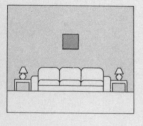

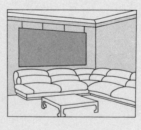

Symmetry?

In a room with a sofa against the wall and symmetrically placed coffee tables at either end, the obvious place for a single picture is the centre. This

would work, perhaps, if the picture was large and low, but a small picture would have more impact as part of one coffee-table group, linked by the table lamp.

Size

A large picture is in some ways easier to manage than a small one that might get lost: rooms can often take a far larger picture than you might think: it

can often make a far stronger statement.

Tricia Guild uses a very large canvas to bridge the awkward gap between the two halves of a knocked-through room.

Pictures plus things

To prevent single pictures from looking isolated, position them close to objects: use them behind table-top arrangements, for example, and make them part of the display.

Let colours and shapes in the picture relate to the elements in the group, and maybe act as a summary of them. Use abstract shapes, or representations: play games arranging flowers near a paint-

ing that depicts them, for instance, or reiterating the theme of the painting in the objects placed in front of it.

Don't be afraid to let objects overlap into the area of a picture: but take

shapes into consideration. In the end it might be a choice between using the picture for the sake of its colour and shape as part of the composition of the group, and letting it be seen for its own sake.

Grouping several pictures

When pictures are grouped, it suggests they are meant to be regarded as a unit; therefore they should not be entirely unrelated.

This does not necessarily mean matching frames, identical size and co-ordinating colours; all that they could have in common is that you like them.

An eclectic approach combining different items benefits from as rich a diversity as possible. The patchwork technique can encompass mirrors, plates and all sorts of hanging objects as well as rectangular pictures. Sometimes this turns into more of a mess than a group. If the answer doesn't come easily, try one of the following approaches:

The split When the pictures are too numerous or awkward to fit into any of the patterns below, split them into smaller units where they *will* cohere as groups, each of which looks good together and has an interesting shape, and use them at separate points on a wall. This is preferable to having an over-large sprawling group, and to spreading the pictures out to fill an entire area.

The shape Make the pictures form a rectangle, square, triangle – or whatever shape suits the architecture of the room. Space in the centre of this shape is acceptable as long as its outer lines are well defined by the edges of the picture frames.

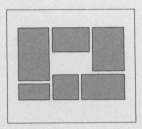

The block When frames and contents are not too different, form them into a block so that they are regarded as a single, large picture. Keep spacing between elements to a minimum.

The line Range all the tops or bottoms of the pictures along one imaginary line, so that they hang from (or rest on) an invisible horizontal. Keep spacing between them to a minimum. Alternatively, have this imaginary line running vertically up the sides of the pictures, or through the centres.

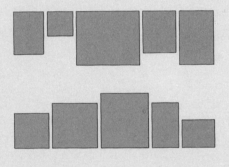

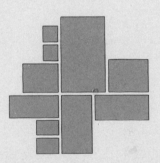

Wooden backdrops

A solution to the problem of small pictures or objects that would get lost on the vast wall space of a studio is to provide them with a framing backdrop. This can both break up the expanse of wall and provide textural interest.

Use old fencing or planking, smooth or rough, butted or not, in the finish that works in the room. Fix it to the wall on battens or (if it is light enough and the wall can take it) hang it from a brass bar. Or make the panel of cork, board or old doors.

Follow the dictates of the room for size, shape and positioning of the backdrop. Pictures and objects can be fixed on with picture hooks, pins or nails. Posters can be pinned on, or for a billboard effect, pasted on with wallpaper paste.

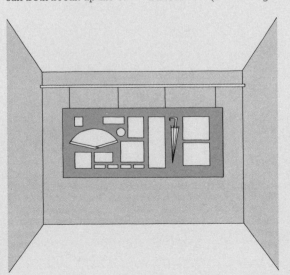

Fabrics worth displaying are nearly always delicate. They respond to loving care but, with the infinite variations of fibres, weaves and dyes, a professional conservator is sometimes needed to advise on the right kind of loving when older textiles are losing their appeal. Such an expert is likely to be found at a museum which deals with textiles, but you should arrange an appointment beforehand.

The advice will fall under one of two headings. Conservation, which means nothing is added or removed – safety through reversible methods; or restoration – reproducing missing parts.

Natural enemies
The greatest single threat is light, both natural and artificial. Not only does it cause fabrics to fade; it damages the structure of their fibres.

Pollution is another foe. Dust and grit literally cut through fabric fibres. So keep delicate textiles away from windows, and line curtains where it is possible.

Excessive dryness and heat also weaken textiles, while damp causes the fibres to rot or develop mould.

The original manufacture too can give rise to flaws. Dyes, especially the blacks and browns of early woollen textiles, can cause fibres to disintegrate (which is why these colours are so often absent from old wool tapestries). Weighted silk is another case where the chemicals did not act kindly. It was a custom, fashionable especially at the turn of the century, to add tin or iron salts to give silk more rustle; in time, the silks deteriorated and split along the folds.

Identifying fibres
Know the fabric you are dealing with before you mend it. The simplest form of identification is to apply the burning test to a small snippet.
Cotton and linen both burn with a yellow flame, leaving a grey ash; cotton smells of burning paper and linen like burning grass.
Wool seldom flares and smells like burning hair, leaving black crushable beads behind.
Silk which shrivels to a small soft blob, smells slightly fishy – unpleasant.

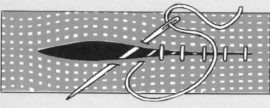

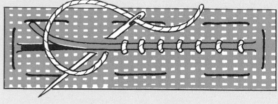

Mending
The most likely trouble spots on tapestries and rugs occur where two colours meet.

If you see a slit, deal with it at once. Sew together the warp threads with button thread. Make small straight stitches across the gap (as above) and try not to split any threads with the needle. A curved needle will help if you are mending *in situ*.

Where the weft threads have worn, leaving the warp threads bare or loose, couch each down to a linen patch, tacked to the back, using stranded embroidery cotton. (Threads are treated individually rather than as a clump, so that the repair will be less obvious.)

Repair cotton, linen, silk and wool fabrics with a thread that matches the thickness of the original weave, or with a fibre withdrawn from the fabric.

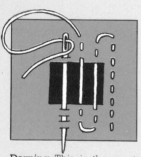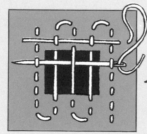

Darning This is the most standard repair, and is advisedly done from the wrong side of the fabric.

Most holes can be safely mended with conventional darning, as shown in the first two diagrams.

If the tear is angular, mend it with a hedge-tear darn, in two stages as shown. To prevent either type puckering, leave the thread slightly loose as you turn to work in the opposite direction.

Hexagonal net Tack the area around the tear to a piece of blue paper (blue because it is easy on the eyes). Cut the tear straight by the thread to give a neat edge and darn in three stages as shown, using a fine thread or one drawn from fabric.

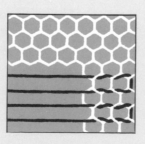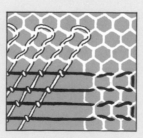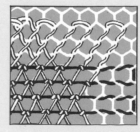

General care

Apart from 'a stitch in time', keeping the item clean and protected from moths if it is in storage is the best advice.

Tapestries, canvas work, rugs, curtains and upholstery should be vacuumed regularly; cotton, linen and lace normally wash well, and if dried with sufficient care seldom need ironing. Avoid it, in any case, on lace, since the heat will flatten the design.

Wool and silk require gentle handling and any item composed of more than one fibre, such as an embroidered cloth or picture, should be treated as for the most vulnerable.

Stains

See chart below.

Treat when fresh, if possible. Use the appropriate remedy on the chart, working from the outside of the stain inwards to prevent the stain from spreading to clean parts.

Stains which have been ensconced in the fabric for years are best left untreated; chemicals are usually the only agents strong enough to remove them, and their strength could damage the fibres.

Cleaning techniques

Vacuuming can significantly brighten dusty tapestries, canvas work, upholstery or curtains – the heavier textile items. To prevent damage to older texules, cover the surface to be cleaned with a piece of nylon monofilament screening, and direct the hand-held nozzle over that.

The nylon allows dust to be sucked up without taking loose threads or decorations along with it. A metre should be sufficient for most purposes, since you can move it along the fabric as you clean. Bind its edges to avoid fraying and wash it occasionally.

If you do not have nylon monofilament, tie a piece of net over the hand-held nozzle instead. Although this may not be as efficient as the nylon, since it should not come into contact with the surface, it will at least provide some protection.

Tempting though it may be, resist brushing the fabric. It only moves the dust from place to place.

Dry cleaning Provided the fabric is reasonably strong and not too old and valuable, you can dry-clean it. Use short cycles on coin-operated machines (the less cleaning fluid the better) and remove anything that could tear the fabric, such as hooks and eyes, applied badges or whatever. Protect items by placing them in a bag improvised from a net curtain.

After cleaning, hang the item in the open air to allow the creases to fall out and the fumes to disperse.

Take valuable items to a specialist dry cleaning firm, or if even that seems risky, to a professional restorer for his advice. Every case is different, but a restorer might have just the trick.

Never use spot cleaners on antique textiles: the concentration of chemicals is anathema.

Hand-washing Some dyes 'bleed', especially those used by the Victorians, so test for colour-fastness before washing by dabbing an inconspicuous corner with wet cotton wool. Test every colour in the weave or embroidery, and all trimmings. If colours run, do not wash.

If it is colour-fast, and old but not inordinately valuable, wash the article flat. Place it, folded if necessary, onto a piece of the nylon monofilament screening, and lower it into hand-hot water. For greater protection, place a second piece of nylon on top and tack the two at the edges. If the water is hard, treat it with a water softener.

Avoid detergents on antique textiles; choose mild products instead, such as Lissapol N (used in a 1 per cent solution), Vulpex (in a 5 per cent solution) or Saponaria (as directed). Dab the suds gently onto the fabric, repeating the wash if the water turns ominously dark. Rinse the final time in distilled water for best results.

Dry flat, right side up, and never hang. For a good drying surface, cover a piece of soft board with blotting paper or plastic sheeting. Smooth the item into shape on top and secure it with brass (rust-free) lace pins. Let it dry naturally but away from the sun. By adhering to these guide-lines, you should not need to iron. But if you do, start off at a low setting.

Bleaches are taboo on old fabrics, as is cleaning them wet *in situ*. DON'T!

Stain	Treatment
Beer	Sponge with 1 part vinegar in 4 parts water.
Blood	Soak in cold salt water.
Coffee, tea, wine	COTTON OR LINEN: Soak in 1 heaped teaspoon of borax dissolved in $\frac{1}{4}$ litre warm water. WOOL OR SILK: Soak in 1 part of 10 volume hydrogen peroxide to 6 parts cold water. Rinse well after about 10 minutes, then wash as usual.
Discoloration from dyes	Difficult to do without removing the fabric's own colour. Treat as for coffee, according to fabric type.
Grass	Soak in surgical spirit.
Grease, candlewax	Scrape away as much as possible, then sandwich the fabric between absorbent tissue paper and apply a hot iron. Use a trichlorethylene grease solvent to remove residue.
Ink, iron-mould, rust	Cover with salt, squeeze lemon juice over and leave 1 hour. Rinse well.
Mildew	Soak in lemon juice.
Tar	Scrape away as much as possible. Soften the rest with glycerine or vaseline. Remove remainder with a clean cloth soaked in surgical spirit using tissue paper above and below to absorb stain.

Once clean and mended, textiles are ready to be put on display or stored.

Storage
There are three basic ways to store textiles – rolled or flat, preferably; otherwise folded.

Carpets, tapestries or woven textiles should be rolled, either around a cardboard tube covered with acid-free tissue paper or a length of plastic drain-pipe (which does not require tissue since the plastic contains no acid). Roll with the right side out and the warp threads going around the tube; cover with a dust sheet tied firmly (but not too tightly) with wide cloth tapes and store the tubes lying down. Never stand them on end (the end taking all the weight could buckle and cause distortion to the fabric) and never use string instead of tapes – it could cut

through the fabric.

Bulky, heavily decorated, bias-cut, awkwardly shaped and very small articles call for flat storage. Wrap the item in acid-free tissue paper, using extra to support folds and shaping. Place each snugly in its own cardboard box (and not in plastic bags, as the item could shift) and label the contents.

Somewhere else keep a photograph, description and note of the repairs, useful in case of theft or further repairs.

Screening from light
Keep older textiles, in particular, out of direct sunlight and spotlights. The least damaging artificial light is tungsten (the average household bulb). Fluorescent tubes, which are next on the list, can be fitted with ultra-violet filters.

Obviously, some textiles will be in line with

windows. You can simply draw shades and blinds, or, in the case of skylights, apply an anti-sun varnish. Dust sheets also help.

Beadwork
Beaded bags and clothes are popular collectors' items. If beads are missing, replacements can usually be found in wholesale specialist shops.

Apply new ones with a beading needle and secure loose threads to prevent further loss.

Where there are large, empty areas, you can fill these with small French knots, instead of new

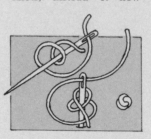

beads. Secure a piece of fabric or net between the lining and surrounding beads, and embroider knots onto this to suit the colour and design.

Repair any three-dimensional beadwork with fuse-wire of a suitable thickness, and string the beads onto this.

Give invisible support to heavily beaded dresses by sewing matching net to the inside, particularly if the fabric is flimsy.

Purses and bags you can display as you like – suspended from hat stands or placed in box frames.

Displayed garments look best on dummies. Prevent them pulling from the shoulder by shifting the strain to supporting tapes. Sew one or two tapes on each side to the inside front waist or hip seam, take them across the shoulders and secure to the same seam at the back.

Costume and uniform
Secure any loose sequins or braid. Clean metal embroidery and buttons with damp swabs, removing buttons first.

Disguise the ravages of moth by inserting cloth of the same colour between the lining and outer fabric.

Traditionally, and very effectively too, costumes are displayed on dummies – ideally with the correct underclothing so that they have the right foundation. Failing this, you can pad with tissue to simulate.

See 'Beading' for other display ideas.

Store uniforms flat, using additional acid-free tissue to protect fabric from buttons, and store other costumes on dummies.

Otherwise you can hang the uniform on a padded coat hanger, stuffing the sleeves and folds with tissue paper.

Reduce strain as for beaded garments and cover with calico tied tightly at the top only. (Never use plastic: it tears and lets in the dust.)

Dolls
Wax and china faces can be wiped gently with cotton swabs and a mild soap solution. Vacuum fabric dolls, and lightly touch with a barely damp cloth, being mindful of painted faces. Wash only if the filling and the paint used for the features are known to withstand it.

Display in glazed boxes or under a large glass dome. Silica gel placed inconspicuously is a good precaution. These are crystals which absorb damp from the atmosphere (the contents in the tiny bag often supplied with cameras and sewing machines). Your camera shop might be able to help you; if not you can buy some from a pharmacist and wrap it up in cotton. Store individually in boxes with acid-free tissue supporting the clothes.

Embroidery
On needlepoint, replace any missing canvas threads with linen ones; patch holes from the back with the same grade canvas, threads aligned.

Simplify surface repairs by mounting the item first Stitch the embroidery right side up with heavy-duty thread to a slightly larger piece of pre-shrunk scrim (matching the grains), which has been mounted first on a frame (as shown). Then re-embroider the

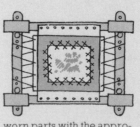

worn parts with the appropriate stitch and thread.

(Replace silk areas, if silk thread is not available, with stranded cotton or D.M.C. thread.)

Fragments can be mounted like pictures.

Stretch a fabric background over a piece of cardboard and lace it across the back as shown. Onto this, sew the embroidery or fragment and

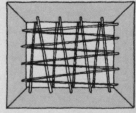

frame it like a picture.

Matching net can be sewn to the back to help support weak areas. Recovering should be left to an expert.

Store rolled or flat.

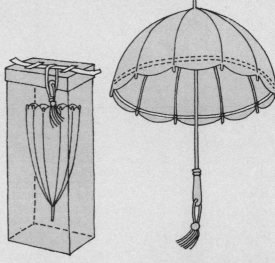

Parasols

Cleaning (except for the removal of surface dust) and re-covering should be left to specialists. Stitch loose trimmings in place with the parasol open.

Parasols can look stunning grouped together, suspended from high ceilings or above stair wells. They work on the floor, too, in repose like drying umbrellas.

Store slightly open with tissue inside the folds. Place in a calico bag and suspend by the handle; alternatively, store upright in a deep cardboard box, keeping the parasol vertical by tying tape to the handle and then through the box top to secure.

Lessen the strain on openly displayed parasols by sewing a matching tape around the perimeter from spoke to spoke slightly tighter than the fabric.

Patchworks and quilts

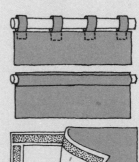

Cover torn or weak patches with matching, fine-meshed net, sewing into existing stitching lines and using the same colour thread and type of stitch – usually running, back or chain. Or, make new patches and slip-stitch these into place.

Sometimes the wadding is missing near tears. Replace according to the original – sheep's wool or blanket in the case of many older ones, or use synthetic wadding. Mend the tear after inserting new filling.

If not using quilts as bedspreads, throw them over furniture. Use smaller quilts as decorative floor mats; hang either type on the wall. Either run a rod through tabs and stitch the top of the quilt to these (top right), sew a 'sleeve' to the back of the lining and run a rod through this (right), or use Velcro (bottom right).

If fabrics run or are quilted, dry-clean rather than hand-wash, and store rolled or flat.

Old shoe collections

Leather, fabric, embroidery, ribbons, metal, braid, beads, glues – all could have been used on a single pair of shoes. Take such shoes to an expert.

On simpler items, vacuum any decorated areas, and apply saddle soap to leather after removing dust. Protect the rest of the shoe when cleaning metal buckles or buttons.

Boots look good lined up near a fireplace or in an entrance way; more delicate items show well in transparent showcases or on shelves.

Store in boxes, with tissue paper to pad the shapes and to protect the leather or fabric from button marks.

Gloves

Use a specialists' leather needle with chiselled point for repairs to kid and hide; linen thread is preferable as it is the strongest.

Display in a box frame, or pegged to a line across a wall if the gloves are not too fragile.

Store boxed, with tissue inside the fingers and the palm.

Fans

Group fans together for maximum impact. Alternatively, frame individually in a custom-made fan case or in a box frame.

Store flat and loosely open with tissue supporting gently. (Kept closed, the folds might weaken; and open, there would be too much strain between the struts.)

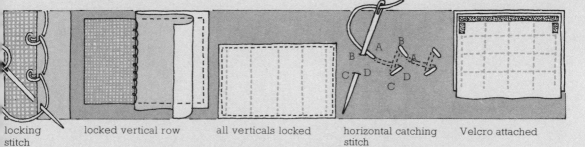

locking stitch   locked vertical row   all verticals locked   horizontal catching stitch   Velcro attached

Tapestry

If you plan to hang unlined tapestries, you should line them first. Send large pieces to an expert.

Smaller ones you can line yourself. Pre-shrink linen or brown holland and cut it to length, allowing plenty for turnings.

Lay the tapestry face down on a flat surface, place the lining on top and pin the centre vertical. Using button thread, stitch parallel lines about 30cm apart. Then stitch horizontal rows across locked tapestry and lining, catching a warp thread of the tapestry between B and C, as shown. Slip-stitch side and top hems and let it hang for a few weeks before hemming the bottom.

Velcro is easy to rig, and can be adjusted so the tapestry hangs well.

Stitch the soft half of the Velcro to the back of the lining through to the tapestry along all sides; nail the rough half to battens, and fix these in turn to the wall. To hang, press the tapestry onto the Velcro.

Alternatively, use the sleeve method described for patchwork.

Store tapestries rolled.

TEXTILES
Window blinds

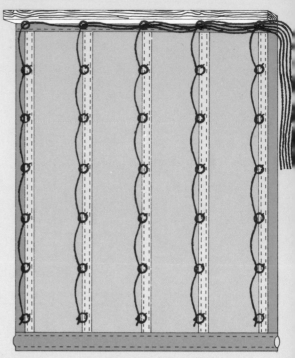

Both blinds look similar from the back when they are pulled down. The flat look and cased batten indicate that this is a Roman blind.

Roman blinds (shades) look like roller blinds when down, but pull up into a series of concertina folds instead of a roll. Gathered blinds look like curtains when down but pull up into folds like those of Roman blinds, but softer; they may also have a frill along the bottom edge which contributes to the soft look.

Both Roman and gathered blinds work on the principle of a series of cords which run vertically through rings on the back of the blind and pull to a common point on one side.

Choose Roman blinds for a tailored appearance or when using a fabric which looks better flat than gathered. Choose gathered blinds for a more feminine effect. Either style is good for windows with side architraves, or for large windows where there is no wall at the sides for hanging conventional curtains. Gathered blinds look best if left partially drawn, so do not use them on small windows.

Use medium-weight cotton furnishing fabric for both types together with a lining for Roman blinds.

Materials
As well as fabric and thread, you will need:
Tape about 15mm wide. Allow one piece, the length of the blind, for every 250–300mm width of blind, plus one extra piece.
Brass or plastic rings 15mm diameter. Allow enough to be spaced at 150–200mm intervals down the blind on each tape.

Wooden batten 25 × 50mm and cut to the blind width, on which to fix the blind.
Screws and wall plugs to fix the batten.
Velcro tape the same length as the blind width, for attaching the blind to the batten; tacks or glue to attach the Velcro to the batten.
Fine cord sufficient to cut into the same number of pieces as there are strips of tape; each piece should

be equal to the blind width plus twice its length.
Screw eyes the same number as strips of tape; choose eyes large enough to hold all thicknesses of cord.
Cleat hook to secure cords when the blind is pulled up.
Screws to fix cleat to the wall.
Stretcher dowel (Roman blind only) 15mm thick and cut to the blind width,

for inserting into a casing at the foot of the blind to help stabilize it.
Pencil pleat tape (gathered blind only) a length equal to the fabric width, to run along top of blind.
Curtain weights (gathered blind only) one weight per tape, to improve the hang of the blind.
Strong thread for attaching rings and Velcro.

Measuring, cutting and joining fabric
Measure the height and width of the window reveal, subtracting 25mm from the width if the blind is to hang inside the reveal but adding 75mm to both height and width if

the blind is to hang outside it. For gathered blinds the fabric should be 1½ times as wide as the reveal to allow for the gathering. For either blind add 100mm to the height and width for hems. Calculate the amount as

for tablecloths (p228, but omit the circle and paper stage); cut and seam widths of fabric.
Frill (gathered blind only) Decide the depth of the frill (e.g. 50mm) and subtract this from blind length. Allow enough fabric to cut

strips twice the frill depth plus 20mm turnings (10mm each) by twice the width of the blind when ungathered.

If the fabric is patterned, cut it so that the design will be consistent; seam the strips together.

Making a Roman blind
Cut and join the fabric as previously described. Cut the lining 100mm narrower than the blind width. Mark the centres at the top and bottom of the blind fabric and lining and, with right sides and side edges together, stitch each side just inside the selvedges of the blind fabric. Press the seam turnings onto the lining.

Match the centre points on the fabric and lining at the top and bottom and smooth out to the sides

until the blind is flat and a border of fabric shows on each side of the lining. Stitch along the top, taking 25mm turnings. Turn right side out and press.
Attaching the tapes Position the side tapes to cover the seamlines of the hems; space the remaining tapes at equal distances of 200–300mm across the blind. Machine-stitch through all thicknesses along both edges of all tapes.
Bottom hem Treating the layers as one, turn up the hem at the foot of the blind

and machine-stitch. Work another row of stitching below this, leaving a space wide enough for the stretcher dowel to be inserted between the two rows of stitching.
Attaching the rings Mark the ring positions on the tapes, starting just above the casing for the stretcher batten and finishing 50mm from the top; leave an equal space of 150–200mm between the rings. It is essential for even-looking folds that each row of rings is exactly

horizontal, so measure their positions accurately.

Firmly oversew the rings to the tape, making sure the stitching does not show on the right side of fabric.
Attaching the batten Decide whether the batten is to be top-fixed or face-fixed. Paint it to match the wall or window frame, or cover it with wallpaper or fabric. Drill the fixing holes through the wider face of the batten, and attach the screw eyes to the batten's underside to

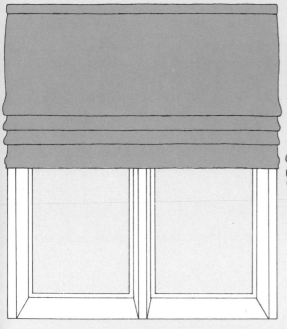

The folds on a Roman blind should be parallel and this means even tension throughout on the cords.

A gathered blind can be simply hemmed at the bottom, as shown, or can be finished with a frill.

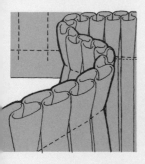

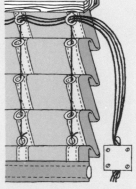

correspond with the tapes on the blind.

Screw the batten in position at the window.

Attaching Velcro Stitch the soft section to the top of the blind. Tack or glue the rough section to the face of the batten.

Threading the cords Decide which side of the blind you wish to have the cleat hook and start threading the cords at the opposite corner.

Unroll the cord, but don't yet cut it. With the blind on a flat surface, tie one end of the cord securely to the bottom corner ring, thread it upwards through all the rings on that tape, pass it loosely

Fix blinds to a face- or ceiling-fixed batten.

across the top of the blind and down to the bottom of the opposite (cleat) side. Cut. Repeat for each tape.

Fix the blind to the batten with the Velcro and insert the stretcher dowel. Starting with the longest cord (i.e. first one threaded), pass it through its own screw eye and

The vertical cords are secured to a wall cleat.

then through all the other eyes across the batten to the side. Leave the remaining length of cord hanging free at the side.

Repeat for the rest of the cords, threading them first through their own screw eyes. Lower the blind; check that cords are taut and even across the top;

knot them at the bottom.

Fix the cleat on the wall. Pull the blind up so that even folds form, and wind the cords round the cleat. Leave a few days to set.

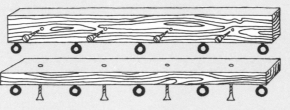

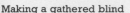

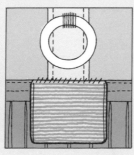

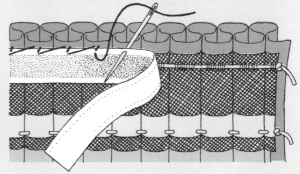

Making a gathered blind Cut and join the fabric as described, and make narrow double hems at the sides and foot of the fabric.

Top and tapes Check the length of the blind and fold over the relevant turning at the top; baste the top hem in position. Attach the tapes and rings as described for Roman blinds.

Attach the pencil pleat tape across the top of the

blind on the wrong side and pull up the pleated tape to the required width. Check that the tapes are still evenly spaced.

Making the frill Cut and seam the strip for the frill as previously described. Fold the turnings to the wrong side all round, mitring corners, and then fold the strip in half with wrong sides together and long edges at the top.

Treating the layers as

one, work gathering (or fine pleating with a sewing-machine attachment) along the top edge of the strip, to fit the bottom edge of the blind.

With the blind right side up, stitch the frill onto the bottom edge (as left) so that the gathered top covers the bottom of the blind by 15mm.

The weights From spare fabric make a small bag to fit each weight, insert the

weight and sew the bag to the tape just above the bottom hem (second left).

Attaching Velcro Place one strip at the top of the blind over the pleated tape. Oversew firmly on both edges to backs of pencil pleats (as above).

Complete the blind as for a Roman blind.

Circular tablecloth

Floor-length circular cloths are a graceful way of dressing up or even disguising a round table, particularly when teamed with a shorter, decorative overcloth. The cutting out for a circular cloth is simplified if you make a paper pattern.

The edges of the cloth may be simply hemmed, bound, faced or scalloped, or could be finished with a fringe or frill.

Choose medium-weight dress or furnishing fabric, lace or tablecloth fabric sold in needlework shops, in a washable fibre such as linen, cotton, or cotton/polyester.

Measuring Measure the diameter of the table and add that to double the table's height to give the finished diameter of the cloth; for the total diameter add a further 30mm for a simple hem, facing or scallops but nothing for a binding. For a fringe or frill, add 30mm for the seam allowance and then subtract the depth of the trimming.

Fabric amount Allow a square of fabric as wide as the cloth's total diameter. Your fabric will almost certainly be too narrow for this; to make it this size you will have to join two or even three widths. Divide the fabric width (excluding selvedges) into the total diameter, round up the figure (if not whole) to the next whole number.

No pattern-match Multiply the number of widths required by the total diam-

eter of the cloth to give the amount of fabric you should buy.

Pattern-matching Divide the tablecloth's total diameter by the length of the pattern repeat, rounding up the answer to the next whole number. Multiply this by the pattern repeat and then this figure by the number of widths required to give the amount of fabric to buy.

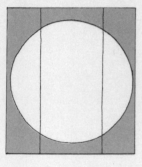

Joining the widths To avoid an ugly seam across the centre of the cloth, join the fabric with a full width in the middle and panels of the required size to each side.

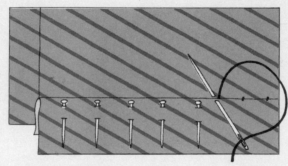

Cutting the widths Start by cutting a length equal to the total diameter for the middle panel. Cut the next length to the same size, first laying the fabric alongside the cut length for pattern-matching and trimming off the waste at the top. Cut any subse-

quent pieces in the same way.

If you are using an even number of widths, cut one of them in half lengthwise parallel to the selvedges. This will be for the outer edge and ensures that there will be no seam in the middle.

Stitching the widths If you are not pattern-matching, pin two widths with right sides and selvedges together. Machine-stitch just inside the selvedge. If you are pattern matching, lay one piece flat, right side up, turn under the selvedge of the piece to be joined on and place the fold over the selvedge of the other piece, carefully matching the pattern (as left). Pin, placing the pins at right angles to the fold; slip-baste. Machine-stitch from the wrong side.

Pressing Press the seam turnings flat, as they were stitched; then open them and press again.

Paper pattern You will need a piece of paper with sides equal to half the total diameter (i.e. the radius), a piece of string slightly longer than this, a pencil and a drawing pin (thumb tack).

Working on a flat surface (into which you can stick the drawing pin) pin the paper to it at one corner (A). Tie the string round the pin at one end and the pencil at the other, leaving the radius between them. Draw an arc between corners B and C, being careful to hold the pencil upright. Cut the paper along this line.

Cutting out Fold the fabric in half lengthwise and then widthwise. Lay it flat and place the paper pattern on top with point A at the junction of the folds. Pin the pattern to the fabric and cut the fabric close to the curved edge of the pattern (i.e. from points B to C).

Remove the pattern and open out the fabric to give the circle.

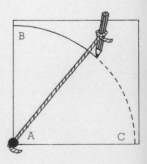

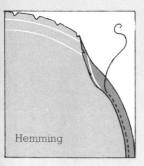

Hemming

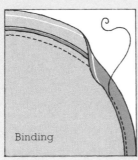

Binding

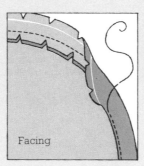

Facing

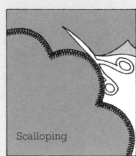

Scalloping

Finishing The tablecloth can be finished in any of the following ways:

Hemming Form a narrow hem round the edge of the circle with 5mm in the first turning and 10mm in the second, cutting notches in the first turning to make

the hem lie flat. Machine-stitch and press.

Binding or facing Cut and join bias strips 40 or 50mm wide from waste fabric and apply to the edge. Press.

Scalloping Work zigzag stitching in scallop pattern

round the edge, leaving a 15mm cutting margin on the crown of the scallops. Trim the excess fabric close to the stitching.

Frill Make and apply a frill as described on p228.

Fringe Turn 15mm onto the right side of the cloth

all round, notching if necessary to make it lie flat. Place the fringe heading over the turning, easing it on the inside edge. Machine-stitch the heading top and bottom.

Lacy overcloth

Choose printed fabric with an overall design of swirling lines or bold floral shapes. Measure a square or circle that will drape over the table-top with a margin of at least 30mm outside the edge motifs. Using tailor's chalk on the right side of the fabric, draw a continuous line around the pattern motifs

for the edge of the cloth, making indentations and scallop shapes as appropriate. Work close zigzag machine stitching along this line all round. With small, sharp-pointed scissors, cut off the waste fabric, cutting close to the stitching but taking care not to cut the stitches themselves.

Applied motifs

Separate motifs can be applied to a plainer background cloth in the same way. Cut the base cloth to the approximate square or circular shape you want. Cut motifs out of patterned fabric allowing a 30mm margin outside them. Pin a motif in position overlapping the edge of the ground fabric with

both fabrics right side up, baste and then work close zigzag machine stitching all around the motif, working through two layers of fabric on the inside edge of the motif. On the right side cut away excess fabric around the motif close to the stitching. Turn to the wrong side and cut away base fabric on inside of zigzag stitching.

Draped lampshades

These are made by draping a fabric square over a coolie hat-shaped base shade, which could be metal, paper or fabric.

Choose a cotton fabric, which will not scorch. Alternatively you could use a square lacy tablecloth of appropriate size.

The sides of the square should be three times the base width of the shade. In the square's centre make an eyelet big enough for the cord to pass through. Finish the eyelet with a metal ring or with buttonhole stitch. Finish the outer edges of the square in one of the methods suggested for tablecloths.

To put the square onto the shade, disconnect the cord at the bottom, thread

it through the eyelet and reconnect it to the foundation shade. Drape the fabric evenly over the shade.

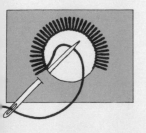

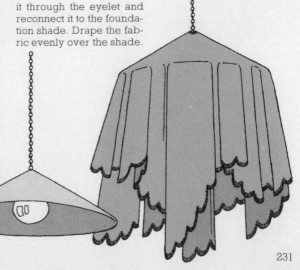

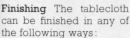

Covering walls and ceilings with fabric creates a comfortable and even an exotic background to possessions. An entire room can be fabric-clad, or one alcove or chimney breast.

Light-weight fabrics such as muslin or cheese-cloth drape well; use them when you want to 'lower' ceilings, or gather them on rods to give a soft, luxurious appearance to walls. Medium-weight cotton fabrics, hessian or felt, and patterned fabrics which look better smooth than gathered, give a more tailored effect when applied in flat panels.

Both gathering and panelling require a considerable amount of fabric. For example, a single wall 5m wide and 2.5m deep would need 10m of 115cm-wide fabric for plain panelling – and 15m for a draped effect. For the whole room you might well use 75m of fabric – more if it has a bold pattern repeat.

Awkward shapes can be particularly extravagant on material; plan for economy but also for appearance; check that joins are not conspicuous.

Fabric on rods
This simple treatment may be used for both walls and ceilings. The fabric is gathered along rods inserted through casings at top and bottom; the rods are attached to brackets on the wall. A lot of fabric is required but the advantage with this method is that the panels are easy to remove and clean.

Taking measurements
Measure the height and width of the area to be covered. Increase the width by half as much again for the gathering and add 10cm (for hems) to the height. To calculate the fabric amount, divide the fabric width, less any selvedges, into the total width required, rounding up the answer for the number of widths needed. Multiply the number of widths by the total length. Repeat for each wall.

Other materials
Two rods (15mm in diameter) as wide as each area. *Brackets* to support rods at ends and at intervals (every join for medium-weight fabrics; alternate joins for light-weight).

Cutting out If necessary, make the end of the fabric straight by pulling out a thread and cutting along its line or by tearing off a small strip from selvedge to selvedge.

Measure the total length required from this straight edge and cut across, making a straight line in the same way. Cut subsequent lengths to the same size.

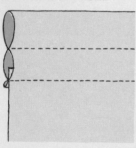

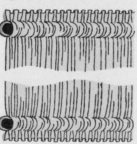

Making the casings If the selvedges are very wide and obvious, turn them to the wrong side and press. Narrow ones can be left.

Turn 50mm to the wrong side at top and bottom of each length and press. Machine-stitch through both thicknesses 25mm from the fold. Turn under the raw edges of the hem for 5mm and machine-stitch to main length. The space between the two machined lines forms the casing.

Hanging Fix the brackets to the wall or ceiling 25mm from the edges. Insert the rods through the casings of each panel in turn and hang the bracket. Arrange the gathers evenly across each panel.

Obstacles Hang the fabric over light switches and power points and accurately mark the area of the cover plate. Cut out to within 10mm of the marking, neaten the edges by over-casting or zigzagging, and work a row of gathering top and bottom. Remove the cover plate, re-hang the fabric and pull up the gathering to fit. Replace the cover plate and screw down tightly so that the fabric edges are gripped underneath.

Above doors and windows Cut the fabric to the appropriate length (you may also have to adjust the panel widths so that a complete one fits).

Above a door, fit the rod so that the bottom edge of the fabric is clear when the door opens. Above a window you can omit the lower rod and cut the panels long enough to form a pelmet. Conventional curtains have to hang inside the window reveal.

Panelled walls
Fabric can be stapled directly into plastered walls, but it is easier to pull it taut if battens are fixed to the wall as a foundation for the fabric.

Neat joins are made by folding fabric around cardboard strips. If the fabric is simply butted, and where staples are visible at the raw edges at top, bottom and corners, conceal them with braid, moulding or with strips of the same fabric plaited (braided) together.

Estimate the amount as for fabric hung on rods, but allow no extra width for fullness, and only 5cm extra length per strip.

Other materials For each wall you need:
Wooden battens, two 15 × 25mm, to fit horizontally along the top and bottom (or above the skirting or baseboard); one batten per panel plus one extra to the height of the wall, measured between the horizontal battens. Allow extra to make frames around light fittings, power points, doors and windows.
Staples and staple gun. Braid, ribbon or *wooden moulding* to cover staples. *Cardboard strips,* 15mm wide to length of vertical battens, for invisible joins.

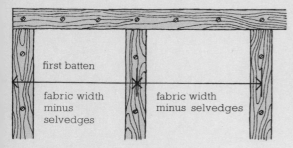

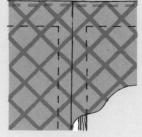

first batten

fabric width minus selvedges

fabric width minus selvedges

Positioning the first and subsequent battens.

Stapling the card strip.

'Invisible' joins.

Fixing the battens Screw the horizontal battens in position using counter-sunk screws. Mark the positions for the vertical battens. If you are covering more than one wall, start at one corner and measure the width of the fabric, less selvedges, between marks. If the last panel is less than a fabric width, plan the first space of the adjacent wall to fit the left-over fabric. If you are covering only one wall, you could centre the first panel and work out to the edges with the remaining panels. Screw on the first and last battens so that the outside edges fit tightly onto the corners. Screw on the intermediate battens so that their centres line up with the marks.

Attach battens to form frames around obstacles.

Hanging the fabric Cut the fabric as described for 'Fabric on rods'.

On the first panel only, mark a point half-way across the horizontal battens, taking the overall measurements from the outside edge of the first vertical batten to the centre of the second batten. For the subsequent panels mark the half-way points from the centre of one batten to the centre of the next.

Next mark the half-way point on all the vertical battens. Place the fabric for the first panel onto the battens, matching the centre of fabric with marked centre points. Temporarily tack at these points by driving the tacks only half-way in. Pull the fabric taut along the top edge to the corners and temporarily tack. Check

that the edge is straight, then staple to the batten 5mm from the top, placing the staples horizontally and about 25mm apart. Remove the temporary tacks from the corners and replace with staples.

Pull the fabric taut to the bottom, keeping the grain straight (you will probably have to re-tack the centre). Pull it taut to the corners and tack there; staple 5mm from the bottom edge of the batten.

Staple along the inner edges of the selvedges down each side, placing the staples vertically. Trim off the excess fabric at the bottom and the selvedge in the corner.

Invisible joins Place the second panel right sides together over the first so that the selvedges align. Temporarily tack at the

top, bottom and centre. Staple at 50mm intervals in between, then remove the tacks and replace with staples.

Place a cardboard strip over the selvedges so that the edge is level with the centre of the batten; staple in place. Turn the fabric over the cardboard and pull taut to the opposite edge. Temporarily tack and then staple. Repeat at the top and bottom. Continue in this way along the wall.

Obstacles Around light switches and power points, or windows and doors, simply staple the fabric to the outer edge of the battens and trim off the excess fabric.

Finishing off Cover all raw edges by gluing on braid or ribbon or by attaching wooden moulding with panel pins.

Draped ceilings
The simplest way of doing this is to let the fabric hang in loops across the ceiling. Twine is passed through the casings on the back of the fabric and fixed to the ceiling at each end.

Taking measurements Measure the length and

width of the area to be covered and decide which way and how deep you wish the loops to hang. Plan the loops to correspond with the fabric width, so that the casings or hooks may be incorporated in the joining seams.

Unless you want very deep, wide loops, make

your panels about 20–25cm narrower than the fabric width. To give the number of panels, divide the estimated size into the room length; if it does not divide exactly, adjust it by a few centimetres until it does.

Multiply the number of panels by the total room

width, adding 10cm per panel for hems and ease.
Other materials
Strong hooks, two per panel plus one extra for last edge.
Non-stretch twine, one piece per panel, 20cm longer than the room width, plus one for last edge.

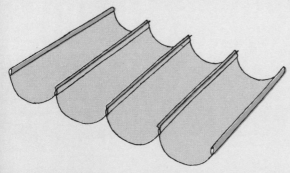

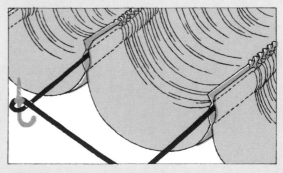

Cutting and joining
Cut the fabric into lengths equal to the total room width. Make narrow hems at the top and bottom. With right sides together, join the lengths along their selvedges, taking 20mm turnings. Work a second line of machining 5mm from the edge to form the casings for the twine. Turn under the remaining sel-

vedges of the outside panels 15mm and stitch.

Screw the hooks into the edges of the ceiling at the corners and then down the length of the room, leaving the panel width between them.

Hanging the fabric Insert the lengths of twine through the casings and through the hems at the selvedges.

With someone to help you, and working on one length of twine at a time, wind each end round a hook, drawing up the twine as tightly as possible so that the fabric is close to the ceiling. When each

length of twine is attached, adjust it if necessary and tie firmly round the hooks.
Obstacles To fit pendent-light cords, simply pierce a hole through the fabric and pass the cord through.

Comfort and efficiency need a combination of two types of light: general light for seeing your way around, and concentrated light for specific tasks and for illuminating specific objects. The two types complement each other. General light is soft and diffused, but rather dull because of a lack of shadow; the sharp light and deep shadow created by concentrated, beamed light give only an incomplete picture which can dazzle with its contrast unless backed up by softer light from another source.

The two complementary types are important for visual pleasure as well as efficiency. Choosing the appropriate fittings and positioning them well can affect the dimensions and appearance of rooms or of passageways – the space – as well as draw attention to objects and displays – the things.

The space Generally, directing light upwards and outwards draws attention to the perimeters and increases the illusion of space, while keeping light localized has the opposite effect. Washing a wall with light seems to increase its size; a narrow room looks wider when light is concentrated on the two smaller walls, leaving the longer ones not specifically lit. Light directed onto a pale coloured ceiling makes a room look higher; conversely, light beamed downwards onto the floor leaving the ceiling in semidarkness focuses attention low down.

This can make a room seem cosy; on the other hand it can sometimes create an atmosphere of gloom, even though the intensity of the actual light is greater than usual. To counteract this 'casino' effect (and to avoid the eye-strain caused by constantly looking from a brightly lit area to darkness) use the odd upward-directed light or wall-illuminating fitting, thus putting into focus other parts of the room.

A pendant immediately seems to establish a new ceiling height, which the eye automatically registers. To make a room seem more spacious, flood the ceiling with light. If you can keep the ceiling clear of lighting hardware, it helps the illusion of sky-like space. But provision needs to be made for alternative forms of lighting to create more intimate atmospheres at times.

A pool of light draws attention to the objects in it and holds them together in a group; this may be the pendant-lit dining table and its immediate surroundings, the table lamp and the objects within its sphere, or an armchair and its adjacent table lit by a beam from a downlight in the ceiling. In a large space, local pools of light create a feeling of intimacy and add interest. The concentration of light that produces this effect may occur where a functional light shines onto a working surface, where an object is highlit for display, or where a beam of light is picking out an architectural element like an archway, fireplace or cornice – or is simply playing on a wall, floor or ceiling. These are not islands of light in a sea of darkness; they are simply areas that are made more interesting by a relative concentration of light.

The things Lighting objects does not necessarily mean the high technology of a tungsten halogen framing projector picking out the exact rectangle of the painting on the wall. It could be the downward light from a table lamp picking out the shapes and textures of a bowl of sea shells, or an adjustable lamp beamed towards a bunch of twigs and making a pattern of shadows on the wall behind. There is a discussion of lighting objects and pictures on pp238–9, but here are a few general points.

Try to light only the objects you want to be lit: use directional light fittings, frame the object in an alcove or position the light source behind a baffle of some kind.

Always have the light fitting glare-free and make sure the beams will not be interrupted when people walk about.

Intense light means intense shadow. Pay as much attention to the position of the shadows as to the light sources themselves. Don't light one piece carefully and then find its shadow falls across – and obscures – another.

Planning

Begin by considering what you want to light, then how you can light it. Bear in mind how and when you may want to vary the effects. Flexibility is vital – of position as well as intensity.

Consider functional light first: for specific tasks like reading and for picking out objects and displays that deserve emphasis. Then look at secondary needs: lighting that will not be wanted all the time, for television viewing, audio equipment, or displays of less interest. Overall general lighting in the background needs to be provided next; finally, add into your planning light fittings that are purely decorative.

Take into consideration the size of the room and whether you want to make it seem more or less spacious, and the colour: dark, light-absorbent surfaces need more lighting than pale, reflecting ones.

While compiling this list of needs and working on possible answers, some overlap will probably occur. General lighting may be a by-product of a directional fitting used to bounce light off an archway or wall. Some light fittings can be positioned to serve more than one purpose. An adjustable directional fitting can provide work light, display light l and bounced background light and is one of the best choices, especially fitted with a dimmer.

Which leads to how much light and when. For different activities and changes of mood, different levels of light intensity must be possible. Never start with too few fittings thinking that it is 'atmosphere': it is more likely to be inefficiency and gloom. Better to have an excess of fittings and not use all of them all of the time. Turn the bright ones off and resort to candles. But dimmers give most flexibility and control.

Dimmer switches allow the adjustment of the amount of light from an individual bulb or from bulbs wired to the same circuit. (It is the flexibility it gives to an individual light fitting that makes a dimmer worthwhile: if less light is required in a room as whole, using less powerful bulbs, turn-ing some light sources off, or redirecting fittings to produce bounced light may be the answer.)

Different types of dimmer control include wall-mounted ones (some with two-way controls), dimmers for table lamps, and dimmers that plug into the wall socket like an adaptor. Variations with photocells switch the lighting on and off at dusk and dawn to fool potential burglars; those with time-lag controls can dim the lighting slowly for long hallways.

The number of lights that can be controlled depends on the wattage rating of the dimmer. Add up the wattage of all bulbs in the light fittings to find their total combined wattage and buy a dimmer that encompasses that rating.

  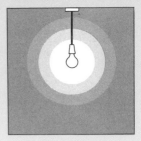

Light fittings can be grouped into three broad divisions by the way they spread their light. Directional fittings give out concentrated beams of light in specific directions; diffusing fittings spread their light in many directions for general illumination, and fittings for indirect lighting reflect light off shiny or bright-coloured surfaces around a room. In practice, these categories overlap, and some light fittings have characteristics of more than one, or can be adapted to spread their light in different ways.

A balanced lighting scheme should contain an even mixture of both directional and diffused lighting, giving the decorative effects required to display objects while providing enough overall light to see by.

Directional lighting Light is concentrated and forced to beam in one direction by an opaque shield or shade, which is often lined with a reflective surface. Directional light fittings are useful for singling out objects and displays from their surroundings, and for highlighting them. The beam of light may be narrow enough to pick out a specific object (hence the term 'accent lighting'), may define a group of objects in a wider pool of light, or may spread light over a comparatively wide area for more general illumination in a room. Because directional light creates pronounced shadows, it throws objects into relief and emphasizes texture. The sharper the angle between the light and a wall ('grazing light'), the more pronounced the texture; as the light is moved away from a wall, the surface seems to flatten.

Indirect lighting
This is achieved by bouncing light off reflective surfaces around the room: a pale-coloured ceiling or wall is the most obvious reflective plane. The light source may be a directional one which is not being used for accent lighting, or may be a floor standard or wall lamp whose V- or U-shaped shade has the opening pointing upwards or outwards.

Indirect lighting is more suitable for decoration and overall background illumination than as a practical source of light: it spreads soft light (which, since it is shadowless, is rather dead) over a limited distance; it is useful to balance accent lighting and to give a soft undertone of light in the background.

Diffused lighting
This category includes the familiar fittings that spread light all round: chandeliers, fittings with translucent shades, and fittings with cylindrical shades that distribute their light upwards, downwards, and sometimes sideways as well: table lamps, wall lights, ceiling surface fittings, pendants, floor standard lamps, nightlights, and some novelty lamps. Their uses range from general background illumination to functional lighting for specific tasks, like reading or eating, and the light source is usually an incandescent filament bulb or tube. These lamps should look attractive, but be functional at the same time. Lamps that are simply visual pleasures, like candlelight used for atmosphere, are luxuries to add only after the lighting proper has been provided for.

Colour
When planning lighting take into consideration the colour rendering of the light source itself – the intrinsic quality of the light glow and its effect on different colours in the surroundings.

Lighting the objects and surfaces in the home both comfortably and accurately is important overall; it is sad when people take the trouble to choose toning colours in daylight and ruin the subtle effect with ill-considered lighting at night. It is also vital to have interesting lighting in monochromatic schemes, since impact is derived less from colour than from texture, and this must be given every chance to stand out. For the first of these considerations it is the colour rendering of the light source that matters; for the second it is more a question of the way the light is positioned.

Most incandescent tungsten filament bulbs producing diffused light have

an intrinsic 'warm' cast; like candlelight, they emphasize yellows and reds. Many fluorescent tubes are 'cold', emphasizing blues and resembling daylight; this is not flattering to most complexions or home decorations, and fluorescent fittings are usually confined to work areas, although some tubes have been developed that produce a warmer, softer light.

To create 'atmosphere' in a room, changing the colour cast of diffused light towards warmer colours is relatively easy: choose colour-coated bulbs, or translucent shades in red, pink, orange or amber (or use lower wattage bulbs). Remember, cold-coloured light in a warm room automatically makes people feel cold. If a room gives the psychological reassurance of warmth, the actual temperature need not be as high.

For more theatrical effects, colour filters on directional lights can pro-

ject colour onto a wall. However, the filters available look unsubtle in the domestic situation. It is a better idea to colour walls in subtle shades and then to bounce white light off the walls.

To create good white light both for reading and for lighting pictures and colours generally, and to sustain it while using a dimmer (most lights yellow as they dim), use low-voltage tungsten halogen spotlights or floods, fitted with 6- or 12-volt transformers.

An effective use of white light is to flood a white-painted ceiling with it, from upward-directed floodlights. The 'daylight' effect is enhanced when not only the light source is concealed – the principle of the up-light – but also the hardware. The extreme heat of tungsten halogen floodlighting fittings means care must be taken in their positioning, and installation should be done by a qualified electrician.

Cables Wiring is unsightly and dangerous; but never run cables under carpets, where they may get damaged by sharp objects or furniture legs. Try to keep portable lamps close to the outlets, or to run cables under permanently positioned pieces of furniture. Run cables around skirtings and door frames, and secure with cable clips.

Lighting track mounted onto or recessed into a ceiling or wall can supply current to a number of fittings along its length, and is one solution to the problem of lighting the centre of a large room: it makes constructive use of the central outlet that most old houses (and many modern ones) are fitted with.

Where concealment is not possible, turn wiring into a design feature: with brass wall light fittings, for example, carry the wiring in brass tubing from the light to the floor. Because it is finished in the same material as the lamp, it will look like part of the design.

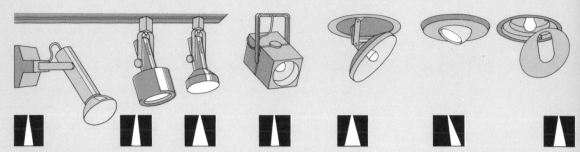

Spotlights True spots produce a narrow beam of concentrated light as in the theatre; most domestic 'spotlights' are actually variations on the directional fitting, incorporating reflective shade linings or using bulbs with internal silvering, and producing beams of light without the intensity and evenness of professional spots.

The more specialized types available for the home include tiny portable spotlights with pinspot beams to accent small details at medium range, and 'framing' spots (see p239). Parabolic reflector spots can provide useful light for reading or sewing as well as for highlighting, since the concentrated beam does not disturb other people in the room with glare.

Spotlights can be wall- or ceiling-mounted, or recessed into the ceiling; they can alternatively be clipped into lighting track to give flexibility of position and angle.

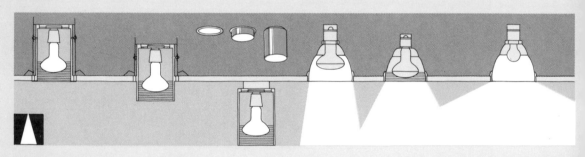

Down-lights are square or cylindrical units whose shafts of light beam directly downwards. They can be fitted onto the ceiling surface, but when recessed into it they become one of the least conspicuous light sources, since their baffles stop brightness from being seen from most viewing angles. Again, the beam width varies: use a narrow beam to define an area, or a wide beam for general overall lighting. And use down-lights alone, in groups, or in rows. But use with wallwashers to avoid a 'tunnel' effect.

Up-lights are down-lights in reverse, beaming light upwards from their normal position on the floor. They may be operated by a foot switch, rather like some standard lamps. Up-lights can be placed under the leaves of large pot plants or put behind furniture to light corners of the room (but not where curtaining or upholstery could cover them and be a fire-risk – or where they could be mistaken for wastepaper baskets).

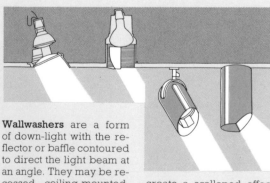

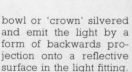

Wallwashers are a form of down-light with the reflector or baffle contoured to direct the light beam at an angle. They may be recessed, ceiling-mounted, fitted on a track, or floor-standing. As the term implies, they wash the wall; when properly positioned the light spills only slightly onto adjacent walls or onto the floor, and does not create a scalloped effect on the illuminated wall. Position the lights about the same distance apart as they are from the wall; the effect is more even the farther the lights are from the wall.

Bulbs To produce their concentrated beams of light, some directional fittings use 'reflector' bulbs, which are partially coated with a silvery material which reflects out of the bulb and concentrates the light output of the fitting. Some bulbs are coated behind the filament internally to reflect the light forwards; others have the bowl or 'crown' silvered and emit the light by a form of backwards projection onto a reflective surface in the light fitting.

Directional fittings, including so-called 'spotlights', often take ordinary incandescent filament bulbs; to produce a concentrated beam, the fitting incorporates a reflecting metal cowl.

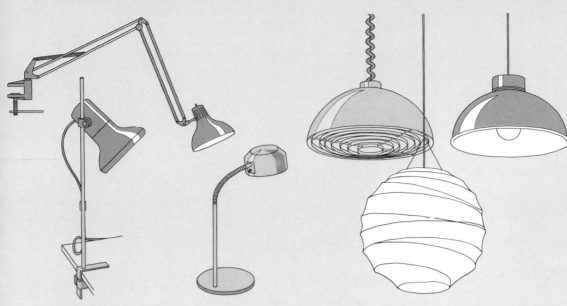

Desk lamps Lighting for close work can come from table or standard lamps, but is usually more efficiently provided by desk, wall and floor lamps with directional fittings: angled, swivelling joints and shades, or gooseneck stems. Like reading lights in aircraft they need to be specifically directed and cause no glare in other areas. Lamps that clip or clamp on save space on the working surface they illuminate. Use this principle for bedside lamps, too. Task lighting can double as bounced lighting: when not being used for work, lamps can be pointed towards a reflective wall or ceiling.

Pendants It is difficult to achieve adequate or interesting lighting from a point unimaginatively placed in the centre of the ceiling. A translucent shade helps to produce useful diffused general light but accents will be necessary to complement the pendant.

A pendant can helpfully make a high ceiling seem lower, but can be obtrusive in a small room. A directional pendant is most useful hung low over a dining table; prevent glare with a fitting which has a shaded bottom, or by vertical adjustment out of eye-level on a rise-and-fall mechanism. Adjust intensity with a dimmer.

Wall lights Unless they have a low output of light, wall lights tend to cause glare; but the low-wattage bulbs that prevent this cause light intensity to fall off about a metre from the wall.

Wall lights can therefore make a room look small; take advantage of this to make a large room seem more intimate. Use them to make a soft, relaxing background light and for decoration. If a wall's surface has an interesting texture, wall lights can emphasize this.

Decorative lamps are good-looking in themselves and increase the general lighting level. They include traditional and modern table lamps whose shades will affect the shape of the beam or the amount of light: an opaque shade emits light at the top and/or bottom, while a translucent one also diffuses some light sideways. The category includes period fittings, and modern 'sculptured' types using light sources encased in semi-opaque glass or acrylic, or built into a design in metal.

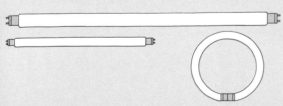
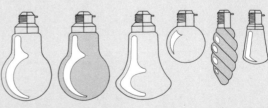

Fluorescent lighting Because it has low power-consumption and casts relatively little shadow, fluorescent light is valued as functional, and is used chiefly in kitchens, offices and workshops. Its limited display use is due to the stark appearance of many of the fittings, and to the cold quality of the light (the very efficiency of the tubes makes them unflattering to complexions and to many household furnishings). However, the tube can be hidden behind a suspended ceiling, a pelmet or a baffle, and a type that gives a warmer, softer light can be chosen.

Bulbs Most fittings giving diffused light take normal incandescent filament bulbs. Pearl (white) bulbs have a coated interior for soft lighting; clear bulbs are recommended for use with opaque shades, and not with translucent fittings where the bulb is visible – unless the spectacle of the naked bulb is part of the design. Candle bulbs are shaped and often coated internally, for use mainly with chandeliers and wall lights. Mushroom bulbs are designed for shallow light fittings and for those where the bulb is exposed. The supplier can advise on the bulb type.

237

Direct lighting from front

Direct lighting from back

Direct lighting from below

Direct lighting from above

Direct lighting from left

Oblique lighting from front left

Oblique lighting from front right

Strong light from top left, plus secondary light

3-D objects
This simple white mask was lit from a number of angles to demonstrate graphically the different efffects produced by moving the light source.

The effects in these examples are exaggerated by the absence of complementary light sources. Similar effects occur with theatrical lighting – and

the moon (which at night is illuminated only by the sun, so appears as a disc or a sickle; rather than rounded like a sphere).

Effects such as these rarely occur in the home, where light would either be bounced off a wall, or come from more than one source. What the examples do illustrate are the effects of glare and dark-

ness brought about by concentrated beamed light: in every instance but one the contrast is so strong that the eye loses more subtle information regarding contours.

Lit directly from the front, the object appears moon-like and flattened. Lit directly from the back, only the silhouette shows. Some angles seem more

informative than others – lighting obliquely from above, for example, seems to achieve the most 'normal' and clear results (perhaps because it is what we are most used to), particularly when teamed with a secondary source.

Lighting plants has two aspects: illumination (for the observer's benefit: to show up plants' shapes and shadows in display), and irradiation (for the plants' benefit: to ensure

healthy growth). Make sure that the heat does not damage the leaves by keeping the light sufficiently far away and by using bulbs of the recommended wattage (p253).

Display-shelf lighting is best planned at the same time as the shelves so that the two can work together. Especially suitable are purpose-built low-voltage miniature 'footlights'

run off a transformer, and miniature spots or strips. Alternatively, strip lighting can be built behind baffles or into lightboxes (see pp172–3).

Lighting vertical surfaces
To define the perimeter of a room, use wallwashers. The light bounced off the wall can supplement task lighting, and the position of the fittings can emphasize or flatten a wall's texture.

A painting or wall hanging calls for more specific accent lighting.

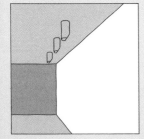

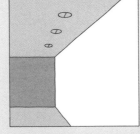

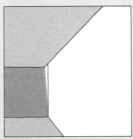

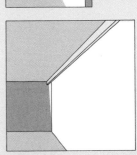

Ceiling-mounted wall-washers have conspicuous hardware. Track-mounted wallwashers are an alternative with a similar effect; use where the the texture of the wall, its contents or the overall effect on the room's shape justify using such noticeable fittings.

Recessed wallwashers achieve the same effect, without the obvious hardware, but need a recess of at least 20cm between the ceiling and the floor above. Or they can be incorporated in a false ceiling (which can disguise an uneven surface and rectify poor proportions).

Recessed track may be either set into the ceiling or created by dropping the ceiling artificially. Because it is set so close to the wall, grazing light emphasizes texture – good or bad. Light intensity is greater at the top, and falls off considerably towards the floor.

Pelmets directing light from fluorescent tubes towards the wall have an effect similar to recessed track, but are easier to install. They look neat when the baffle is fitted right across the room from one wall to the other. Light intensity is most pronounced at the top.

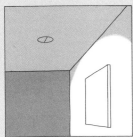

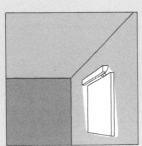

Strip lighting can be fitted on the picture frame itself or held proud of the wall. Choose a bulb that gives as accurate a colour rendering as possible. Light too close could damage a fragile painting: take advice on lighting valuable works. The light intensity is not even – it is greatest at the top (but this could suit some subjects).

Wiring for wall-mounted lights is often difficult to conceal; with a picture rail it can be combined in the hanging hardware – run it along the rail and down the chain or rod.

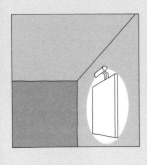

Wallwashing by a directional ceiling fitting or an up-light casts a beam that is neither intense nor even in the general direction of the painting (again it could be effective with some subjects – maybe suggesting a shaft of sunlight striking the picture). Beware with a dark picture on a pale, reflective wall: the wall around the picture could reflect more light than the canvas itself, achieving the opposite of what was intended. A darker-coloured background could help to bring out the qualities of the picture.

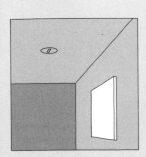

Framing spots project straight-edged beam shapes to light the precise rectangle intended. Much light is lost in the fitting – the farther away the picture, the less intense the lighting; so use in low background lighting conditions to show a canvas at its best.

Parabolic reflectors help to concentrate the light thrown back out of a crown-silvered bulb into a fairly even beam with low-intensity dazzle at oblique angles.

Tungsten halogen bulbs produce a white light that shows the colours of the pictures accurately.

LIGHTING / Displays

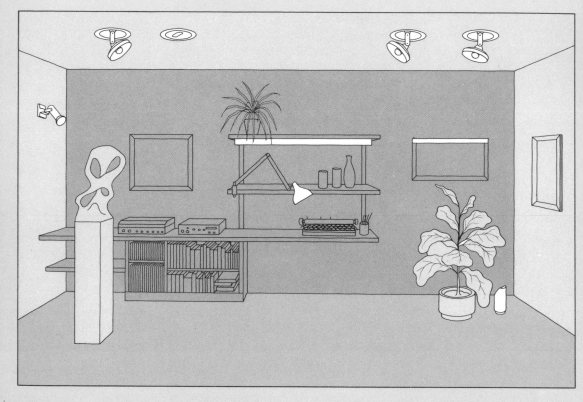

As much as extra space or planned storage, lighting can make multi-purpose rooms. These drawings demonstrate how a variety of types of fittings can be used for display.

The light fittings include a wall-mounted spotlight, a desk lamp clamped to a shelf, a strip light under one shelf, an up-light in the right-hand corner, and parabolic spots and a recessed framing projector in the ceiling.

The contents of the room that need lighting are displays on the shelves, pictures on the walls, a piece of sculpture on a plinth, the work surface and the audio equipment.

Other parts of the room might be used for dining or relaxing, so that the wall area illustrated would occasionally serve as a backdrop for activities such as these.

The pictures show planned lighting rather than actual effects – light beams are not in fact as concentrated as they appear diagrammatically, and spill out over adjacent areas. In addition, light is bounced off reflective surfaces and is generally diffused.

Flexibility
It is always better to have too many lighting fittings than too few, so that the desired effects can be achieved without too much effort: they need not all be used simultaneously. If it is not possible to provide a light fitting for every purpose, plan for flexibility. Choose fittings that can be used in different ways.

A spotlight located on the ceiling is not the answer to every prayer simply because it can be adjusted: how often is one repositioned unless it is within easy reach? But at least spotlights represent an improvement on what they so often replace – the ceiling pendant from the inevitable central ceiling rose. Even if the spot is only repositioned to show off the Christmas tree once a year, at least the potential is there. A pair of spotlights in this position, or a track if it suits the room's architecture, is a greater improvement.

Switching
When planning rooms where the lighting will be varied to suit different moods or functions, switching is important. Have two or three different circuits so that a whole scheme of lighting can be put on at once – and a whole look or atmosphere can be created at the touch of a switch. Within the circuit you can always adapt and change – and turn off – individual items, but awkward groping for light switches is eliminated. The systems (or some of them) can be fitted with dimmers. On entering the room, the programme for working or relaxing or dining can be selected instantly.

Wiring
One of the strong points in favour of the room set illustrated is the absence of trailing cables (only the up-light and the desk lamp are not built-in; the cable for the lamp is easily contained in the shelving supports). This not only prevents tripping but also improves the streamlined appearance of a room.

Alternatives
Most rooms would work well with only a selection of these fittings. One or two directional fittings could be positioned so that their light could be used on the work surface, could illuminate the art objects or could be directed to the wall to give off bounced light. A wallwashing up-light could be used to light one of the paintings. The shelf displays could be lit by miniature spots; or the strip lighting could be especially designed for growing indoor plants.

Accent lighting concentrated on individual objects creates a dramatic but not particularly comfortable effect. The darkness is not dispelled by such limited lighting, and even the objects themselves would benefit from a higher degree of overall lighting – so that the eye is not dazzled, and so that more detail is revealed. But this arrangement would be a pleasant background to a down-lit dining table in another part of the room, or to fireside reading; low-key accent lighting is a reminder that the remainder of the room exists.

Functional lighting provided by directional fittings needs to be complemented by other lighting so that the eye is not dazzled when it looks away from the work surface. Not-too-specific lighting elsewhere achieves this; light from the display shelf, for example (provided the source is hidden behind a baffle), would reflect off the wall and illuminate the room gently.

The angled desk lamp could be turned to the wall when not in use on the desk surface, to create bounced general light, or could be turned towards a plant or object.

Washing the wall with light from a number of fittings – not necessarily a line of wallwashers – illuminates things less specifically than accent lighting does, and certainly not as dramatically.

Because the whole wall is lit, individual items are not picked out and there is a danger of their importance being reduced to that of the lowest common denominator. In addition, the areas of shadow below shelves and work surfaces may obscure objects of interest – or simply create pools of darkness.

The main effect is to make the room look larger and lighter overall.

It was once so simple to choose a paint for interior work – oil-based gloss for all woodwork and water-based emulsion (latex) for walls and ceilings. The only dilemma lay in the choice of colours.

Paint technology has advanced so far that we now have specific paints and specific finishes exactly suited to the type of material on which they are to be used, and the type of wear they will get.

The paints most commonly used in interior house painting are either oil-based or water-based. Recently, the oil vehicle in oil-based paints has been replaced by synthetic resins that are odourless and more quick-drying.

Paints are now more generally categorized by the finish they give when dry than by the vehicle in which the pigments are suspended. To describe the many intermediate finishes between matt and gloss, manufacturers use various terms: eggshell, silk, satin, semi-gloss. The glossier the finish, the more easy it is to clean. Although many matt emulsions claim to be washable, it is simply not as easy to remove heavy grease stains without marring the texture. In general, glossy surfaces are more hardwearing, but many modern emulsions are just as resilient.

Opaque paints	
Type	**Description**
Gloss	Oil-based, hardwearing. (Alkyd resin the normal additive.) Available in degrees of shine – matt, silk, etc. For use on woodwork and metal.
Emulsion	Water-based. Finishes include matt, eggshell, silk. For use on walls and ceilings. Can be used on woodwork, but without the durability provided by gloss. For increased durability, available with vinyl or acrylic resin.
Non-drip	Both gloss and emulsion available in this form. Contents jelly-like, as opposed to liquid; do not need stirring. If stirred by mistake, leave to set.
Specialized paints	
Enamel	High quality, durable gloss for surfaces subject to rough treatment – e.g. toys.
Fire-retardant	Emulsion with fire-resisting quality. For use on polystyrene (styrofoam) ceiling tiles, where flammability a high risk. Reduces (but does not prevent) spread of flame. Can also be used on timber, hardboard and chipboard.
Aerosols	Most paint types available in aerosol cans. Suitable for small jobs only, since expensive. Particularly useful for wickerwork. Work in a well-ventilated room, or outside with a cardboard enclosure to shield the wind from spraying paint everywhere. Shake container well and angle as directed. Articles should be placed horizontally if possible, to avoid drips. A series of thin coats, left to dry, is preferable to one thick coat.

Walls and ceilings
Use either a 200mm or 225mm brush, or a similarly sized roller or paint pad. Use a small brush first for corners and other awkward places. Paint a wall or ceiling working away from the window.
Plaster surfaces Fill small holes with cellulose filler, big ones with plaster.
Bare plaster Seal with a coat of plaster primer or a water-thinned coat of emulsion, and then apply one or two topcoats of emulsion.
Painted plaster If the surface is already matt, simply apply one or two coats of emulsion. If the surface is gloss, sand it down to flatten the shine and to give the paint a better ground, then apply one or two coats of paint.
Papered surfaces Many problems can arise when applying paint to papered surfaces: the surface of the paper may not accept paint very well; colour from the paper may bleed through the paint, or the solvents in the paint may dissolve the adhesive holding the paper to the wall. Test a small area first for any blistering, colour seeping through or failure to adhere. Small bubbles usually dry back, but if large blisters or any other of the above symptoms appear, strip the paper.
Non-washable paper It is usually advisable to strip such paper if it is heavily soiled, as stains may bleed into the paint. There are commercial wallpaper cleaners in paste form, but they are expensive and time-consuming. If the paper is clean enough, test patterned paper for colour showing through if it is to be painted with a pale emulsion. If it does show through, apply a coat of primer sealer and leave to dry for 24 hours before painting.
Painted or washable paper Wash with a solution of household detergent, then rinse with a damp cloth and allow to dry before painting.

Metal
Iron and steel are prone to rust, which must be removed before painting. Small rust spots can be rubbed off with an emery cloth, larger areas wire-brushed by hand or with a wire-cup brush fitted to a power drill. Wear goggles to protect your eyes from flying particles. Treat rust spots with a primer that inhibits rust. Apply primer to bare metal – universal primer or metal primer such as zinc chromate. Finally apply undercoat, and then gloss. Painted metal should be rubbed down and cleaned thoroughly with detergent.

Plastic and fibreglass
Clean surfaces and rub with fine-grade wet-and-dry paper to give a key. Apply primer (thinned alkyd gloss paint) and topcoat of gloss.

Painting woodwork

Tools Rollers and pads leave an impression of their own texture; don't use them on wood unless covering large areas or creating a matt finish, and always use brushes for a high gloss finish. Suitable brushes range in width from 12mm for cutting in at edges next to other surfaces, to 75mm which is the optimum width for use on large flat surfaces.

New woodwork

Check wood is sound, rot-free and dry. Fill all holes and blemishes with plastic wood filler, leave to dry and sand smooth. Then knotting, primer and undercoat are applied, in that order, before the top coats. Let each coat dry before applying the next.

Knotting Shellac knotting is dabbed or brushed over any knots or resinous patches of bare wood. It seals in the resin which might otherwise bleed through the paint.

Primer This adheres to the untreated surface to provide a sound base for the paint. Primers are sometimes referred to as sealers since the sealing of porous surfaces is part of their function. They also prevent any possible chemical reaction between the surface and the paint; for example, oily woods can prevent an oil-based paint from drying properly. So-called 'universal primers' for use on any surface are not as effective as those intended for woodwork.

White or pink wood primer is suitable for general use on all timber surfaces. Aluminium wood primer is intended for hardwoods (oily) and resinous surfaces. Acrylic wood primer is for interior timber only, and is extra-quick drying.

Undercoat Water-based paints (sometimes thinned for economy) normally serve as their own undercoat, but specially made oil-based undercoats are available to provide a good ground for oil-based paints since these are more expensive and do not provide a good base when thinned. Use the same colour undercoat as the intended topcoat, and for best appearance and durability apply two layers of undercoat.

Topcoat This is traditionally a gloss finish on wood. A second coat can provide an even better-wearing, better-looking gloss finish. See also 'High-shine finish' p244.

Painted woodwork

If existing woodwork is well coated with a sound film of paint, do not remove the paint. If it is gloss, rub it down with sandpaper to flatten the shine and give a better ground for the new paint. If a change of colour is involved, apply a new undercoat; if the same colour, apply the new topcoat directly.

Stripping paint

Paint that is cracking, flaking or blistering must be removed, if necessary back to bare wood. It is generally better to work first on awkward places and mouldings and then on flat surfaces.

Chemical stripping is only really suitable for use on relatively small areas, as the chemicals are expensive and give off unpleasant, and sometimes toxic, fumes. Use a jelly type which will cling to surfaces that are inclined or vertical. Wear protective gloves. Dab on the chemical with an old brush, allow time for the paint to rise in blisters, then scrape off.

Blowtorch Play the flame across the surface until the paint melts and wrinkles: just supply enough heat to lift the paint into blisters and strip off with a scraper immediately. Do not let the flame rest on any one spot for any length of time or the wood will char. If the intention is to leave the wood in a natural finish, take off the final layers of paint some other way, as scorch marks can be difficult to sand away.

Machine-sanding Use a drum sander or a paint and varnish remover fitted onto an electric drill, the plain disc attachment or the more unusual types – the orbital or the flailing-arm. Industrial sanders with built-in vacuum cleaners can be rented to tackle large areas like wooden floors. Do not leave too long on one area or slice at an angle.

Preparing stripped wood If chemicals were used, clean the surface with white spirit or solvent. However the wood has been stripped, rub the surface with sandpaper to remove any small nibs of paint. After knotting and priming, fill holes.

Clear wood finishes Hardwoods, with their attractive colours and grain formations, are usually given a clear finish. Since varnishes and seals are less durable than paint, at least two coats will be needed; sand before each. (See table.)

Natural wood finishes	
Type	**Description**
Oil varnish	High gloss finish.
Polyurethane varnish	Quicker-drying than oil type. Hard, protective film. Available in gloss, eggshell and matt finishes. Can also be used over any paint as protective layer. At least two coats are needed; on floors apply three coats. Various transparent tints available for changing the colour of wood.
Polyurethane clear varnish	Very expensive, but resists abrasion, water and chemicals. Can also be used over emulsion-painted floor, where floor paint was not used because of limited colour range.
Sealers	Available in various shades; one brush coat seals surface and leaves matt finish. Further coats build up a high gloss finish. Toughened sealers available for floors.
Coloured preservatives	Stains wood various shades at same time as protects against woodworm and rot. For floor boards and other exposed structural timber.
Wood stains	Water-based easier to use than oil-based. Wet bare wood with water, let dry, and then rub with medium fine sandpaper. Dust, and apply the dye.

PAINTING / Effects

Having put the right paint on the right surfaces, ensuring their durability and well-being, treat some larger areas as backgrounds – as a painter considers his canvases.

Even without colour changes, dramatic effects can be created merely by variations in finish: gloss-coated cornices in a matt-painted room; mouldings highlighted by a different finish; shiny, reflective corners muted by a matt treatment.

More daringly, try paint-on-paint: in pictures, stripes, lettering, friezes. See what results you can get from disregarding the rules and stretching the boundaries of the orthodox.

Consider the wall pictured on the jacket of this book. Tradition would dictate that it be planed and sanded down smoothly, the joints hidden and gloss paint applied to give a burnished finish.

In fact, the rough-hewn wood, pinned to a batten framework, was painted with matt emulsion; when that dried the wood on either side of the join was covered with an oil-based stain in a deliberately uneven line.

This simple, neat trick gives texture and character to large areas, using cheap timber attractively. Covering such a surface with gloss paint would be much more expensive and more arduous.

On furniture with recessed detail in the wood the same sort of contrast can be used to effect – highlighting the detail with the oil-based stain. If the item is to receive heavy wear use oil-based egg-shell gloss as the base, instead of emulsion.

Antique finish After priming and applying an undercoat to a wooden surface, cover with an oil-based satin-finish gloss. Apply a contrasting colour of the same paint to any detail (carved work, say) and, before completely dry, wipe some off in those areas which would be expected to wear most with time and use. Once dry, use a brush or cloth pad to apply a clear glaze of one part linseed oil to three parts turpentine (or white spirit). This dries quickly, so to give it a 'streaky' effect – to match the worn look of the paint – glaze only a few square inches at a time and wipe a cloth across it immediately. For the best effect, confine 'streaking' to central areas, leaving surrounds glazed. When dry, coat with a clear varnish or white shellac.

High-shine finish The surface must first be filled and sanded impeccably before any painting. On wood, apply primer, sand, and re-fill any imperfections. Then, using topcoat as undercoat, apply at least five coats of high gloss, sanding with fine paper (and dusting off) after each coat has dried. Using this process on walls is a mammoth task as you *must* use brushes, even for the first few coats, since rollers impart too uneven a texture. The principle is the same, but use emulsion instead of primer, and wet-and-dry paper for glasspaper.

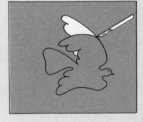

Stencils

Stencils are cut-out shapes of patterns in paper or card for use in painting ready-made designs onto surfaces. Motifs can be bought at art shops, or you can make your own. The sort of stiff oil-treated cardboard used for office files makes excellent stencil paper.

To transfer an existing design onto a stencil rather than draw one freehand, lay some tracing or waxed paper over the design and draw the outline with a sharp pencil.

Shade this line with soft pencil so that when you turn it over, place it on top of the stencil paper and pencil firmly over the outline, it will transfer onto the stencil paper. Pin or tape it to a thick piece of board and cut the shape out with a craft knife.

Make sure the background paint is clean and dry. Fix the stencil to the surface with masking tape. You can use either side of the stencil and thus can reverse an image from left to right. Apply paint with a dabbing action around the outline of the stencil (brush strokes might encourage paint to seep under the edges). Press the stencil flat as you paint.

Use a stencil brush for an opaque cover. For a blotchy effect – suggesting clouds or water – dab on paint with a piece of foam rubber.

If more than one stage is needed for a design, allow each to dry before doing the next. When stencilling designs with more than one colour, work on larger areas first, and then apply the finer details with an artist's fitch.

Peel the stencil away before the paint is totally dry to avoid breaks in the lines, but when it is at least touch-dry to prevent smudging. Any smudges should be cleaned off immediately with the appropriate solvent – as should both sides of the stencil after use.

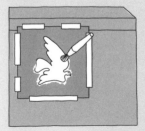
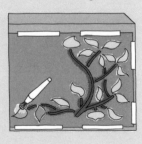

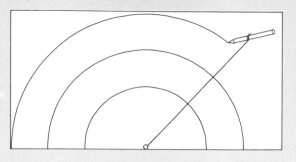

Straight lines

Use strips of masking tape to define lines. Make sure surfaces are clean and dry before the tape is put in place, particularly if applying successive lines of different colours.

As with stencils, remove tape when paint is touch-dry to avoid smudging and broken edges.

Steady-handed people can simply cut in straight lines with an artist's fitch. Again, wait for each strip to dry before painting the adjoining one.

Circles

To draw a circle make two knotted loops at the ends of a piece of string. Put one loop over a pin fixed firmly at the centre of the design, and the other round a pencil. Adjust the length of the string to the required radius of the circle, and describe it, keeping the string taut at all times.

If the design is to consist of concentric circles, shorten the string progressively for each. Paint alternate roundels, and when these have dried, fill in those in between.

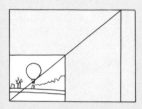
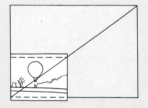
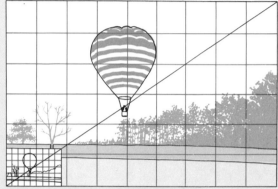

Murals

Scale up a smaller design – your own, an image from a photograph or an illustration from a magazine. It is easier to use an original with roughly the same proportions as the wall.

To get a more definite idea of proportion, draw a scale model of the wall on tracing paper (perhaps using the wall measurements in metres and making the model in centimetres). Place the original at the lower left hand corner of the model and draw a line across the diagonal of the image (as shown), continuing the line to a point where it meets either edge of the 'wall'. A line drawn vertically down from this point represents where the edge of the mural would lie. This will give you an idea of the size of borders to use if the mural is to be centred on a wall space.

If it is more important that the image fills the wall, it will be necessary to crop the original. To do this, draw a diagonal line across the model of the wall and place it over the image so that they are aligned at the left. The point where the diagonal crosses the right side of the image gives you a point from which to construct a box giving the area of image that can be used. Move this area over the image to decide on the appropriate crop.

Construct a grid over the area of image to be used (or on a tracing of it). 25mm squares are usual; use a smaller grid for intricate designs. Pencil a similar scaled-up grid on the wall, and then pencil the design on the wall, working one square at a time. Paint as for stencils.

Designs on glass

To decorate windows or glass panelling, use artist's oil paints or ordinary oil-based gloss paint.

You can draw your design freehand onto the glass, or a simple trick is to place a design you wish to copy on the other side of the glass – held in position with masking tape – and 'trace' it through. If it isn't big enough you can scale it up, in the same way as for wall murals, onto a large piece of drawing paper, and then put that behind the glass.

After the paint has dried, give it a protective layer of oil-based varnish.

Most effective glass decoration can be achieved by taking simple shapes – often dictated by the dimple indentations on frosted glass – and repeating them for an all-over pattern. Larger shapes can be finger-painted for an interesting finish.

Mirrors Apply the paint directly again as for glass, or you can use some of the signwriting techniques described below.

Signwriting tricks

Signwriters use an epidiascope to project and enlarge images onto the surfaces they have to paint; an alternative is an ordinary slide projector.

Another trick is to use the grid/mural technique to scale up small designs onto a large sheet of paper. Perforate the outlines of the design; place the paper in position over the area to be painted – securing it with masking tape – and use a sharp pencil to dot through the perforations, transferring the outline to the surface to be painted. (On glass, dab the perforations with emulsion.)

Finally, specialist art shops sell a tracing paper with one side coated with blue or red powder. To use this, first dust off the powder until it is almost 'bald' (otherwise it might smudge the paintwork); then fix the paper with the powdered surface against the surface to be painted. Place the illustration against the tracing paper and shade over the outline to transfer the powder. Then, outline in pencil and remove the powder.

There are two basic ways to put a shelf on a wall: buy a proprietary system comprising slotted strips and brackets or clips (with some you also get the actual shelf) or obtain the materials and build the shelf from scratch.

The essential thing is flexibility: this is provided for in the proprietary systems, and can be built in to home-made shelving, especially by taking advantage of some of the fixtures shown overleaf.

The basic principle of most proprietary shelving systems is the same – though the details vary slightly. Slotted uprights are screwed to the wall, the brackets are locked in place at the chosen height and the shelf is either fixed to the brackets or laid loosely on them.

The uprights and the brackets are mostly of aluminium or steel. The finish may be white or satin aluminium; or a choice of anodized silver or gold, enamelled black, brass, bronze or colours. You might prefer to choose a finish first and then look for a system that includes it.

Shelf material supplied is usually veneered or plastic-faced chipboard, or may be metal or glass. Systems supplied without shelves accept most materials popularly used, including different types of wood. Choose the finish that suits the environment, and the material whose strength is appropriate to the intended use of the shelves.

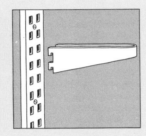
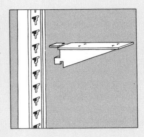
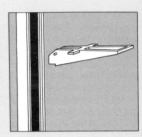

Standard-and-bracket

The uprights The popularity of these systems is largely in their flexibility. Some systems are available with only one size of upright; when planning for the future it would probably pay to buy longer uprights and more brackets than are needed immediately. Or add extra sections to short uprights to create more shelves. Conversely, trim uprights with a hacksaw to fit an exact space.

Uprights can be fixed to a solid wall without problems. Some manufacturers either include screws and wallplugs in the kit or recommend screw sizes. Usually the screws are of sufficient length to give a good wall fixing: the threaded part of the screw must extend into the brick (plaster has no holding power). Remember that the screws are the only thing preventing a complete collapse. Don't use screws shorter than 40mm.

Cavity walls require special fixing devices, not all of them suitable for the chosen shelf system: check with the manufacturer's instructions for the recommended type, or take the uprights along to the shop for advice.

There are two types of upright. Some have regularly spaced slots into which the brackets locate, allowing shelf heights to be selected fairly closely. Other types have a hollow channel in which the brackets can slide up and down to be fixed at any point – important where exact shelf positions are required. The latter type is slightly easier to fit because all you have to ensure is that the two uprights are vertical and correctly spaced; the brackets can be adjusted later to make the shelf horizontal. With the slotted type you have to make certain that the slots on both uprights line up when fixing them to the wall.

The brackets There are slight variations in the styling of brackets, but little to choose in the way they slot in. The length is important since it governs the depth of the shelf material: it should overlap the end of the bracket slightly, or be cut to fit exactly inside a lipped edge. In complete packages, the shelves will be of a predetermined depth to fit varying bracket depths.

Some systems have brackets which can be slanted either upwards or downwards: useful for storing an item which might roll off a shelf or for some displays – like magazine stands in stores.

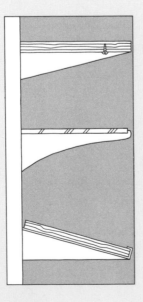

Shelf material Unless it is supplied with a shelf kit, you have to buy shelving material. Natural hardwood is strong and excellent for high-quality appearance, but expensive.

Manufactured boards (chipboard, blockboard and plywood) are popular choices because of their availability in a number of different standard depths and lengths. Veneered or faced chipboard is marginally stronger than plain chipboard, which requires more support and has to be painted. Plywood and blockboard are also stronger than plain chipboard, but are much more costly. Glass shelves can be bought from glaziers with the front edges and sides or all four sides polished.

Metal shelves are supplied with some proprietary systems. Metal sheeting can be used but continuous support would be needed on the back and sides. You would also have to cut the material with a hacksaw and add lipping of some sort to protect the sharp front edge, or file it smooth. Thin, cheap plywood and hardboard also require continuous support on the back and front edge (use wall-fixed battens at the back). Even then, these materials quickly bow.

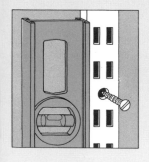
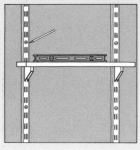
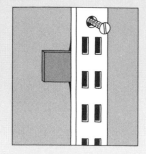
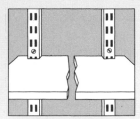

Fixing uprights

Position the first upright, drill a hole, insert a plug and loosely insert the top screw into the wall. Use a spirit level (or a plumbline) to get the upright perfectly vertical, then insert the bottom screw loosely. Insert any intermediate screws that are necessary.

Insert pieces of cardboard behind the uprights to pack out any undulations in the wall (see third diagram). Tighten up all screws. (If more than two screws are used per upright, wallplugs must be inserted in the exact position of each hole before the top and bottom screws are tightened and the upright is finally secured.)

Place a bracket into, say, the third slot from the top. Fix another bracket into the other upright in the matching slot. Lay a straight-edge (or the shelf) between the fixed upright and the other upright (hand held). Place a spirit level on the straight-edge to check that the shelf will lie horizontally, and adjust the unfixed upright to the vertical. Mark off the screw hole positions in the wall for the unfixed upright. Drill holes, insert plugs, position and fix second upright as before. If more than two uprights are used, fix the end two before any intermediate uprights.

Preventing movement

Unless the standards are set into an alcove, there is a risk of people knocking into a shelf and dislodging it. In some systems the shelf is screwed to the bearers or held in place by lipped brackets. One method of preventing movement is to cut slots in the rear edge of the shelf for the standards to fit into. For this, have the shelf slightly deeper, so that the front edges of the shelf and its brackets line up as intended.

'Bookcase' strips

An alternative type of slotted metal strip takes not brackets but clips: one for each corner of the shelf. Instead of being mounted on the face of a wall, the standards here are secured to facing walls, like those in an alcove, or to the side panels of a bookcase. Secure the strips as for standard-and-bracket systems, making sure that the slots in all four strips are perfectly level so that the shelves will be horizontal.

The metal strips and the clips both come in various finishes.

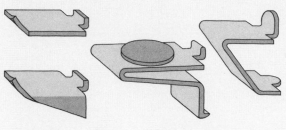
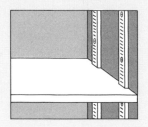

Appropriate clips can be chosen for the required strength. Some clips can be secured to wooden shelves; others have pads which prevent glass shelves from slipping.

The clips are fairly unobtrusive under the shelves, but there are three possible ways of making the fittings neater – at the expense of more complicated installation. One is to sink the metal strips into rebates cut into the uprights, where these are wooden, so that they don't stand out. At the same time rebates can be cut underneath the shelf to conceal the clips.

An alternative is to cut slots in the ends of the shelves to accommodate the vertical strips; this incidentally also increases a shelf's stability.

Loadbearing

The loadbearing quality of a shelf depends on the shelf material, the type and number of supports and the distance between them, and the wall fixings used. Clearly a glass shelf of any type should not be expected to house more than a collection of lightweight ornaments or some paperback books. For heavy loads you will need a thick, well-supported, manufactured board. The table indicates various materials, and the maximum distance between supports. But the manufacturer of a shelf system should be able to provide some guidance.

The best position for the brackets is about one-sixth or one-fifth in from each end of the shelf. For maximum strength, site the brackets immediately under a screw used to fix the upright to the wall.

It's probably worth remembering that shelves make handy dumping grounds and the load they are intended to take is invariably exceeded over the years: it is worth while building a sturdier shelf than you think you need.

Manufacturers generally specify the sort of load a shelf will take. A light load would be ornaments; a heavy load a collection of large books or records.

Maximum spacing between shelf supports		
material	thickness	distance
wood	16mm	0.5m
	22mm	0.8m
	25mm	1.0m
plywood	16mm	0.75m
	25mm	1.0m
blockboard	16mm	0.5m
faced chipboard	16mm	0.5m
	25mm	0.75m
glass	6mm	0.25m
	10mm	0.5m
acrylic sheet	12mm	0.5m

Adjustability can also be built in to the shelves a handyperson designs at home. One way of doing this is to imitate a proprietary system based on a series of equally spaced holes drilled into uprights in which pegs of various types are positioned. Another way is to design shelves with additional bearers equally spaced up the length of each side panel and with the shelves themselves not fixed so that their position can be altered. Finally, it is possible to use a framework of scaffolding, or even a ladder, to give a 'high-tech' style, but to make the shelves secure they need to be designed to fit snugly and securely in place.

Materials for the shelves are the same as those discussed on the previous two pages.

Peg systems

The principle is that each shelf rests on four pegs, one at each corner. The pegs are plugged into holes drilled into wooden uprights: these may be the two sides of a cabinet or four separate pieces fixed to a wall or forming a frame. The holes, usually of uniform 6mm diameter, are spaced at equal intervals (often 50mm) up the length of the uprights, and became an unobtrusive part of the design. It is an easy matter to lift the shelf off the pegs and reposition the pegs at a new height.

There is a wide range of choice in the type of peg available, whether do-it-yourself or ready-made; various sizes, styles, shapes and materials cater for different types of shelf material and function.

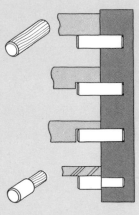 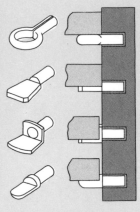 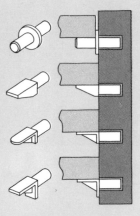 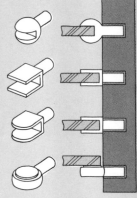

Dowels 6mm wooden dowelling can be cut to length and simply tapped into the holes. The ends can be rounded to improve their appearance. The shelf can simply rest on the dowelling, or can be rebated to conceal either half its depth or the complete peg. Plastic or rubber sleeves can slip over the projecting end.

Metal or plastic pegs When using proprietary metal or plastic pegs, it is advisable to line the hole with a metal or plastic sleeve to give a more secure fixing.

Steel pegs in various finishes may be spade-shaped or eyelet-shaped to hold wooden shelves.

Plastic or nylon pegs (available in various colours) may be rounded like dowelling or spade-shaped with a flat surface to support the shelf from underneath.

Pegs for glass Special pegs are designed to prevent glass shelves from sliding off: transparent plastic pegs are unobtrusive, but metal ones often suit the styling of glass shelves.

Pegs may have slots into which the glass shelf slides to be held securely. Alternatively, pegs may have a cushion or pad.

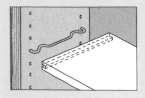 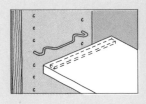  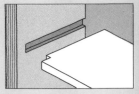

Wire supports

The uprights at either end of the shelf are drilled with a series of holes as for peg systems, but a length of shaped wire is used at each end of the shelf instead of a pair of pegs. The distance between the holes is determined by the width of the wire support – manufacturers make them for several shelf depths.

Shelf rebates are made at either end of the shelf to take the wire. The groove usually runs the whole depth of the shelf, and is small enough to be almost unnoticeable; if the groove is not taken to the front of the shelf the wire is completely invisible.

Housing joints

For a very strong joint, using either wood or manufactured board, cut a groove in the end support panels to receive one shelf edge.

A series of grooves cut at regular intervals into the uprights would permit flexibility of shelf position, but accurate cutting is essential with such joints for the sake of both appearance and fit.

(A neater shelf – but one that isn't adjustable – is made by using a stopped housing joint which conceals the edge of the shelf from the front.)

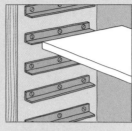

Battens

A similar system can be achieved without cutting grooves into the uprights, but by fixing a series of battens at regular intervals to the side panels. Accurate positioning is important, but less complex cutting is needed. The pattern of battens becomes part of the design of the piece (as in some proprietary plastic systems) and for this reason the finish needs to be good-looking.

Depending on the length of shelf, it may be necessary to continue the battening along the back wall as well as along the sides for support.

Metal supports

Angled metal strip supports of extruded aluminium or mild steel can be bought with holes predrilled for fixing to the side walls of a recess or cupboard. They perform the same function as wooden bearer battens: cut them to length with a hacksaw and provide a bearer across the back wall as well as the sides if necessary.

The appearance of metal strip supports is less attractive than wood, but the system makes excellent use of storage space: instead of shelves, filing trays or baskets with lipped edges can be run along the metal channels.

Two simple methods for locating shelves on horizontal supports: screwed-in battens and V-shaped grooves.

Scaffolding

Traditional builder's scaffolding has now been redesigned and adapted for use in shops and homes. It is possible to buy tubes in a variety of diameters together with a wide range of connectors, and to have finishes other than the traditional galvanized steel.

Because of the chunky scale of even the smallest scaffolding systems, desk tops and shelves incorporated in them need to be of substantial thickness, for both practical and aesthetic reasons.

Shelves need to rest on horizontal members, and have to be locked into position to prevent lateral movement (see above).

Alternatively cut a quarter-circle out of each corner of the shelf so that it fits snugly into the upright tubes (bottom left).

Or cut a corner section from underneath the shelf at each end to enable it to fit snugly over the horizontally supporting tubes. It's more secure to drill through the tube and bolt the shelf into position (bottom right).

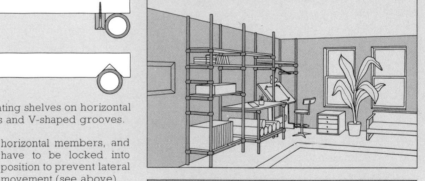

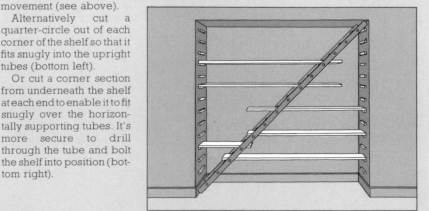

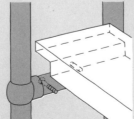

Ladders

It is possible to work shelving variations on the scaffolding theme using ladders – actually secondhand ladders, or structures made from dowelling fixed at regular intervals into a softwood batten to make a climbing-frame type of upright. An old aluminium ladder wedged or secured into position at an angle in an alcove can take one end of a shelf (fixed with a batten or a groove in the shelf's underside) – its other end could rest on a bearer batten on the wall.

MAKE SOMETHING OF IT

Cast-offs can be a great aid to cheap and cheerful home-making – from doors that came off when two rooms were knocked into one to hessian feedsacks discarded when the cows were fed.

These and other items are candidates for interesting recycling ideas. The doors could become a free-standing screen, the feedsacks a rug on the floor.

Use old chimney pots (and large flower pots) for *jardinières*, umbrella stands, uplighters. Make coffee tables out of barrels, packing cases, giant flower pots, cable reels, galvanized rubbish bins

and wine racks. Hang a bread basket over a light bulb to provide a lamp shade. Use a single riding boot (filled with sand, or its stretcher) as a door stop.

Do the materials discarded from larger projects in your home (or those in someone else's home but now in the skip outside) have any potential? Or the shop fittings from a local store that is closing down?

Shop fittings
If discarded items are sitting outside awaiting disposal they are fair game, but if things have not reached this stage yet ask

the owner what his plans are. It is no secret that shopfittings fetch high prices from antique shops, but the prices should be lower at source.

Bookstores or newsagents will be a good source for old racks which can be put to the same use for your magazines.

Butchers might have old chopping blocks or marble surfaces that can be made into tables; meat hanging hooks and their support bars are the other items to look for.

Old-fashioned milliners sometimes have beautiful old plaster head forms that were used in window displays and if the hats

were made on the premises there might be wooden blocks as well.

Tailors will have dressmaking dummies and possibly old wooden shelving systems where the fabric lengths were stored.

Pharmacists have apothecary jars and interesting wooden boxes with brass knobs on top.

Carpenters, printers and almost any other type of shop employing craftsmen contain a gamut of gadgets – from simple wood block planes to book binding presses.

Old-door screen
Hinge together two or more doors to make a screen. Remove all old furniture (hinges, locks and handles); fill the holes left with wood filler and sand smooth. Saw wide doors in half lengthwise and plane and sand the edges smooth.

Panelled doors can be left as they are, or the faces of the door halves can be disguised by pinning on hardboard cut to the same size. Before attaching any hardboard, make a saw cut the depth of the panel recess between the top and bottom panels to give an air channel to prevent the hardboard from bowing out. Smooth the edges flush with the door.

To finish with fabric, cut the hardboard to fit and stretch fabric over it, stapling the edges on the wrong side and mitring the corners. Then pin the hardboard in place.

Mark corresponding

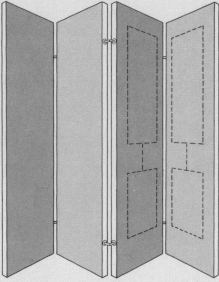

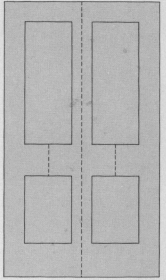

positions for the hinges on each section of the screen, about 30cm from top and from bottom, and fix in place. Soss or concealed hinges are preferable.

Finish the surface by painting (see p244) or with *découpage* (p219).

Other ideas Use doors as trestle-table tops. Cover panelled ones with hardboard; plain doors can take laminated plastic, simulated leather and all kinds of fabric finishes, which look better if halfround wooden mouldings are fixed to the edges.

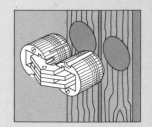

Hessian feedsacks
These can be made into stuffed seats and floor rugs, good as temporary measures before the real items arrive.
Seating Make a pouffe from two feedsacks: line

with cotton and stitch together with strong thread, leaving an opening for a filling: polystyrene beads make a good texture.
Rugs The more sacks, the bigger the rug. Open up the sacks, iron them flat

under a damp rag, stitch them with strong thread to the size you want and line if necessary; hem the edges. To keep it from sliding underfoot, back the rug with foam carpet underlay about 75mm

smaller all round than the finished size of the rug. Turn over the hemmed edges, mitring the corners, and stick the turnings to the underside of the underlay with fabric adhesive.

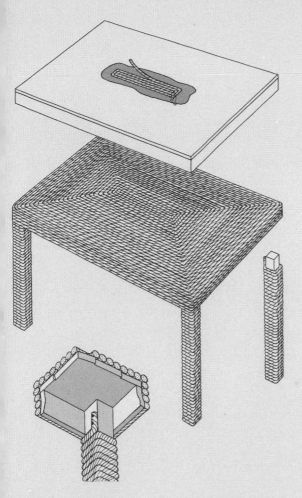

required for a table (it will not be cheap), first measure the area of the top surface. The rope needed is equal to the area of the table divided by the thickness of the rope. Add to this the length needed for the top edge (the perimeter times the depth, divided by the thickness of the rope). Top and edge should be one length; allow extra for knots. Estimate rope needed for the legs (separate lengths for each) by the same formula as the top edge; allow extra for starting behind table edge.

Whip the end before you begin, to prevent fraying. Start with the table top; drill a hole in the centre (if the table is square or circular) or at a point equidistant from three sides of a rectangle. The hole should be large enough for the rope to pass through. Knot it (with a figure-of-eight) underneath to secure.

Apply clear contact adhesive to the top of the table, a little at a time, following the line the rope will follow. Wait for it to dry, as directed by the manufacturer, and stick the rope in place. Start off in a spiral (and continue this formation for circular tables), straightening it

into corners as the rope reaches the table edges. Keep the lines of rope as close together as possible. Pin the rope (because on tables it is subject to knocks) at 10cm intervals using small brass tacks.

Try not to leave a gap between top and edges. About 12mm away (if the rope is that thick) from the final corner on the last lap, drill a hole and feed through the end of the rope. Knot as before and pin securely out of sight.

Now do the legs, one at a time. Start from behind at the top, where the leg is concealed by the edge. Nail and glue the end and run it down to where the leg begins to show. Wrap it horizontally around the leg, gluing and pinning as before. Continue to the base and finish by nailing and gluing to the inside of the leg.

Other ideas Also cover with rope or string lamp bases, picture frames, oil drums to make table bases and empty tin cans for storage or waste paper.

Rope-covered objects
Tables with a deep drop edge and a regular shape are ideal for this cover-up which is useful to disguise a bad surface. Inevitably, some will show through, though, so it is advisable first to paint the surface the

same colour as the rope.

Use good-quality sisal or nylon nautical line, preferably of a thickness that divides evenly into the depth of the table's top edge (12mm is a standard gauge).

To estimate the rope

Chimney-pot uplighter
Set a chimney pot in a bed of ready-mix cement, passing a length of tubing under the pot to take a power cable and embedding a wooden block for a bulb carrier.
Meat-grinder lamp
Drill a hole for the cable (keep clear of the mechanism; or lock the handle with a block of wood). Wedge the bulb carrier in position and use thick wire to hold the lampshade (you could use a cheese-grater). Clamp the grinder to a shelf or surface.
Tin-can uplighter
Drill a hole for cable and fit a rubber grommet. Bolt an L-bracket inside to support a bulb carrier. For

the baffle make two wire profiles to hold slats cut from an old Venetian blind across the top of the can.
Parasol pendent shade
Screw an eyelet into the end of the handle and thread over a cuphook fixed to the ceiling beside the light fitting. Adjust the cable so that heat from the bulb will not damage the parasol.

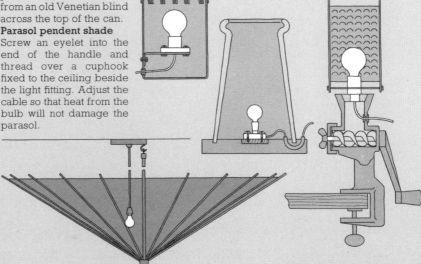

PLANTS / Care

It takes plants to bring a room to life. Think of them as living furniture, to be chosen by reference to size, shape and colour. And like good furniture, they need loving care.

Plants are worth – and often get – whole books to themselves. The advice here covers only the rudiments of keeping them healthy and looking good.

Plants need nutrients, a specific temperature range, an energy source and rest.

There may seem to be good domestic reasons for keeping the curtains closed for a week – but plants cannot live without light; watering routines should take account of the fact that over-watering in winter disturbs a plant's rest. If in doubt, practise benign neglect: a plant makes it obvious when it needs special care.

Watering

Over-watering is destructive and it is a mistake to water according to a diary-set routine. You can tell if a plant needs water by sticking a forefinger into its soil to the first joint. Water only if your finger-tip emerges dry.

The great danger is waterlogging. Take the plant pot off its saucer and add water (lukewarm, preferably) until it begins to run out of the bottom. Or, to save lifting the pots every time you water, line each saucer with aquarium pebbles (they are uniformly sized and sterile).

Holiday provisions Do not expect plants to survive if you cannot guarantee 10°C (50°F) in your absence. With that assurance, give a neighbour a watering brief; or try one of the following methods.

Before leaving, water all the plants (according to the finger-test requirements) and then group them together in your shadiest room. Surround them with bowls of water to increase the moisture supply. Otherwise, water the plants, wrap each in a clean plastic bag and place them in a shady spot. This is particularly good for the moisture-lovers.

In the cooler months, when the soil can be damp for weeks, ensure that the plant is not over-watered.

The plants to choose

Delicate ferns do not flourish in oppressive central heating; tropical plants cannot take winter fluctuations of temperature in draughty homes.

So hardy plants are the safest: Philodendrons, *Tradescantia*, English and grape ivies, jade-tree or money plants. While maidenhair ferns are too delicate for an erratic household climate, Boston ferns (*Nephrolepsis exal-tata*) are more tolerant, given plenty of moisture and a position in bright shade.

For minimum care requirements, choose cacti – but only if they can be in sunlit windows.

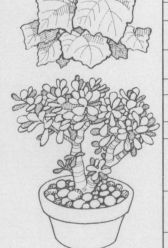

The easy plant guide		
Plant	Best situation	Special tips
Aspidistra	Cool, not sunny.	Keep pot-bound.
Chamaerops excelsa	Cool, semi-light.	Water sparingly in winter, well in summer.
Chlorophytum comosum	Anywhere sunny.	Keep moist.
Fatshedera lizei	Cool shade.	Can be trained to climb.
Ficus elastica	Cool, bright shade.	Don't over-water. Roots need space.
Helxine soleirolii	Moderate, sunny.	Trailing plant.
Monstera deliciosa	Warm, sunny	Train aerial roots to grow around stake covered in damp sphagnum moss.
Neanthe bella	Average, bright shade.	Easiest dwarf palm to grow: minimum attention.
Pandanus sanderi	Warm, light shade.	Keep moist.

Humidity
Since many indoor plants came originally from tropical climates or damp forest floors, they need as much as possible to live in similar conditions. Even if the plant is not tropical, it needs humidity to replenish what it loses through transpiration.

The various ways to replace it are by spraying the leaves regularly (if the plants are in dry environments), by keeping the plants on pebbles (as described in 'Watering') or, if they are true moisture lovers, by treating them to a weekly 'sauna'.

Plants that respond well to the steam bath include ferns, palms, dwarf bananas, Swiss cheese plants and prayer plants. Put a 5–8cm layer of aquarium pebbles in a deep tray. Pour boiling water over the pebbles and place the plants on top to breathe in the steam.

Light
The process by which a plant converts light into chemical energy and then, with water and carbon dioxide, produces the simple sugars that build its roots, stems and leaves is called photosynthesis. Light is the vital nourishment link, but how much?

The natural habitat often provides the best clue. If the plant is tropical (abundant foliage overhead in its original habitat with sunlight filtering through), give it bright shade. Cacti need maximum sunlight.

The individual plant will indicate quickly enough whether it has sufficient; if it looks good it probably has. Try to find the right position without too much shifting around: disturbance is bad for plants.

Artificial light Natural light is not always essential. Some plants can survive just as well near a light bulb, a good remedy for a windowless corner.

Ordinary fluorescent tubes do the job satisfactorily (combine a 'daylight' strip with a 'cool white'). Otherwise there are light strips and bulbs specially designed for lighting plants – expensive, but the blue and red rays they emit are what the plants need to flower and stay green. The standard wattage required is 60 to 100. Flowering plants should go underneath the centre of the light; foliage plants, which need less light, can go at the sides. The distance between the light and the plant, the type of plant, the exposure to the light – these are salient factors. Start with smallish plants closely arranged, with the light source about 30–45cm above and switched on for 12–16 hours a day.

If the leaves turn yellow more light is needed; if they shrivel, less. The light will make the leaves transpire more, so keep the plants on pebbles and check their watering needs frequently.

If lights look unsightly, use pelmets to cover strips, shades for bulbs or a hooded arrangement like that on the trolley.

Pinching growing tips
This checks vertical growth and promotes bushiness by encouraging more leaves and lateral shoots. Do it only during the active growth period (spring-summer) and start while the plant is small.

With tweezers, remove the tiny new leaf that is the growing tip. The foliage plants you can pinch include avocado, *Coleus*, *Fatshedera*, *Heptapleurum arboricola* and *Tradescantia*.

The flowering plants are geraniums, begonias, *Impatiens*. Pinching the new leafy growth gives a stronger flower as well.

Post-winter facelift
After a dry winter in central heating or near the fire, even the strongest plants show signs of wear.

Examine both sides of the leaves, the stems and top-soil for insect life. Isolate any infected specimens and refer to a comprehensive plant guide for treatment techniques.

The first-aid kit for the others comprises a bowl of tepid water, a bag of cotton balls, manicure scissors and a wastepaper basket. Cut off the dead dry leaves, or the yellowing edges. Clear away the dead debris from the soil.

Swab both sides of each leaf on a large-leaved plant with a damp cotton ball, supporting the other side with your open palm. (Use a new ball for every leaf to make sure pests are not spread.)

You can increase the shine with a water and milk solution (4 parts to 1) – but watch out for streaking, which can occur if dust survived the swabbing. Use proprietary 'shiners' sparingly: they can give an *ersatz* finish.

If hairy-leaved plants look matted, do not wash them; gently 'comb' them with a baby's hairbrush or a shaving brush.

Plants can be displayed to perform any number of visual tricks. Use them to set off good architectural features, to camouflage bad ones, or – as room dividers – to become part of the architecture itself.

With their wide variety of shapes and colours, plants provide pattern as well as structure. Use them to add form to areas of solid colour or to complement furnishing fabrics.

Make similar use of decorative containers (cachepots), letting the room and the look of the plant determine your choice – be it oriental-looking cane or bamboo for palms or turn-of-the-century ceramic for aspidistras.

Massing plants makes an important contribution to their display. Clustered together they produce more visual impact than if shown individually; this is especially true of small plants.

A practical bonus is that, by virtue of their proximity, each can draw upon the moisture given off by its neighbours' leaves.

Cactus displays
Create a unique landscape using different varieties of cactus in a glass or acrylic sheet container. (Laboratory tanks are inexpensive and attractive glass containers.)

Choose a container that is about 4cm deeper than the tallest of the cactus pots to be used. Make sure that the container is clean both inside and out, and then spread a layer of pebbles on its base. Arrange pots of varying heights, shapes and sizes to make an interesting display. Where required, build up the pebble layer so that the tops of all the pots are level.

Leave sufficient space between pots so that each specimen is clearly visible. Too close an arrangement also cuts down on essential air circulation and encourages rapid spread of any pest or disease.

Finish by pouring in fine sand to cover the pots. It then looks as if all the cacti spring from the same soil.

Cacti (and the glass containers) do present a hazard, particularly where small children might stumble over them. Choose a site carefully.

Moveable plants
A good way to cope with plants that need constant strong sunlight, with the minimum of effort, is to group them together on a food (or surgical) trolley. Just move the cart to follow the sun.

Staging Place the plants on the steps of stairways or improvise other supports to make an interestingly shaped grouping. Inverted clay pots and acrylic sheet cubes of varying heights are two types of base that work well since both can be portable.

Uniformity in the type of support (and not too many different types of plant) prevents the arrangement looking fragmented.

Size in its place
Although larger plants may be expensive, they demand much less attention than clusters of different varieties of plant.

Among the best types of plant to use in splendid isolation are: *Ficus benjamina*, *Ficus lyrata*, *Howeia belmoreana*, *Chamaedorea erumpens*, *Crysalidocarpus lutescens* and *Rhapis excelsa*.

In modern settings, the large plants that strengthen sleek lines are *Yucca aloifolia*, *Dracaena marginata* and *D. fragrans* 'Massangeana', *Euphorbia canariensis*, *E. tirucali* and *E. ingens*.

Revival and camouflage
Those plants that are missing leaves or showing an unseemly amount of stem can be doctored or camouflaged.

Top-heavy if leggy plants have abundant and healthy top growth (rubber plants often grow this way), they can be put into a deep, wide basket, so that only the healthier parts show. If more leafiness is required, surround them in their baskets with small bushy plants elevated on pots or glass jars.

To get the best effect from this type of scheme use plants with a common shape or leaf form.

One-sided Plants growing to one side can be rotated a quarter turn each day to help them regain fullness of growth. Alternatively, take advantage of their asymmetry and display in a corner.

General malaise Sometimes plants just look as though they have gone through a bad time. There are no real symptoms, just a sorrowful air. As long as there is no sign of disease, try them somewhere new or in the company of other plants.

Staging plants in a basket (right) for either camouflage or display.

Rooms with a view

Plants can dress up a plain window or hide an unpleasant view.

Pots of plants, particularly trailers, can even act as 'curtains'. The more there are, the more privacy they will give. *Rhoicissus* 'Ellen Danica', *Asparagus sprengeri*, *Helxine soleirolii*, *Chlorophytum*, *Hedera*, *Philodendron scandens* are all suitable.

For an informal look, hang them at different levels and use varied species. Stand tall ones in front of the window and let them interplay with the trailers to give even greater cover.

You can also place them on shelves in the window frame. Look for plants that complement the design scheme, and display one variety of foliage plant with one type of flowering plant: for example, trailing ivies interspersed with cyclamen in winter – geraniums in summer.

Window colour

A host of flowering plants grow best near windows. Aim for colour to last the year. African violets flower all year round in warm sunny places. Hyacinths can be 'forced' to flower at any time. Keep them in a warm place while in bloom. Geraniums flower in midsummer, chrysanthemums flower in the summer and in autumn, cyclamen in autumn. Water by standing the pot to soak.

Window-sill herbs

These look and smell wonderful in a kitchen, and are incomparably superior to their dried counterparts in cooking. Start with small plants rather than from seed. Mint, sweet basil, parsley, marjoram, chervil and thyme are among the most hardy.

Plants as architecture

Rows of plants can be used to divide up space in large rooms – to act as 'walls' or to define areas used for different purposes. Make walls from upward-growing varieties of plant; place them on a low free-standing shelf, or arrange them in similar containers on bases of varying height (see 'Staging' opposite).

To enclose a particular area or to make a way from one area to another, you can also hang plants from the ceiling. Suspend trailing plants from a skylight or from an exposed ceiling beam.

Hanging a plant or two is also a useful device for 'lowering' a ceiling, or for bringing life to a long, brightly lit hallway.

Watering Always ensure that there is a water retainer underneath each hanging plant.

An easy way to water plants above head level is to put ice cubes on the soil (the chill will have gone from the water by the time it reaches the roots).

Try using a plastic squeeze-pump bottle with a long feed tube; or lower the plants on a system of pulleys, using cords and cleats.

Plants chosen as room dividers should be light and delicate to make a leafy screen – not an impenetrable jungle. Graceful candidates for the job include the tall specimens of umbrella plant, grape ivies, fiddle-leaf figs, and Fatshedera, a cross between *Fatsia japonica* and *Hedera* (ivy). Since the light in the centre of a room is often poor, choose varieties that will find the position suitable.

FLOWERS

Arranging objects is one thing; arranging flowers is quite different. Their short-lived beauty contrasts with the permanence of most of our possessions.

Set aside traditional notions of stylization, since flowers arranged formally lack the natural look that they should be able to contribute to an interior.

Try to display them as they might grow – which could mean using lots of them – and position them as they might be seen growing, bending naturally, not ramrod-stiff. But don't consider the natural state as sacrosanct. Experiment – don't be afraid to cut stems short, for instance, to achieve the shape that works best for particular flowers and containers.

Make extensive use of foliage. The greenery can provide the shape of the arrangement while the flowers lend their colour.

But not all arrangements need foliage. Some flowers, like daffodils, roses and daisies, look better without. Arrange them so that their blooms are the main thing showing (the common mistake is to leave the stems too long).

Flowers should be as much a part of the room as the furniture, adding colour and decoration and making a display that works effectively in the setting at all times. When the flowers change, the whole feel of a room can change with them.

For reasons of economy, some people only have flowers when entertaining. Whatever the occasion – or lack of it – consider the function the flowers have to fulfil. If they are for a dinner-table centrepiece they should be unobtrusive and not block lines of sight; at a party where people will be standing, arrangements should be high and bold.

Choosing flowers

For the serious flower lover the right source of fresh flowers is as important as the right butcher is to the ardent cook. Some florists buy from private gardens; look to them for unexpected species and the individuality of flowers grown by the bed rather than by the acre.

A garden full of flowers is the best (and cheapest) source of both flowers and foliage. But in the unproductive months, and throughout most of the year for city dwellers, a good florist is the chief source – providing not only a wide choice of fresh flowers, but professional advice. Street stalls are often a false economy: the flowers are usually the ones the florists rejected and, being outside, they are exposed to the damaging effects of weather and pollution.

Spotting quality Leaves should be green and crisp-looking and the blooms half-open. Tight budded flowers may not open after cutting; if they are wholly opened, the petals will soon drop. (The one exception is the chrysanthemum, which should be wholly open when bought.)

Another measure of freshness is the pollen; if it is powdery, it means the bloom was nearing its end when cut; compact pollen with tinges of green indicates a much longer life.

Finally, examine stems. Avoid any that look slimy. **Foliage** in arrangements can provide the basic shape and reduce the need for several flowers – thereby cutting costs. Choose the foliage after deciding on the flowers.

Use, say, three types of greenery in an arrangement, particularly if the flowers are mixed. Eucalyptus looks good with flowers in pastel shades; shiny-leaved foliage works with most flowers.

Natural selection

Early morning and just before sunset are the best times to pick flowers out of doors. In the garden, take a bucket of water and plunge the stems into it; use warm water if the flowers look limp.

Country walks Pick only those wild flowers that are not protected species. As a bucket would be cumbersome, take a polythene bag with a damp newspaper in the bottom and place the stems in that. Seal the top of the bag and keep it out of the sun while transporting it home.

Types of flower With so many types to choose from, the best way to simplify classification is by type of stem. As a general rule, the tougher-looking ones last longer, the more graceful are easier to arrange. Flowers such as tulips or roses have leaves large enough to provide their own foliage so that no other greenery is required. For mixed arrangements you can choose flower colours, petal shapes and textures which either harmonize or contrast.

Artificial flowers Don't be afraid of using fake flowers – either on their own or in combination with real flowers. Quality ones (like those made from silk) look good, and real enough to fool anyone; they also reduce costs after the initial expense of purchase.

Stem treatment

Cut flowers live longer if their stems are treated so that they can absorb moisture freely and breed as few bacteria as possible in the water.

To minimize decomposition, which encourages bacterial growth, remove all leaves that would be submerged; but leave the top ones so that the process of photosynthesis can still take place.

To facilitate the absorption of water, treat stems as follows.

Tough or woody stems Cut at an angle and remove any thick bark at the base. Hammer the base with a wooden mallet or slit with florist's scissors. *Roses* Remove bottom leaves and thorns. Roll in bunches in greaseproof (wax) paper to straighten the stems while soaking. *Lilac and Helleborus* should soak in hot water. *Carnations* should be cut at an angle between leaf joints, and placed in warm water to soak. Hammer only if the stems are tough.

Bleeding stems (poppies and poinsettias) Seal the cut ends in a flame.
Soft stems Cut at an angle. *Daffodils* and other soft-stemmed spring flowers that exude sap lose most of this if they are left overnight to soak. This sap will decompose and foul the water if not allowed to drain off.
Tulips can be rolled in bunches in greaseproof paper to help straighten the stems as they soak, but many people prefer to let them bend. Save the leaves for foliage and wrap their bases in damp tissue paper.

After treating the stems as described above, soak the flowers in a deep bucket of water for at least two hours in a cool, dark place.

When cutting the flowers to their final length for the arrangement, treat the stems again in the prescribed manner. However, stems already hammered need only be split for arrangement.

Containers

These are as important to flower arrangements as frames are to pictures. Aim to enhance the flowers by choosing a container that makes a statement with the flowers. Perhaps the colours will tone, or a metal container, say, will provide background contrast. Have a wide choice of shapes, sizes and textures to complement different types of flower.

If the container is particularly worthy of display, arrange the flowers to work with its shape and colours.

On the other hand, if the container is purely utilitarian – a tooth mug by a hospital bed, for instance – disguise it with flowers that trail in front. In such a case, the container has no other purpose than to hold the water and keep the stems together.

Ideally, for an arrangement to look natural, the top of the container should be splayed. It should be large enough for the flowers to fit comfortably without being jammed, but not so large that they are difficult to keep in place.

Before making any arrangements, ensure that the container is clean inside and out.

Metal containers Protect the metal from corrosion by arranging the flowers in a glass jar and placing that inside the container.

Basket containers Use a glass jar, as above, or line the inside with heavy-duty polythene. Use a sheet large enough to fill the container entirely, so that the container rather than the polythene will take the brunt of the water pressure. Leave a generous allowance of polythene at the top; turn it under and secure it all the way round with transparent tape.

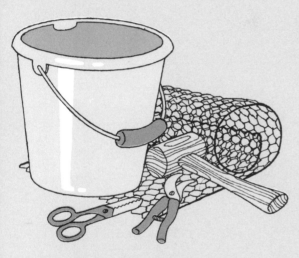

Tools and materials

Secateurs for cutting tree or shrub branches.

Florist's scissors with slightly serrated edges for cutting both flowers and chicken wire. These are available from hardware shops, garden centres and some florists, and are preferred for their jagged cut which breaks up the flower stem in a way that helps the flower absorb water.

Deep bucket for soaking the flowers.

Wooden mallet for hammering the stems.

Chicken wire Positioned so that it lies smooth across the top of the container, this makes the most natural-looking arrangements and gives more flexibility of display than using it crumpled.

Transparent tape On glass vases, where other holders would show, criss-cross this over the top and insert flowers through the gaps between the strips.

Watering can with a long narrow spout for topping up the water after flowers have been arranged.

Arranging flowers

If a flower holder is needed, prepare the container accordingly. Then fill it with cold water. If using foliage, arrange this first, starting in the centre with the highest and working outwards with any trailing branches at the edges. Then insert the flowers. Most should stand slightly proud of any foliage so as not to get lost.

Assess stem lengths by eye, or by holding the stem against the outside of the container. Do not cut too short too early.

In an arrangement that will go against a wall, put the tallest flowers at the back, larger-headed ones in the centre and the more delicate blooms at the edge.

Display and after-care

Keep flowers away from sources of heat, draughts and direct sunlight.

Flowers last longer if the water is fresh and plentiful, so keep it topped up. If the water is dangerously murky and the arrangement can take the disturbance, remove the flowers, clean out the container and refill with fresh water.

Snip off flower heads as they die. Resuscitate wilting flowers by removing them and snipping off a piece of stem (see 'Stem treatment'). Re-slit woody-stemmed flowers and roses and plunge them into warm water; when this has cooled return the flowers to the arrangement.

With proper care, a flower arrangement can last as long as six weeks, but ten days is a healthy average.

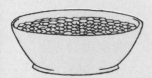

GLOSSARY

Because both products and the people who use them nowadays travel all over the world, here are some definitions of terms and materials that are referred to in the Back-up pages and that are sometimes known by different names.

Acetone Solvent useful for removing fresh excess adhesive, varnish, lacquer and waxes. Also effective in removal of deep-seated greasy stains. Colourless, highly volatile and inflammable petroleum derivative, to be used and stored very carefully as it is powerful and fast-acting. Never use in a confined space or near a naked flame.

Acrylic resin Viscous liquid which hardens on exposure to air to produce a clear light-weight plastic that is strong and hard-wearing. Used to fill in chips and holes in ceramic and glass material. Sold in various proprietary forms; some especially pigmented for particular use. Also used in solution in acetone as an adhesive.

Alkyd paint Type of paint, usually gloss or semi-gloss, in which the usual oil vehicle has been replaced by an odourless, fast-drying synthetic resin. Rapidly replacing oil-based paints, particularly as the interval between coats is shortened. Thinned like an oil-based paint with thinner or turpentine.

Ammonium acetate Used in aqueous solution to clean porous ceramics, as it has the bleaching power of ammonia but is safe and non-toxic, and evaporates too rapidly to seep into the material.

Anhydrous lanolin Water-free variety of fat from sheep's wool, used to give a protective coating to metals and other materials corroded by atmospheric moisture.

Baseboard see **Skirting board.**

Batten (Cleat) Long, narrow strip of square-sectioned wood used to reinforce surfaces, particularly flooring and doors, and as framework, e.g. for attaching fabric to walls.

Benzene Solvent for a wide range of substances including grease and oil and synthetic resins. Good for removing heavy soiling, particularly on fabrics. Colourless highly volatile and inflammable liquid derived from petroleum. Sold as 'Benzol'. Never use in a confined space or near a naked flame.

Benzine Mixture of liquid hydrocarbons derived from petroleum or coal. Used as a solvent, primarily in dry cleaning.

Blockboard Board suitable for cladding, cupboards and shelves. Made by gluing together under high pressure strips of softwood up to 25mm wide between sheets of veneer.

Carbon tetrachloride Liquid solvent particularly effective in removing grease and oil stains from clothes and other textiles. Colourless, highly toxic chloroform derivative, not to be used in confined spaces. Although non-flammable, it should not be used near heat or a naked flame as it can break down to more dangerous constituents.

Carborundum Extremely hard material (silicon carbide) used as an abrasive on tough surfaces like masonry and gemstone.

Cerium oxide (ceric oxide) Fine, pale yellow powder used as an abrasive to remove scratches from and polish ceramic and glass.

Chipboard (Particle board) Coarse, lighter form of hardboard

suitable only for internal use. Made by bonding chips of softwood and resin together under high pressure.

Cleat see **Batten.**

Crocus powder Red variety of iron oxide used as a coarse abrasive powder, particularly for removing scratches from and polishing metal and glass surfaces.

Denatured alcohol see **Methylated spirit.**

Epoxy putty Putty used for filling chips and holes in non-translucent ceramic and in metal. Made by mixing epoxy resin adhesive with pigment to get a good colour (titanium dioxide for a good ceramic white) and, sometimes, with kaolin as a binder. Sets very slowly on exposure to air (gentle heating speeds the process) but gives an extremely tough finish and adheres strongly.

Epoxy resin adhesives Group of adhesives made from synthetic resins. Characterized by their strength of bonding, toughness and resistance to wear. They can be used on almost all types of material. Clear varieties also resist discoloration, and are accordingly the most popular type of adhesive in use today. Commonly supplied in two parts – resin and hardener – which are mixed together just before use.

Foxing (Fox marks) Discoloration, normally yellowish-brown stains, of the paper of old books, usually caused by damp.

French chalk Available in solid form to mark fabric for cutting, or as a powder which absorbs grease and thus makes an excellent dry stain-remover. A form of soft talc (soapstone), it is also used as a dry lubricant and as a mild abrasive.

Glycerine (Glycerin or glycerol) Water-soluble solvent useful for removing stains and effective in removing rust and tar. Colourless, sweet viscous liquid, a by-product in soap manufacture, it is also useful as a lubricant on metal and glass.

Hardboard Board used primarily as a lining for both walls and ceilings. A heavy board made from pulped softwood bonded into sheets at high temperatures and under high pressure. Generally one side has a smooth finish, but it can be bought with both sides finished. It can also be bought tempered with oils and resins which make it tougher and less absorbent.

Hydrochloric acid Highly corrosive acid used in dilute aqueous solution to clean metals and remove very stubborn stains. Hydrogen chloride, a gas at normal temperatures, readily dissolves in water to form this fuming toxic acid also known as 'spirits of salt'. A mixture of this and nitric acid, *aqua regia*, can dissolve the 'noble' metals – gold and platinum.

Hydrogen peroxide Strong oxidizing and bleaching agent useful for removing stains on delicate materials which other solvents might damage. A clear, heavy liquid which is unstable and decomposes readily, it is normally supplied in aqueous solution in dark-tinted bottles.

Jeweller's rouge A fine-powdered red variety of iron oxide used primarily as an abrasive and polish on metallic surfaces.

Kerosene see **Paraffin.**

Lacquer Used to give a high-gloss protective and decorative coating to wood and metal surfaces. Originally a term reserved for the sap of the lacquer tree, it is now used for any of various other clear or coloured, synthetic (cellulose) or natural (shellac) resins in volatile vehicles used to give a similar surface coating. *See also* **Varnish**.

Linseed oil Used mixed with turpentine (eight parts to one) to make a varnish that gives a particularly tough protective coating to hardwood surfaces. A brownish-yellow oil produced by crushing the seeds of flax, it can also be used as a varnish on its own.

Liquid paraffin (liquid petrolatum, mineral oil, liquid wax) General lubricant and mild solvent, a clear, odourless, tasteless liquid distilled from petroleum. Primarily used medicinally as a laxative.

Magnesium silicate Normally available as a powder used in a water paste to clean marble and ceramic surfaces. It is the mineral commonly known as talc, in its natural granular form it is known as soapstone, and in its fine-grained variety, French chalk.

Mat *see* **Mount**.

Methylated spirit (Denatured alcohol) Powerful solvent used to strip varnishes and to clean heavily soiled materials. It is a mixture consisting mainly of ethyl alcohol rendered unfit to drink, and thus exempt from liquor laws and taxes, by the addition of toxic methyl alcohol (wood spirit) and various other substances including a violet dye to make it visually distinctive. It is highly inflammable, and should not be used in a confined space.

Mount (Mat) Border of cardboard or other material surrounding a picture within the moulded frame to give visual contrast between the picture and frame.

Nitric acid Powerful oxidizing agent used in dilute aqueous solution to clean metals and glass and to remove some types of stain. A colourless, fuming, highly corrosive acid, formerly known as *aqua fortis*.

Oxalic acid Mild acid used to clean copper and to remove many types of stain from materials including paper, wood and fabric. Usually supplied in crystalline form, it is highly toxic and to be used with great care.

Paint thinner *see* **White spirit**.

Paraffin (Kerosene) The solvent most commonly used to remove oil and grease. A derivative of petroleum, it also serves to soften corrosion such as rust, to facilitate subsequent removal.

Particle board *see* **Chipboard**.

Pumice powder A very fine abrasive for polishing. Useful on fragile or easily scratched surfaces, like glass, as the more the powder is used the finer the abrasive particles become. Derived from a porous lightweight form of volcanic rock.

Rebate (Rabbet) Cut or groove along or near the edge of a piece of wood, usually in the form of a rectangular recess, which will allow another piece of material to fit into it.

Rubbing alcohol *see* **Surgical spirit**.

Silicone polish Polish with a synthetic base used to give a coating to surfaces where the protective element is more important, as it is highly resistant to temperature changes and to moisture.

Skirting board (Baseboard) Moulding used along the bottom of an interior wall to fill and finish the join between the wall and the floor.

Soundpost (Soundboard) Board within a musical instrument, particularly one of the violin family, which forms the top of the resonant chamber.

Surgical spirit (Rubbing alcohol) Another denatured form of alcohol similar to methylated spirit, used principally for medicinal purposes like cleansing wounds. Since it does not contain any dye, it can be used as a solvent or cleaning agent in circumstances where there must be no risk of discoloration. Various unpleasant-tasting compounds are added to the alcohol, instead, to render the spirit unfit to drink.

Turpentine Thin volatile oil obtained from the sap of pine trees. Possibly the best solvent for most paints and varnishes and generally used as a good-quality paint thinner. It is expensive, however, and turpentine substitute or white spirit is normally used in its place. It is highly inflammable and to be handled and stored with care.

Varnish Natural or synthetic (polyurethane) resin in an oil or spirit base, used to give a hard, smooth, high-gloss protective coating, primarily to wood and metal surfaces.

Veneer A thin layer of high-quality wood or other material used to cover and give a finer finish to coarse base material like inexpensive wood or board.

Wallplugs Cylinders of softwood or plastic inserted into holes drilled in wall plaster so that screws driven into the holes have material on which to grip. They are available in a wide range of sizes to match all types and sizes of screw.

Wet-and-dry paper Abrasive paper on which particles of carborundum have been bonded with resin. Used dry, it is just like ordinary glasspaper or sandpaper; used damp it gives a fine, smooth finish most suitable for preparing painted surfaces for the next coat. Available in several grades.

White spirit (Paint thinner) Solvent obtained from distillation of petroleum, used as a substitute for turpentine. It is inflammable, and to be handled with care.

Metric measures and equivalents				
Length				
1 millimetre (mm)				= 0.04 inches (in)
1 centimetre (cm)	=	10mm	=	0.39 inches
1 metre (m)	=	100cm	=	1.09 yards (yd)
Weight				
1 milligramme (mg)				= 0.02 grain
1 gramme (g)	=	1000mg	=	0.04 ounces (oz)
1 kilogramme (kg)	=	1000g	=	2.20 pounds (lb)
Volume				
1 litre = 0.22 UK gal = 0.26 US gal = 35.19 fl oz				

INDEX

ACKNOWLEDGEMENTS

The Author and Publishers gratefully acknowledge invaluable assistance from the following people and organizations:
Chris Ashton/Heritage Antiques; Peter Boswell; Peter Burian/Peter Burian Associates; Stuart Cropper/Grays Mews Market; John Dickinson/designer and interior decorator; The Drury Tea & Coffee Co Ltd; David Ehrhard/Psycho-Ceramic Restorations; Roy Flooks; William Galbraith; Philip Geraghty/Homeworks; Major and Mrs Henry Gibbs/Wycombe Cane; Tricia Guild; Chris Halsey/Designers Guild; David Jessel; Bob Milne/London Lighting Co Ltd; The Monmouth Coffee Shop; Richard Rooney; Bruce Wolf.

Typesetting
Servis Filmsetting Ltd, Manchester; Photoprint Plates Ltd, Essex.

Origination
Gilchrist Bros Ltd, Leeds.

Printing
Smeets Offset BV, Weert, The Netherlands.

Editorial Contributors and Consultants
Mary Adams (Flowers: 256); Tony Babarik (Plants: 252–5); Julian Calder (Photographs: 215); Valerie Davies (Textiles: 224–7); The Decorative Lighting Association (Lighting: 234–41); Roger Dubern (Pictures: 216–19); Ian Elliott Shircore (Bottle collections: 209); Lindsay Graham (Textiles: 228–33); Rose Gray and David MacIlwaine/Home Stoves Limited (Stoves: 205); David Griffith (Tin ephemera: 204); Ruth Harris/Homeworks (Make something of it: 250); Thom Henvey (Furniture surfaces: 210); John McGowan (Painting: 242–5; Shelving: 246–9); Nicky Seymour (Miscellaneous: 212); Anna Southall and Rica Jones (Pictures: 214).

Illustrators
Venner Artists: 39; 94–5; 96–7; 104; 114–15; 116–17; 118; 120; 122; 124; 126; 128–9; 130–1; 133; 134–5; 136–7; 138–9; 140–1; 142–3; 150; 153; 156; 159; 160–1; 163; 166–7; 169; 170–1; 172–3; 178; 184–5; 186; 188–9; 190–1; 192–3; 195; 196–7; 198–9; 216–17; 218–19; 220–1; 222–3; 235; 236–7; 238–9; 240–1; 244–5; 246–7; 248–9; 250–1.

Ivan Ripley/Anglo-Continental Artists: 202; 204–5; 207; 209; 213; 214–15; 224; 226–7; 228–9; 230–1; 232–3; 252–3; 254–5; 257.

Photographic credits
b=bottom c=centre
l=left r=right t=top

Cover: Bruce Wolf; 1–4: Bruce Wolf; 7: Scoop/Transworld Features; 10–11: Bill McLaughlin; 14t & b: Bruce Wolf; 15t: Michael Dunne; 15b: Bill McLaughlin; 16t: Ron Sutherland; 16b: Julius Shulman; 17t & b: David Cripps/Elizabeth Whiting & Associates; 18: Leonardo Ferrante; 19tl: Henk Snoek; 19tr & b: Jessica Strang; 20t & bl: Jessica Strang; 20br: Jerry Tubby/Elizabeth Whiting & Associates; 21t & b: Jessica Strang; 22tl: British Tourist Authority; 22tr & bl: Emmett Bright; 22br: Malcolm Lewis; 23: British Tourist Authority; 24t: Bruce Wolf; 24b: Emmett Bright; 24–5: Jessica Strang; 25t: Jessica Strang; 26t: Jessica Strang; 26b: Bruce Wolf; 26–7: Jessica Strang; 27t: Jessica Strang; 27c: Bill McLaughlin; 28t: Michael Dunne; 28b: David Cripps/Elizabeth Whiting & Associates; 28–9: Henk Snoek/Law & Dunbar-Nasmith; 29t: Jerry Tubby/Elizabeth Whiting & Associates; 29br: Tim Street-Porter/Elizabeth Whiting & Associates; 30t: Tim Street-Porter/Elizabeth Whiting & Associates; 30b: Scoop/Transworld Features; 31tl: Jessica Strang; 31tr: Christine Hanscomb; 31c & b: Tim Street-Porter/Elizabeth Whiting & Associates; 32–3: Bruce Wolf; 33tl: Robin Guild; 33c: Mike Peters; 33bl: Margaret Murray; 33br: Popperfoto; 34t: Elyse Lewin/Transworld Features; 34b: Schöner Wohnen/Camera Press; 35: Jessica Strang; 36t: Für Sie/Camera Press; 36b: Jessica Strang; 36–7: Schöner Wohnen/Camera Press; 37tl: Bill McLaughlin; 37tr: The Picture Library; 38t: Brigitte Baert; 38b: Nelson Hargreave; 39: Jessica Strang; 42: Femina/Camera Press; 43t & c: Bruce Wolf; 43b: Michael Dunne; 44t: The National Magazine Co Ltd; 44b: Michael Nicholson/Elizabeth Whiting & Associates; 45t: Robin Guild; 45b: Tim Street-Porter/Elizabeth Whiting & Associates; 46t: Bruce Wolf; 46b: Schöner Wohnen/Camera Press; 47t: The Picture Library; 47b: Michael Nicholson/Elizabeth Whiting & Associates; 48: Brigitte Baert; 49t: Robin Bath; 49c:

Michael Dunne; 49b: Bruce Wolf; 50t: Robin Bath; 50b: *Schöner Wohnen*/Camera Press; 51t: Bruce Wolf; 51c: Michael Dunne; 51b: Emmett Bright; 52t: Emmett Bright; 52b: Bruce Wolf; 52–3: Bruce Wolf; 54t: Michael Dunne; 54–5: Bruce Wolf; 55tl & tr: Jessica Strang; 55cl: *Schöner Wohnen*/Camera Press; 56t: Jessica Strang; 56b: *Schöner Wohnen*/Camera Press; 57t: Ruslan Khalid; 57c: Jessica Strang; 57bl: George Wright; 57br: Robin Guild; 58tl & tr: Crafts Council; 58c: Jessica Strang; 58bl: Crafts Council/K. Cosserat; 58br: Robin Guild; 59tl: Robin Guild; 59tr: Art Directors Photo Library; 59c: Christine Hanscomb; 59b: Paul Brierley; 60t: Bruce Wolf; 60b: Emmett Bright; 61t: Robin Guild; 61c: Michael Nicholson/Elizabeth Whiting & Associates; 61b: Tim Street-Porter/Elizabeth Whiting & Associates; 62–3: Bruce Wolf; 64: Bruce Wolf; 65: Christine Hanscomb; 66t: Bill McLaughlin; 66bl: Spike Powell/Elizabeth Whiting & Associates; 66br: Elyse Lewin/Transworld Features; 67: Bruce Wolf; 68: Michael Dunne; 69t: Jerry Tubby/Elizabeth Whiting & Associates; 69b: Brigitte Baert; 70t: The Picture Library; 70b: Rolf Benz; 71t: Elyse Lewin/Transworld Features; 71c: Bruce Wolf; 71b: *Schöner Wohnen*/Camera Press; 72t: Michael Boys/Susan Griggs Agency; 72c: Bruce Wolf; 72b: Robin Bath; 73: Bruce Wolf; 74–5: Bruce Wolf; 76t: George Wright; 76–7: Bruce Wolf; 77t & b: Bruce Wolf; 78t: Bruce Wolf; 78b: *Schöner Wohnen*/Camera Press; 79tl & tr: The Picture Library; 79b: *Schöner Wohnen*/Camera Press; 80t: Elizabeth Whiting & Associates; 80b: Bill McLaughlin; 81t: Elizabeth Whiting & Associates; 81c: *Für Sie*/Camera Press; 81b: *Schöner Wohnen*/Camera Press; 82t: Fotofass; 82c: Michael Nicholson/Elizabeth Whiting & Associates; 82b: Bruce Wolf; 83t: Spectrum; 83c: Michael Nicholson/Elizabeth Whiting & Associates; 83b: Bruce Wolf; 84–9: Bruce Wolf; 90t: Scoop/Transworld Features; 90b: Brigitte Baert; 91: Robin Guild; 92t: Angelo Hornak; 92–3t & b: *Schöner Wohnen*/Camera Press; 93t: Angelo Hornak; 94t: Michael Boys/Susan Griggs Agency; 94b: Saporiti; 95: Bruce Wolf; 96: Bruce Wolf; 96–7t: Jessica Strang; 96–7b: *Over 21*; 97t: *McCalls*/Transworld Features; 98t: Emmett Bright; 98b: *Schöner Wohnen*/Camera Press; 99tl & tr: Emmett Bright; 99b: Bruce Wolf; 100–1: Bruce Wolf; 102t: *Schöner Wohnen*/Camera Press; 102b: Bruce Wolf; 103t: Michael Dunne; 103bl: Jessica Strang; 103tr: David Cripps/Elizabeth Whiting & Associates; 104t: Bruce Wolf; 104b: Brigitte Baert; 105t: Michael Dunne; 105b: Bruce Wolf; 106: Scoop/Transworld Features; 106–7: Scoop/Transworld Features; 107t: Mike Peters; 107c: Bruce Wolf; 107b: *Schöner Wohnen*/Camera Press; 108t: Emmett Bright; 108b: Sam Lambert; 109t: Emmett Bright; 108–9: Carla de Benedetti; 110t: *Femina*/Camera Press; 110b: *Schöner Wohnen*/Camera Press; 110–11: The National Magazine Co Ltd; 111t & b: Bruce Wolf; 114t: George Wright; 114–15: Bruce Wolf; 115: *Schöner Wohnen*/Camera Press; 116: Michael Nicholson/Elizabeth Whiting & Associates; 117t: Syntax Films; 117b: Bill McLaughlin; 118t: Bruce Wolf; 118b: *Over 21*; 119tl & tr: Jessica Strang; 119b: Bruce Wolf; 120t: Elizabeth Whiting & Associates; 120c: Julian Nieman/Elizabeth Whiting & Associates; 120b: Jerry Tubby/Elizabeth Whiting & Associates; 121tl: Tim Street-Porter/Elizabeth Whiting & Associates; 121tr: Jessica Strang; 121b: *Brigitte*/Camera Press; 122t: Jessica Strang; 122b: Tim Street-Porter/Elizabeth Whiting & Associates; 123t: *Schöner Wohnen*/Camera Press; 123b: Michael Nicholson/Elizabeth Whiting & Associates; 124t: *Femina*/Camera Press; 124b: Leonardo Ferrante; 125: Bill McLaughlin; 126: Jessica Strang; 126–7: Brigitte Baert; 127tl: Michael Dunne; 127tr & b: Jessica Strang; 128t: Jessica Strang; 128b: *Schöner Wohnen*/Camera Press; 129t: Bruce Wolf; 129b: *Schöner Wohnen*/Camera Press; 130t: Bruce Wolf; 130b: Julius Shulman; 131t: Mike Peters; 131b: Scoop/Transworld Features; 132–3: *Schöner Wohnen*/Camera Press; 133t & b: Bruce Wolf; 134t: Jessica Strang; 134b: Scoop/Transworld Features; 135t: *Schöner Wohnen*/Camera Press; 135b: Bruce Wolf; 136: *Tout Faire*/Sungravure; 137tl: Michael Dunne; 137tr: Brigitte Baert; 137b: Emmett Bright; 138t: Michael Dunne; 138b: Bill McLaughlin; 139t: Bruce Wolf; 139b: Leonardo Ferrante; 140t: Scoop/Transworld Features; 140b: Tim Street-Porter/Elizabeth Whiting & Associates; 141t: Mike St Maur Sheil; 141b: *Schöner Wohnen*/Camera Press; 142t & b: *Schöner Wohnen*/Camera Press; 143t: Zefa; 143c & b: *Schöner Wohnen*/Camera Press; 146t & br: *Femina*/Camera Press; 146bl: Emmett Bright; 147: Christine Hanscomb; 148t: *Schöner Wohnen*/Camera Press; 148b: A. de Vernisy/Transworld Features; 149t: Emmett Bright; 149b: Bruce Wolf; 150t: *Schöner Wohnen*/Camera Press; 150b: Emmett Bright; 151t: Scoop/Transworld Features; 151c: Brigitte Baert; 151b: *Femina*/Camera Press; 152t: Jessica Strang; 152b: Elizabeth Whiting & Associates; 153: Brecht-Einzig Ltd; 154t: Brigitte Baert; 154b: Bruce Wolf; 155t: Boffi; 154–5: Saporiti; 156t & b: *Schöner Wohnen*/Camera Press; 157t: *Schöner Wohnen*/Camera Press; 157b: Julius Shulman; 158l: Michael Nicholson/Elizabeth Whiting & Associates; 158r: Leonardo Ferrante; 159t: Scoop/Transworld Features; 159b: Emmett Bright; 160t: Bruce Wolf; 160b: David Cripps/Elizabeth Whiting & Associates; 161: *Femina*/Camera Press; 162t: Elizabeth Whiting & Associates; 162b: Interlübke; 163t: *American Home*/Transworld Features; 163b: *Zuhause*/Camera Press; 164t: Jessica Strang; 164b: Bruce Wolf; 165t: Tim Street-Porter/Eliabeth Whiting & Associates; 175bl: Scoop/Transworld Features; 165br: *American Home*/Transworld Features; 166t: Julius Shulman; 166bl: Emmett Bright; 166br: Sam Lambert; 167t: Julian Nieman/Elizabeth Whiting & Associates; 167c: Michael Nicholson/Elizabeth Whiting & Associates; 167b: Bruce Wolf; 168t: Tim Street-Porter/Elizabeth Whiting & Associates; 165bl: Scoop/Blessing/Richard Himmel ASID; 168b: Clive Helm/Elizabeth Whiting & Associates; 169t: *Femina*/Camera Press; 169c: Emmet Bright; 169b: Brigitte Baert; 170t: Elizabeth Whiting & Associates; 170b: Jessica Strang; 171: Bruce Wolf; 172: Tim Street-Porter/Elizabeth Whiting & Associates; 172–3: Brigitte Baert; 173: Tim Street-Porter/Elizabeth Whiting & Associates; 174: Geoffrey Frosh/Elizabeth Whiting & Associates; 175t: Elyse Lewin/Transworld Features; 175b: Transworld Features; 178t: Bruce Wolf; 178b: *Schöner Wohnen*/-Camera Press; 179: Jessica Strang; 180t: Bruce Coleman; 180–1: Michael Nicholson/Elizabeth Whiting & Associates; 181tl: Elizabeth Whiting & Associates; 181tr: Brigitte Baert; 181b: Bruce Wolf; 182: David Cripps/Elizabeth Whiting & Associates; 182–3: Scoop/Transworld Features; 183t: *Over 21*; 183b: Bruce Wolf; 184t: *Brigitte*/Camera Press; 184b & 184–5: *Schöner Wohnen*/Camera Press; 186: Bruce Wolf; 187t & b: Emmett Bright; 187c: James Mortimer/Transworld Features; 188t: Interlübke; 188c: *American Home*/Transworld Features; 188b: *Tout Faire*/Sungravure; 189t: Camera Press; 189b: Brigitte Baert; 190–1: *Schöner Wohnen*/Camera Press; 192t & c: *Schöner Wohnen*/Camera Press; 192b: Robin Guild; 193t & b: Bruce Wolf; 196: Interlübke; 197tl & tr: Interlübke; 197b: Transworld Features; 198t: Brigitte Baert; 198b: IMS/Camera Press; 199t: IMS/Camera Press; 199b: *Schöner Wohnen*/Camera Press; 238t: Peter Kibbles.